WAL
LEGEND OF

SEORAS WALLACE

Ist Edition

Published in 2019 by Wolf and Wildcat Publishing

ISBN Paperback: 978-1-9999170-8-1
Ebook: 978-1-9999170-9-8

A CIP catalogue copy of this book can be found
in the British Library.

Published with the help of Indie Authors World
www.indieauthorsworld.com

IndieAuthors
World

www.facebook.com/InDiScotland

Wolf & Wildcat publishing
Associate: Jade Macfarlane
+44(0)7766 584 360
www.wolfandwildcat.com
www.facebook.com/Wallace.Legend
Clan Wallace PO Box 1305 Glasgow G51 4UB Scotland

Dedicate to the memory of a great clansman…
RIP
Paul Hayde

Acknowledgements

Big thank you for the writing support from
my hard working family and friends

Special thanks to:

Maire Petterrson

Kerstin Kilpatrick Stråhlesköld

Knights Celeres Nordica.

- Älskade Piraten -

About the Author: Seoras Wallace

After a career in the film industry spanning over thirty years, in such films as Highlander, Gladiator, Rob Roy, Braveheart, Saving Private Ryan and many more. In 1997 following a serious horse riding accident, Seoras turned his valuable experience to becoming an author, and parallel to his professional life. Seoras has also served as acting chief executive of the Wallace Clan Trust for Scotland.

"An experience like no other," said Seoras, "One of the constants in my vocation has been the revelation of private or secretive documents and accounts from many unusual sources that gave me a wholly different perspective of William Wallace, that shaped him as a man who became a nations Iconic patriot and world hero in the eyes and hearts of many. At first I used to think that the information I witnessed was too incredible to be true, but when certain parts of that narrative repeated from different sources, another story from the academic norm began to emerge. Growing up in a remote west coast village, that was extremely patriotic and nationalist, I was taught from the clan elders at an early age the family legend of Wallace, but that too did not match the publicly available narrative. On my many travels around the world, especially after the release and success of the film Braveheart, people would often say upon hearing my account, "You should write a book about the Wallace." "I have always replied that no one would ever believe it, but following my accident, I decided to leave the family legacy as a fact based fictional narrative for my family and future generations, almost as a historical bloodline diary. The epic account I have written about the Life and Legend of William Wallace has been an inspiration and brought to me a newfound love for the man, the people and the country he fought for. Many who have been test reading the epic series as it developed, have a constant response that stands out more than any other comment, "Seoras, I've researched what you've written, and it's true…" My reply has always been… "Naw… it's just fiction!"

5

Machars Obhainn Mòr

A dark and foreboding night falls as William and Fiónlaidh walk off the battlefield and into the Gallóbhet camp, where she leads him to a large obhainn mòr. He notices the outer cover of the obhainn is made weatherproof by layers of greased highland bull-skins, hair-side out, hair-tip down, all secured by square netting weighted down with a necklace of heavy round boulders hanging as a beaded skirt.

On entering the obhainn, William is greeted by a low ochre light emanating from two large glowing peat fires. As he looks around the interior, it reminds him of his obhainn back in glen Afton, but this obhainn is much larger in size, yet it is lighter in construction, using long thin willow stalks as cross-members and double-bound hazel ribs for supports. The inside roofing and walls is lined with deerskin tile, turned hair-side out and hair-tip down, allowing any water penetration to fall away to outside run-off channels. Long wooden stey racks run alongside the flimsy looking structure walls, holding léine, leather battle-jacks, and a variety of other textile and leather war garments, all drying from the incessant damp of the season in the radiant heat from the central fires. Fiónlaidh says, "This is our Machars obhainn mòr for the night Wallace," she points towards the far end of the structure, "and that wee leather door over there goes through into the seomra uisge beg." (Little water room) William is surprised when he observes many men and women going through the wee leather door, completely naked, he watches curiously as they push back a small leather flap-door which releases great plumes of steam. As individuals enter, they close the flap behind them to seal off whatever is inside the little appendix. "Take off your haubergeon and léine Wallace." requests Fiónlaidh "I'll take you to the seomra uisge beg where we may share an Glanadh." (The Cleansing) William enquires, "Is that where those Gallóbhet and Ceitherne are going at the end of the obhainn?" Fiónlaidh replies as she undresses. "It is... Hang all your leather armour and léine on the stays over there, then they'll all be dry by the morn."

They both quickly disrobe and hang up their damp garments on the stey racks; then they approach the little flap-door of the seomra uisge beag. Fiónlaidh stoops low and pushes her way through the little doorway; William gets on his hands and knees and follows close behind. He pushes through the small opening then stands up in a dense, steam filled area of the obhainn, but the scalding heat that greets him instantly sears his face neck and chest, the shock causes him to draw involuntary breath, with the steam almost scorching the lining of his lungs.

Fiónlaidh laughs and pulls him downwards by the hand. "Stay down before yie cook ya big daft lump. The steam is at its hottest nearest the bender, (Apex), so its best to sit on the floor and get accustomed to the wet heat first." William obediently sits cross-legged on thick flooring made from matted river reeds set upon many layered rush leaf bedding. As he settles down, he hears the faint sounds of Uliann bagpipes and clarsach's play soothing music outside. He peers around the small room and can see that other people sitting similarly to him, others lay prone while their partners use small pieces of split willow to scrape the sweat off the skin with slow thoughtful strokes, cleansing the grime of the campaign away from each others bodies. William attempts to speak as he catches his breath, "I've heard o' these places Fiónlaidh, but I've never experienced one before." Laughing, Fiónlaidh says, "That's likely why all you townies smell so feckn bad." They both laugh as they relax and savour the luxury of the seomra uisge beg.

A second door flap opens and a young female Ceithernach enters, carrying red-hot stones on a large wide mouth platter gathered from a bellows fire just outside. Using tongs, she places the hot stones like a little pyramid in the centre of the seomra uisge beg. Next, she pours a little scented water onto the hot stones that instantly produces scalding steam profusely in reaction, producing a sweet scented hot mist. She removes the cooling stones from a previous pile then takes them away for re-heating. It isn't long before William and Fiónlaidh are dripping wet with a sheen of sweat emanating from their opening pores caused by the steam, coaxing all the dirt and stale oils out from their bodies. Reaching into a small leather satchel nearby, Fiónlaidh removes two fist size linen bags packed full of sphagnum moss, previously saturated with viscose wort-oils natural limes, vinegar and other scented aromatic herbs. "What's that?" enquires William. Fiónlaidh replies, "These are my Magha bags, the potion inside is called Cúr na ré. Now Wallace, you just lie face down till I'm ready."

William lies face down, closes his eyes and smiles, enjoying the faint sound of music in this opulent luxury in the middle of no-where near a freezing stinking bog, surrounded by thousands of warriors intent on savagery and killing. He laughs at the thought; then he opens his eyes and looks around and sees Fiónlaidh tying her long red-blonde hair back behind her head. She smiles as she picks up the Magha bags, dips them into a churn of hot water, then she rubs them vigorously together in her hands to produce a large mass of scented creamy foam lather. She places the Magha bags on his shoulders and begins to body-wash him with the rich textured Cúr na Ré. William relaxes and savours the intimate sensations, accentuated by her caring touch as she kneads and coaxes the aches and pains away from his body. Her gentle and expert application sends him into a near state of catatonic bliss. After what seems to be a luxurious eternity of exquisite pampering, William sleepily sits up and watches Fiónlaidh as she dips the two little bags back into the warm water once more.

"Cúr na ré… Foam o' the moon?" says William "That's a beautiful name for that creamy stuff Fiónlaidh, the monks in Paisley use something similar when they wash, but it burns your feckn skin off and nips your eyes out… they call it soap I think." Fiónlaidh laughs, then she pushes him over onto his back. "Right Wallace, your for a much overdue an Glanadh big fella, for as handsome as yie are, you smelling like an auld sow's pisser, does yie no great favours at all." Somewhat embarrassed by her comment, William lay motionless while Fiónlaidh begins to rub the little bags of Cúr na ré in a gentle circular motion all over his body, reminding him of when he was a child, when Wee Maw used to wash both him and wee John in an old oak tub in front of the roaring fires of ach na Feàrna. He soon loses himself in the cleansing and serenity of Fiónlaidh caressing his body with the creamy lather.

When she has finished her ritual, William cleanses Fiónlaidh in turn, thoughtfully making her cleansing as relaxing and as pleasurable for her as he had found the experience to be. As William tends meticulously to her cleansing pleasure, he cannot ignore how lithe her body is, how beautiful she is, and the feeling of exhilaration by her trust in him to be cleansing her so intimately, yet so right in its tribal innocence. William eventually completes his task, then they both sit upright on the rush mats cross-legged to endure the steam cleansing a little while longer, till all the sweat is again running freely from their pores as rainwater from a broadleaf. "Right…" says Fiónlaidh "Close yer eyes." Dutifully William closes his eyes, a few moments pass before he begins to feels what could only be described as a, chilling, sweet sensation on the top of his head begin to trickle ever so slowly down his neck, face back and chest… "Oh my feckn Aicé Fiónlaidh, what are you doin' to me… this is pure amazin'." Fiónlaidh smiles and replies with a cheeky smile, "I just dipped the Magha bags into freezin' water then I slowly squeezed them out above your head." William says, "That was an amazing sensation, indescribable…"

"C'mon Wallace…" says Fiónlaidh as she stands up and shakes him by the arm, "Follow me, we're goin' to the dippin' bowrie, what's next is even better." With both her small hands, she grips William firmly by one of his, then, using all her might, she pulls him to his feet and leads him towards a small door to exit the seomra uisge beag.

Much to his surprise, he finds himself standing outside in the freezing winter's night; naked as the day he was born. Nearby Gallóglaigh and Gallóbhan sitting around the bellows fire nearby, appear equally surprised and greatly amused to see his giant naked frame and covered in a thick layer of Cúr na ré… "Follow me Wallace," shouts Fiónlaidh. He watches as she laughs then runs a short distance and jumps into a freezing water-filled bowrie beg (Little water dam) *'Naw…'* he thinks to himself, *'I cannae do this…'* But instinctively he runs and jumps towards the dam, even though everything in his mind is screaming *'Don't do it Wallace… it'll be feckin*

11

freezin and ahm gonnae feckn die...' Plunging into the bowrie beside Fiónlaidh, he instantly goes under the surface, where the sub-zero chill of the water is instantaneous, but not as he had expected... Surprisingly, it's refreshing and sensational. As he bursts back through the icy cold surface gasping for breath, Fiónlaidh laughs at him as she washes the Cúr na ré from her hair and body. William laughs too, then he stands up calmly, but he quickly sits back down in the bowrie up to his neck, as the water feels much warmer than the air temperature above surface.

"I don't believe this..." exclaims William, "It's freezing, middle o' winter, with snow slush and ice all around us, I'm naked in a bowrie... yet my body tingles all over with such a clean heat... and it feels great." Fiónlaidh grins, "If I'd told you beforehand, you wouldn't have believed me." William is amazed at the sensations rippling through his body, every inch of his skin tingles from the soles of his feet to the top of his head. He also feels immense inner-body warmth, despite the freezing temperature around him. "This doesn't make any feckn sense," exclaims a delighted William, "there's snow on the ground, ice hanging from trees, an army across the plains who'd wish to kill me... yet here I am enjoying myself naked in a bowrie beg with you ma bonnie wee Gallóbhan... with only the light from the moon and stars above, how amazin' and bizarre is this?" They both look to the heavens to see a full moon with a vibrant quicksilver ring, and not a cloud in sight. The twinkling stars do indeed shine brightly for them this night.For a long time, they both gaze at the heavens, oblivious to the freezing air that surrounds them.

As the cold finally sets in to their bodies, they wash off the last of the creamy Cúr na ré, then Fiónlaidh says, "Right Wallace, lets get back inside, we've one more cleansing to do." They clamber out of the bowrie and run as fast as they can for the seomra uisge beag, once inside, they settle down to repeat the ritual of an Glanadh. After lathering his body, Fiónlaidh picks up two small split willow sticks to use them like fat-skinning hide blades and begins to scrape the Cúr na ré away from his skin. Carefully and thoughtfully she scours every inch of his body, removing all the oils away. "Sit up Wallace," commands Fiónlaidh. William sits upright, then very slowly, she pours freezin cold water on top of his head once more, letting it trickle down to wash away the remaining Cúr na Ré. "Oh my feckn Gods Fiónlaidh, the sensations o' the cold water running down ma body... how do you explain this to someone who's never experienced the cleansing?" He looks at his Gallóbhan friend and is struck by her stunning beauty. Seeing his glance, Fiónlaidh giggles and flushes.

Slightly embarrassed, he looks away when he notices Faolán and Graham sitting directly across from him. He watches Graham gently scraping the Cúr na Ré away from Faoláns full breasts... She looks back over at William with a disarming smile, shockingly he feels a pang of jealousy and the need to be cleansing with Faolán... it doesn't make sense, but he can feel the urge. Her smile is so beautiful and the pull to be with her is immense. He shakes his head and lies back down on the matted floor, wondering what on earth happened to his emotions at that moment. He can't help but think about this sudden spark and unexpected connection with Faolán, yet he couldn't go to her, he can't, even though every fibre in his being is telling him she wants him too.

Dispelling the thought, he glances at Fiónlaidh, picks up the willow sticks and begins to ritually cleanse her with the same care she had shown to him earlier, soon, all thoughts of being with Faolán fade away. On completion of the second cleansing, they repeat the bowrie plunge before returning to the area from which they had originally disrobed. Fiónlaidh reaches into a large barrel by the door, grabs handfuls of dried sphagnum moss and bunches them tightly in each of her tiny fists; then she vigorously rubs the moss all over his body.

"Don't just stand there gawping at me Wallace, grab some o' the dry sfaggy and start rubbin' me too, it soaks up the water and creates a heat in your skin to bring out the moss' special healing balm that gets into all the small scratches and cuts about your body, it keeps all the bad blood and skin maladies away." For a moment William stands motionless and in sheer bliss, totally enjoying these amazing sensations. "Get feckn goin' Wallace," says Fiónlaidh "I don't want to freeze here drying you…" Laughing, William grabs two handfuls of moss then frantically they begin to rub each other all over with the moss, laughing at the bizarre and humorous end to the ritual cleansing of the seomra uisge beag.

Satisfied they're both disinfected and thoroughly cleansed. Fiónlaidh pulls a large mantle robe from a nearby stey rack and hands it to William, he feels the material's soft texture as it glides over his skin. Fiónlaidh says, "It's made from beaten nettle fibre and hemp stalk." William examines the texture and the intricate weave of the robe that has obviously been painstakingly woven and perfectly embossed with ancient knotwork patterns, totemic birds and animals from the Galloway Gallghàidheilab culture. Equally impressive is the embroidery colours in vibrant reds, greens and blues that stand out from the pastel background of the robe. The silk-smooth material brushes his skin as he wraps it around his muscular body. William grins with the continuing pleasure, clearly enjoying the rare sensation of such soft warm texture against his skin. "Awe…" says William, "this material is so soft and warm." Fiónlaidh laughs, "Just like your big feckn head then…" Fiónlaidh puts her arms around

William's waist and pulls a card-pleated belt tight and ties it in a slipknot; then she wraps herself in a mantle, clasps him by the hand and leads him through a small adjoining doorway and back into the main obhainn.

For a brief moment everyone resident in the obhainn looks at him, many smile and nod as a welcome then they continue with their chatter and doings. William peers through the dim light while moving through the obhainn, he sees many of the Gallóbhet are sleeping, some talk quietly, others are making love. He can feel the warmth of the peat fires, so comforting and evenly radiant throughout. His attention is drawn to a group sitting quietly singing a Ghaeltacht Ceantrachd puirt-a-beul, a form of mouth music, where nonsensical words and guttural sounds are chosen for their rhythmic qualities and note patterns to create a beautiful vocal form of song, emulating the instrument and the musical movements each individual may play. His thoughts are interrupted when Fiónlaidh points to a thick pile of fine-brushed lambskins on a large crib. She says, "We sleep here…" William smiles when seeing the ermine-like pelts with a large bull-hide cover that's to be their crib.

Dropping her mantle, Fiónlaidh climbs in between the soft fleeces then she quickly pulls them over her head. William takes off his mantle and climbs in beside her. She pops her head out from under the covers, giggles "You sleep on my left side Wallace, I need a draft stopper and you may be all of that to protect me from the chilly fae this eve." Crossing over the top of Fiónlaidh, William lays down beside her. She sits up again, reaches into a nearby bag and removes small pottery phials filled with sweet oils then proceeds to pour a little of the contents into her cupped hand, then she rubs her hands together and begins to smooth the oils all over her body, neck and face. Completing her preening, Fiónlaidh begins to rub the sweet scented oils into William's shoulders then proceeds to massage his entire body, leaving nowhere untouched or unscented. Suddenly, Fiónlaidh laughs. William opens his eyes… his deep contentment and Elysian peace is shattered by the interruption. He enquires, "What's so funny?" Fiónlaidh smiles coyly, reaches down and clasps his manhood. She glances at him with a gorgeous twinkle in her bright eyes.

"Well Wallace, now that I hold him in my hands… I can see that your wee fella is up and fair ready to play, though I should say, the big fella… And if this is meant to be our last night on this earth, we may take pleasure and make love as we please as the goddess would wish it." Fiónlaidh giggles, "And if your wee fella won't, then it's a beautiful sleep and rest we may share in each others arms this night." William laughs, for he is filled with a sense of contentment in natures blessing to be chosen by Fiónlaidh, so happy to accept the judgment of this beautiful Gallóbhan Aicé, be it to sleep in the arms of one so beautiful in heart and soul, or to make love with a shared passion for a moment in time as Anam Álainn.

Soon, Fiónlaidh completes William's cleansing then she dries her hands and wipes the oils from her fingers on his night mantle. Giggling, she quickly dives back under the pelts, pulling the fleeces and top hide over their heads then clings tightly to his warm body, Fiónlaidh affectionately presses her warm body against his as she wraps her leg across his thighs, lays her arm across his stomach and pulls him close. William feels her warm soft breasts push gently against his chest, the cleansing and the heat from her warm svelte-like skin soothes his mind as he pulls her close in comfort. With her head resting on his chest, he senses the sweet, scents she had applied earlier. Closing his eyes, William hears the delightful sounds of the puirt-a-beul music in the background, infusing a deep sense of peace and harmony in his heart. He lay in a blissful peace for a few moments then he pops his head out from below the skins to peer into the shallow darkness of the obhainn. He looks around at all the renowned and feared Gallóbhet warriors; some are fast asleep, while others gently comfort their partners or simply sit and chat quietly.

The stillness and quiet of the obhainn is complemented by the gentle puirt-a-beul harmonies and faint musical sounds of Uliann pipes, clarsachan and psalteries being played outside the obhainn by the wonderfull folk of the Machars Ceàrdannan Gallóbhet. Smiling, William thinks *'This couldn't the same ignorant savages so feared in Scotland and beyond for their brutal and merciless fighting skills... It couldn't be...'* He laughs to himself while savoring these moments in this blissful heaven. With the sweet aroma of smoldering peat and aromatic scents filling the air, he thinks this experience is more akin to a woodland haven from the nurture Fae in one of Wee Maw's legendary fairy tales. He lay back down, tired and happy that some peace has came to him after such a tragic and heartbreaking few days.

As he relaxes, he feels Fiónlaidh's warm breath against his skin... she whispers "Wallace..." William eagerly senses a notion of lustful romance... "Aye Fiónlaidh, what are yie thinkin'?" Fiónlaidh enquires, "Ahm thinkin'... what happened to your face?" William laughs out loud at this unexpected question. "I'll tell you the in morn bonnie Fiónlaidh." She whispers, "Oidhche math spiorad càirdeach." William whispers, "Oidhche math sùilean geala." (Goodnight-bright eyes) Contentedly, He wraps his arms around her, both so very warm and snug below the soft silken weaves fleeces and heavy bull-hide that traps them both in the warmth, as though protected inside the motherly womb of natures Elvin queen. He yawns and closes his heavy tired eyes as both he and Fiónlaidh's souls descend towards a deep sleep, so very much welcomed.

Hazily, William opens his eyes and looks all about his surrounds; he can see it's still dark outside, though a low light glimpses through the obhainn doors, indicating it is near sunrise. He realises he's slept for many long hours and knows he could sleep for many more in such glorious comfort… then he feels a movement from the warm soft naked body of Fiónlaidh as she snugly backs into him. She whispers in a sleepy voice, "Are you awake Wallace?" he replies in a whisper. "I am… Fiónlaidh… I just don't ever want to get up from this wee haven o' luxury." He pulls her close, sensing the delightful sweet scents of the aromatic oils. This comfort and peace he feels with Fiónlaidh he's not felt in a very long time. The two erstwhile companions are so much at peace holding each other close, sheltering and hidden together from a cruel unforgiving world in their warm nest, once again they begin to doze off…

A little while later, he wakes to hear Fiónlaidh giggle: he can feel she is gently pushing back into him, slowly gyrating her hips back and forth. He closes his eyes and whispers, "This is so beautiful…" He embraces Fiónlaidh with a care, thinking of how peaceful and happy he feels to be simply holding her and to feel her naked warmth. Without warning and much to his consternation, he feels the stirring of lust manifest in his loins. It isn't long before it becomes blatantly evident the intense heat between her thighs makes his passion slightly embarrassing for him, and amusing for her…"Sorry about this…" he whispers pathetically, "but the wee fella has a mind of his own." Fiónlaidh giggles and raises her leg slightly that his manhood can rest between her thighs, she gently closes her legs, "There yie go Wallace, your wee fella can rest in peace there awhile… and if he goes back to sleep, so be it."

Fiónlaidh giggles again as she gently pushes back into his groin, then she cradles his manhood with one hand, pressing it against her hot full lips, reaches behind her, grasps his hip and pulls him close. William feels a rush of immense ecstasy as he enters her, the intensity of shared sensations make them both moan with the heightening pleasure, their pulsing hearts beat as one, sending waves of pure bliss through both of them in a shared passion. They lay still for a moment, not moving, just savoring the intensity and sheer excitement flowing through their bodies before the involuntary rhythm of lust begins to carry them along in a passionate embrace...

Suddenly, a feminine voice now familiar to William calls out... "Master Wallace... Master Wallace..." Alasdair, the odd looking little monk, is desperately searching for "Master Wallace..." William moans, "Awe naw, for fucks sake... not now Alasdair, please... not now..." There are shouts and curses from everyone in the Gallóbhet obhainn from those who are disturbed and awakened by the little monk in his noisy thoughtless search for William. Again he cries relentlessly "Master Wallace..." Alasdair peaks his head fully through the Obhainn door as William groans and sits up, he hears Fiónlaidh chuckle under the covers, for they are still fully coupled together. William waves at Alasdair to be quiet, but little Alasdair will not go away without an answer. "Master Wallace... Master Wallace..."

"AYE Alasdair," replies William tersely, "what the fuck do yie want?" Alasdair clasps his hands joyously and calls out "It's at the behest of the Master's Bailey and Coinach. They have sent me on an errand to enquire if you would wish to be joining them for break fasting vittals?"

"What?" enquires William, "It's still feckn dark outside?" Meanwhile, Fiónlaidh has slipped from their passionate coupling and turns her mischievous attention to William's manhood by applying her soft warm mouth and hot tongue with great skill to his Wee fella, much to his consternation while he is trying to have a bizarre dialogue with an odd looking little English monk. William looks around, picks up a small bag at the side of their crib; feels that it's weighty, then throws it at little Alasdair, who deftly avoids the missile. William growls, "Fuck off Alasdair... Can yie no' see that I'm busy?" Alasdair enquires; "Does this mean you do not require any morning vittals master Wallace?" Throwing back the covers, Fiónlaidh glares at Alasdair. She deliberately leaves nothing to the imagination... then she says, "Now do yie understand ya wee religious bastard, now go on, fuck off... or you're next, and ahl fuck yer tiny wee ginger brains out?" Aghast at such a wanton sight of such perverse fornication, Alasdair squeals in a high-pitched voice and runs out of the obhainn in a flux.

William laughs and looks into the beautiful bright eyes of Fiónlaidh, "So me bonnie wee Sùilean geala... you truly are a bahn sídhe then? One look from you and men run away screaming for their God to help them?" Fiónlaidh smiles "Aye, that I might be..." she begins to move sensually once more, pinning him to the soft warm fleece and straddling him in the same movement. She looks into his eyes, then enquires, "Wallace, was that a wee man or an ugly wee woman?" William laughs, "Ahm glad ahm no' the man that will ever have to find that out..." Fiónlaidh gently bites William on his lower lip and pulls the covers back over them, slowly and passionately reclaiming her love union with her spiorad càirdeach. (Spiritual friend) Fiónlaidh groans with pleasure, "Wallace... if yie know what's good for yie... don't you dare stop..."

MacDougal's Opinion

Later that morning, William and Fiónlaidh walk towards the Wallace Obhainn's where Coinach and Bailey sit eating morning vittals. A young man sits with them singing and playing music on a psaltery. "Fiónlaidh…" says William. She reaches up with one hand and presses a finger against his lips, "Wallace, ma bonnie spiorad càirdeach… in gaining you as a good friend and companion, I'm truly grateful, and I'll not be forgetting you. The Goddess has sure blessed us both with love for a moment in time, but me and my Gallóbhan sisters must be returning to the Rhinns and Machars with much haste." William enquires, "Your leaving right now?"

"Aye," replies Fiónlaidh, "I'm away back to my home near Dùn Reicheit. I've two sons there I long to see, and they need their mother." William enquires, "They've no father?" Fiónlaidh replies, "Naw, he's long gone to Tír nan Óg by the hands of the Norman's." Feeling a little saddened hearing this, William looks down at this small petite Gallóbhan wildcat. "Will we ever meet again mo sùilean geala?" Fiónlaidh looks up at him with a mischievous smile, "Wallace, may that which you believe in always take care of you and yours… and your lively wee fella." With a cheeky smile, Fiónlaidh reaches down and gives his wee fella a gentle squeeze. William laughs, for he admires the pluck of Fiónlaidh, but their parting is tinged with a little sadness that he's met someone so compatible, both in physique and sense of nature. Though Fiónlaidh is near half his size, he knows in his mind and heart they are well matched, for Fiónlaidh is a real woman in his eyes… but he also knows they must part and resume different lives. "And you too Fiónlaidh," sighs William "You take care, for I will no' forget you neither, ma bonnie wee warrior woman… my sùilean geala o' the Gallóbhan." Fiónlaidh smiles and joins Eochaidh Gunn who has brought their horses.

As he watches them leave, Fiónlaidh turns and calls back to him "Here Wallace my spiorad càirdeach…" Fiónlaidh throws a little bag over to him. He catches the small bag, recognising it as the one he threw at Alasdair earlier that morning. He opens it up and sees many small stones with Oghamic script engraved upon each stone, he looks up and calls out, "What's this?" Fiónlaidh laughs, "It's a Norman's nut-sack my grandmother cut from him when he tried to visit rapine upon her."

The shock of hearing this information makes William involuntarily throw his hands in the air and drops the bag to the ground. He tentatively picks up the little bag and throws it back over to Fiónlaidh, "I thank you for the intended gift Fiónlaidh… but the memory of meeting you is more than enough to carry me forward with good fortune." Fiónlaidh catches the Norman's nut-sack and smiles disarmingly, then she blows him a kiss, whereby he feigns to catch it and place it against his heart. He notices Fiónlaidh's bright eyes glint one last time. She brushes her long wiry red-blond lion's mane from her face and smiles as she and Eochaidh turn their horses and canter toward the camp of the Gallóbhan. Waving his 'spiorad càirdeach' farewell. William walks over and sits beside his friends where Bailey enquires, "Here Wallace, do you want some fine ale?"

"Naw," Sighs William, "I think I had enough yesterday… Fuck aye, all right then, ah will. Anyways, how are yiez doin'? Did yiez both get a good sleep?"

"Yes actually, I did," replies Bailey, "we had a great night, and by the looks of you, wee Fiónlaidh has put the spring back in your step too." Coinach says, "The wee Fiónlaidh that just left yie Wallace, she's one of the most prolific assassins o' the Gallóbhan." William raises his eyebrows in surprise. Bailey comments with a smile, "She's their number one assassin I believe, that's what Lihd said." William laughs, "Funny that, Fiónlaidh said the same about Lihd, and added that she was also her Ceithernach lover." They all laugh heartily as they sup their heather ale. William says with a grin, "Aye, they're fine bonnie lassies the fightin' Gallóbhan o' the Machars. Coinach quips, "Especially when they leave their lethal weapons at the door." Bailey enquires, "Did you have time to meet any of her kinfolk?" William replies, "Aye, ah did. Fiónlaidh took me round to meet some of the Gallóbhet at their training grounds early this morn, they showed to me their fighting weaponry… fuck, those fellas and lassies sure know how to fight a war." Bailey enquires, "Did you see their famous halberd's or bardiche?"

"Aye," replies William, "though they call them a spartaxe… some of those things have six foot long ash shafts with narrow curved blades about half an arm's length long, feck me, those are lethal. Some have hooks on the back side of the axe for ripping into men and horses to pull them to the ground or just plain gut them, no messin' about with those fella's." Everyone agrees while supping more ale, then Coinach enquires, "Did yie see any o' those Gallóbhan ring spears close-up?" William grins, "I did. Those things are unbelievable, you would have no chance of survival if one of those got into yie." Bailey smirks on seeing the fresh glow in William's demeanor. "It looks as if you have been doing more than just making friends at this supposed battle." William smiles, "Aye Bailey, those wee Gallóbhan sure have a good attitude to the crib as well as the fight, but I do like their fightin spirit and how they organise. It's a bit like us on the hunt, with each Gallóglaigh or Gallóbhan having two youngsters they call a Ceithernach. Their duties are to carry the armour and to be lookin' after their Sparr commanders kit, prepare camp, doing the cooking and fixin' things that needs fixin' Apparently in battle, the Ceithernach carry at least three ring spears while another Ceithernach uses long-darts dipped in shit…"

"Aye, they have shields made from tree bark too." says Bailey "I've never seen that before, I tried sending an arrow through one and it just bounced off, same with a sword strike…" Drinking more ale, Bailey enquires, "Are you thinking of joining the Gallóglaigh?" William thinks a moment, then he replies, "D'yie know Bailey, that might no' be such a bad idea, me you and Coinach could form our own Sparr, ma uncles Davey and Joanie are Gallóglaigh from the Rhinns and Machars… we could ask them about it the next time we meet." Bailey enquires, "Did you say, a Sparr?" William exclaims, "Fuck Bailey, Were you no' feckn listening to Fiónlaidh yesterday?" Bailey sighs, "No, not really, I was too busy watching Lihd's bum… She's gorgeous boyo."

William laughs at Baileys honest reply, then he continues "Anyways, the Galloway Gallóbhet normally fight at the front o' the King, the lead Sparr hammers the enemy with long-darts and arrows, with all their blades and tips dipped in black blood or shit before they fight, a bit like how we stood with Faolán yesterday when Fiónlaidh pissed on the arrow-heads, they do the same with the ring-spears or javelins too. What a mess o' yer life those fuckin' things

24

could do to a fella…" The young man sitting beside Coinach playing his psaltery, laughs "That has the making of a fine ballad." Coinach offers an introduction, "Wallace, this fella here is Alain o' Annandale, he's a minstrel. He came up here to make lyrics about the battle, though I don't think there'll be much to be singing about this day… the battle that never was maybe?" William shakes Alain's hand. "I've been hearing your music all morning Alain o' Annandale, it sure did sooth the beast o' these plains I reckon."

"It's good to meet you too Wallace," replies Alain "Most people call me Alain a'Dale… Its easier to remember me by." William says "I reckon the chords you graced us with this morn were much better than the screams o' death that may have been our choral song this day. Alain smiles, "Aye, ah prefer it so myself. I'd rather sing about the love and beauty of a good woman." William grins, "Ah couldn't agree more."

The hustle and bustle of both armies breaking down their camps is nearing completion when Alain Wallace and a group of knights approach. "William, a moment with yie. I'd like to introduce you to some auld friends o' mine, this fella here is Alexander Scrymgeour, the Constable o' Dundee and this is Robyn Hodde MacGilchrist, Lord of Loch Sloy, nephew to the Earl of Lennox." Shaking hands upon introduction, William thinks it seems like only yesterday he was home in the peaceful solitude of hunting the Wolf and wildcat forest with his father. Now he reflects on the terrible sights of inhumanity he has witnessed, the massacres, how he has looked into the tortured twisted faces of men, women and children, all senselessly murdered and mutilated in the most barbaric of practise, and for no purpose nor reason that he will ever understand. Now he's meeting people of importance who offer him respect by the merit of his name, but he's beginning to feel extremely disturbed in his thoughts.

Alain says "William, Bishop Wishart wants you and the other scout Ceannard to join us in his pavilion soon, you're to report directly to him and convey all that you've seen, but first we must go to the main gathering for God's blessing."'God's blessing' thinks William. 'Where the fuck was God when the families of the Marchal and Torquill needed him.' William speaks to his father, "Dá, what I've seen at the Corserine and Dunveoch has left me cold… yet when I tell you of these things, I fear that you're not understanding why I'm not crying like a wain or running home to hide below ma crib. Dá, I need an answer as to why I feel so detached in my heart."

Looking at William sympathetically, Alain replies "Your feelings son, I can only say it's as nature requires it to be for your very survival. It's right you should have conflicted feelings in a time of great upheaval such as this, but you will surely lose your wit by too much thinking. Now tell to me Scrymgeour and MacGilchrist here what you may reveal to the Guardians, for talking it out and sharing your witness gives men the mettle to suffer more easy all evil things that happen." William relays everything he had seen at the Corserine sheilin.' Hearing the detail of the massacre clearly disturbs the three elders, Alain utters, "I thought Marchal had maybe took his kinfolk glen Afton for safety…" William replies, "Naw, Coinach and wee Affric are the only two that survived, and poor Affric… she's in a bad way Dá, ah don't know yet if she'll live through her injuries they are so bad."

"Is she here?" queries Alain, "Naw," replies William, "she's back up at Glen Afton being nursed by Mharaidh, Auld Jean and Katriona. We took Affric back there first then made our way here as fast as we could, that's the reason why we were so late getting back." Alain walks over to Coinach sitting nearby and looks directly into his eyes, "We'll find who did this Coinach, and we will make them pay dearly."

"I'll find them," states Coinach tersely, "no matter who's with me." William speaks, "We found auld Torquill Fletcher and his sons bodies too Dá. They had been hung by the neck and shot full o' their own arrows, we found them at the Dalqhaut flow a few miles behind the Pact camp. Then we met with the massacre o' his folks in their sheilin' up at Dunveoch, it was the same terrible butchery there as befell Marchal's clan. Dá, we need to go back to Dunveoch and cremate the bodies, for we had to leave them out in the open where we found them." Alain exclaims, "Fuck... all of Fletchers people gone too?" MacGilchrist says "We must to tell the Guardians of this Alain, they'll know what to do... for we cannot have bands of young Ceitherne scattering abroad to be seeking the Blood tax, not now, especially as we have a brokered peace with the Pact." The meeting is interrupted by a heralds call, "To Council... The Guardians require your presence my Lords." Alain says, "Walk with me boys."

As they make their way over to Wishart's pavilion, Alain continues, "William, we know there were bands of English mercenaries roaming Galloway and slaying all who would resist the Pact, but de Brix denies they are anything other than Gallóbhet bandits from Galloway that are the cause of this wanton carnage. Such is the vigour of the commissioner's perpetrating this evil by leaving none alive, it's ill upon us to prove otherwise." William enquires, "Who commits such terrible atrocities Dá? Does anyone know?" Alain shakes his head, "We only know there are mercenaries from border marches in England who vantage here in the disarray. Hardy caught a band of English cutthroat's, but Faoláns Gallóbhet tore them to pieces before anyone could find out who their masters were, or who sent them." Coinach rages, "I don't give a fuck who they are, I'll find them... by my life I'll find them, with or without any bastards help, Bishop or no fuckin' Bishop." Alain glares at Coinach with steely cold eyes and is about to say something, when William speaks, "Dá, It was Coinach's whole family that these bastards visited with their murdering trade... and ah tell yie, such brutality I've never before witnessed or could ever have imagined, even upon the slaughter of the animals, I tell yie this too Dá, I'm wie Coinach... for I too cannot go back to peace knowing that these foul murderers are still out there."

Alain knows in his heart, that he would say and do as William if such tragedy had been visited upon his own people, but he has to quell Coinach's rage first, so much more than his personal tragedy depends on this peace treaty meeting with success. "My condolences and my own feelings of great sadness may be of little comfort to you now Coinach, but my hand and my sword is yours should you need them in pursuit and apprehension of the perpetrators of these evil Deeds." Coinach drops his head and looks away as tears of grief and emotion fill his eyes... Alain puts his hand out, "Coinach... your mother and father were as close as family to me in my hour of need. I could do no less for you."

Accepting Alain's hand, Coinach says, "I can't waste any more fuckin' time here though Alain, I now know my life's mission, and that is to save others from the pain that now eats and tears away at my heart and soul... and that is to kill de Percy." Alain looks on sympathetically, "We cannot know yet for sure who is behind this evil Coinach, come with us and we will speak with the Guardians, tell to them first hand what you know and what you've seen. If the Pact can be proven to be behind this base treachery, then we must surely bring to justice the murderers of your father and your Clan." To calm Coinach down, his kinsman Sean Ceàrr walks away with him towards the pavilion. Alain, William, Bailey, MacGilchrist and Scrymgeour look at each other, each privately trying to understand Coinach's feelings should the same nightmare reality of his world be placed upon them. Scrymgeour, a powerful and respected chief says, "A bad business Alain, but I fear this day is not the end of the matter, it's but only the beginning." Alain replies, "We should heed the Guardians words and enforce what they decree. We'd better go to them for they'll be getting impatient." They all walk toward Wishart's pavilion in deep discussion when Young Andrew de Moray exits the pavilion with one of his men to greet them. William is surprised to see the size and physique of the man beside Moray.

"Madhainn mhath Moray." says William. "Mornin'" replies Moray, "Wallace, this my kinsman Iain Beag a' Moireach… or Little John as the English call him, he's master hunter and lead scout to Robyn Hodde MacGilchrist. He's also my fathers head tacksman for Strathearn and Avoch." Iain Beg is an extremely powerful looking giant of a man, with his long brown hair tied back in the way of the forest hunters. He's dressed in full dark woodland green léine, haubergeon and brat. On his back he carries a great longbow and hanging bare on his back, is a beautiful and most ornate pleat-forged Claymore. While Iain Beag and William make conversation. It's noticed by many onlookers that both these two young men of obvious prowess, are equal in height, muscular and athletic stature… fighting giants by any other words.

"For fucks sake Moray…" whispers Bailey, "Would you look at the size o' those two, they're like brothers who've been overfed oats since birth, could you imagine those fella's wanting your porridge and you sayin' no?" Moray scrutinises William and Iain Beag. "You're right there Bailey, I think we've just brought the giants o' Fianna Legend together, those two are the embodiment of Finn McCuil and Ben an' Donner." The impromptu meeting is disturbed when they hear Scrymgeour call out, "You youngblood... over here, quickly. The Guardians are waiting for all the Ceannard scouts to come in to the pavilion." The group quickly make their way towards Wishart's pavilion, Bailey talking with Moray. William and Iain Beg, the two erstwhile giants, are in deep discussion, followed by a surly Coinach and Sean Ceàrr. Upon entering the pavilion, the Ceannard are ushered to the sidewalls, where William looks around at all the gathered magnates lords and knights.

A young chieftain standing beside William; speaks to him quietly, "I don't think they'll be taking our witness this day." William looks at him and enquires, "And why no'?" The young chieftain replies, "These fuckin' nobles care little for the lives o' the Sillers, Crofters and simples o' Galloway and more about their own fat lardy fuckin' arses remainin' in a life o' fuckin' luxury." William smiles as he examines the wiry looking man. Experience of battle is obviously no stranger to this young chieftain. William also notices this chieftain's dress is an unusually dark maroon léine and brown leather battle-jack, with armoured sleeves and iron vambrace. His long brown hair is plaited and flowing into the hood of his wolf-skin mantle. It appears to William this man is likely a Galloway or Gallóglaigh chieftain. He also notices an Anam Crios hanging by the chieftain's side when the strange chieftain makes introduction, "Sibhdaidh (shiffday) MacDougal from Morrison mòr's Birlinn fleet o' Jura and Dounarwyse... at yer fuckin' service."

The likeable warrior grins, "Chieftain of the Blackfoot Gallóglaigh, great-grandson of Fergus the high chief o' Galloway, bastard son o' Ragnhild Dubhgall o' the isles." Breaking into a grin, William shakes the hand of the likeable MacDougal. "William Wallace, son of Alain Wallace the kings hunter o' the Wolf and wildcats."

"Pleased to meet yie Wallace. Some fuckin' mess this, eh?" MacDougal lifts a horn full of whisky to his bearded lips and takes a long satisfying drink of the contents. William enquires, "Do you know what's going on? For I don't, and not one person I've met can explain to me anything I fully understand?" MacDougal replies, "For fuck's sake Wallace, it's easy enough... One Norman fuck is challenging another Norman fuck for the throne o' Scotland, and all because they both claim descent from Kings Malcolm and auld Fergus. But their main claims is as the two great-grandsons of David the Earl of Huntingdon. Dyie see John Balliol over there, he's the grandson of David's daughter Margaret. Robert de Brus... he's the grandson of Isabel, Margaret's younger sister. There, now yie know all yie need tae know about this fuckin' guddle." Grinning at this succinct and concise reply from MacDougal, William enquires, "So why do they pick such a remote land as Galloway to fight their battles?"

"Ah'll tell yie then Wallace, it's because the two Norman fucks responsible for all o' this shite are the lords o' Galloway and Annandale respectively." MacDougal groans, "Those two Norman bastards gained their lands by dowry to steal a foothold in Scotland. They did it by marrying ther' arses into the old blood o' the Cruathnie kings female lineage, all just a fuckin' sham for gain. Aye Wallace... fine women wasted they all are, born from the loins o' Fergus of Galloway and his feck'd up warring sons Gillie Brighde and Uchtred, but that's typical Galloway brains in action for yie..."

"What do yie mean?" enquires William. MacDougal replies, "When the Norman's first came here, they married their sons into the offspring o' the chiefs o' Galloway, Carrick and the Annandale to gain land for their feckn heirs." MacDougal points across the pavilion, "See that cunt Baliol over there; his fathers marriage was to Devorguilla MacDowall, royal heiress and successor to Uchtred mac au Fergusa, that's how that Norman prick became Lord of Galloway."

MacDougal takes another sip from the deer horn cup then passes it to William, "Across the plain over there sitting on his skinny fuckin' arse like an old dried up spinster is Rober' de Brix. His son Robert Brus' wife is Marthoc, the Countess of Carrick, she's also an heiress and successor to Gilla Brìghde mac au Fergusa, that's how that Norman prick became Lord of Carrick… fuck, he's so fuckin' soft in the head, Marthoc had him thrown into her dungeons Until he promised to marry her, now he wants to rule the fuckin' realm, ah don't fuckin' think so… the pair o' useless Norman bastard halfwit cunts."

"What?" Exclaims William. MacDougal continues, "Uchtred and Gilla Brighidh were the sons o' auld King Fergus, so this land belongs to us his offspring, no' those Norman bastards." William enquires, "So is it Baliol you favour?" MacDougal replies, "Ah'v no' made ma mind up, yet…" William appears puzzled, "Why no'?" MacDougal spits on the ground, "Because I'm related to both of those Norman bastards through ma great-grandfather king Fergus, his foundling bastard son was ma fathers father, a right mean bastard." William tries hard not to laugh, "You've Norman blood runnin' through yie then?" MacDougal replies indignantly, "Naw, fuck off Wallace, the blood went out the way, no' in. Likely the same as your friends Douglas and Graham… and most o' the fuckin' nobility o' Scotland I wager." William says, "An Irish friend o' mine once told me that if we're ever without King, then the Norman's would fight like starving wolves to gain power here, and all of us native Scots would be the sorry meat of their famishin' play."

"A wise man…" replies MacDougal, "if Brix and Balliol do fight out their difference in Galloway, the winner will acquire the mass levies of the defeated challenger from England and Ireland then bring them in to reinforce their claim, and whoever gains the pledge of the fighting Gallóbhet… that would surely be the end of it for Scotland." Puzzled, William enquires, "But what about the maid of Norway?" MacDougal laughs, "Ach for fucks sake Wallace, do you really believe that wee soul will ever be allowed to make it to Scotland alive? She'll never set her wee Norwegian arse on the throne of Scotland? Where have you been hidin' ma sad wee simple country boy?"

William is stunned at what he is hearing from MacDougal; but it reinforces what Andrew Moray had told him in confidence the night before. William's reaction is noticed immediately by MacDougal, he says, "Ach don't be minding me Wallace, It's this fine Jura craitur that's doin' the talking, just think o' me as a mouthy Gallóglaigh Bastard, but most definitely no' a theivin' Norman fuck… or me and you will be havin' words." William is curious, "An auld fella told me the fleet of Morrison mòr and the MacDougal's drove the Norse out of Scottish waters at the battle of Largs, was that your folks that day?"

"Aye it was us," replies MacDougal, "Fuckin' Norse warriors can kiss ma arse." William laughs, he likes this wild cursing isleman. Before he could say anything more, the heralds blow their clarion call to order. The Guardians, Bishop Wishart, David, chief of the Grahams, Lord Comyn of Badenoch, the Black Douglas and Duncan the earl of Fife, enter the pavilion and take their seats at the head of an enormous table beside the most imminent magnates lords and knights of Scotland. "Call to order…" barks the speaker of the council. William whispers "Good to be meeting you MacDougal," MacDougal replies, "Aye, you too Wallace." The noisy assembly is brought to order as Bishop Wishart prepares to speak.

All in attendance focus their attention on the renowned
Bishop of Glasgow, a friend to both de Brix and Lord Baliol,
trusted implicitly by the Guardians and many leaders of
the Pact as the voice of reason. All present will hang on
every word Wishart will utter, for they know him to be of
impeccable integrity, a man of his word and man of honour.
Standing proud, Wishart delivers the treaty in detail…

*"The Pact, under the leadership of Rober' de Brix, Lord
of Annandale and Robert Brus Earl of Carrick, have agreed
to withdraw their forces from Galloway and from the shire
of Dun Fries. Henceforth, they will retire to their respective
borderlands in the Annan Dale and those other territories
belonging to the Earl of Carrick. Lord Brix will return
to Whittle in Essex. My Lord Graham, commanding the
Guardian army of the borders will escort lord de Brix and
his English allies to his boundaries in Annan dale and my
Lord Moray will escort Robert Brus Earl of Carrick and sir
Richard De Burgh the earl of Ulster with his Irish allies to the
Turnberry castle boundaries in the west. Lord Comyn and
Sir Alain Wallace of Glen Afton will escort de Longueville,
the Capetians and Corsairs back to Baile na h-Uige that they
may return to France. Lord Douglas will escort lords John
and Edward Baliol to the English border where they shall
then retire to castle Barnard in Yorkshire. All are agreed to
settle this dispute by future negotiation under oath. I am
heartily pleased to be telling you all that no blood will be
shed this day on Scottish soil. There will be no contest of arms
for the throne of Scotland. All Royal debate and contentions
shall be decided by impartial arbitration, Scots law and God's
will. All are foresworn on oath before God this day to raise no
arms except in defense of life and liberty…"*

A great sigh of approval raises in the air as Wishart
continues, "Fellow countrymen… the pestilent disaster of

civil war has been averted this day, we should take heed of how perilously close it was that war had came to us. Much delicacy must be yet be employed by every one gathered here and by those who serve you faithfully, for any single spark may still set this realm alight, from which we may never recover. I do thank you all for your devotion to your duty. Your presence here alone is testament to your courage and fastidious honour my lords. We shall now pray..."

"Fuckin' load o' shite," whispers MacDougal, William tries not to laugh at MacDougal's thoughtful outburst during the solemn prayer. McDougal continues, "In my opinion, this scunner of a rankle should be settled right here right now Wallace. I'll tell yie this... a bitter winter battle will seem but an itch no' worth fuckin' scratchin' compared to what's gathering in the black hearts of de Brix and his treasonous fuckin' Pact." William Looks at MacDougal and whispers, "What dyie mean?" MacDougal continues, "I don't trust that chicken shit Wishart... he plays fast and loose for his own gain." William exclaims, "What the fuck are yie talking about MacDougal?" Surprise at MacDougal's comments distracts William during the solemn prayer, he senses silence... then he sees his father glaring at him. The council concludes their prayers then begin their detailed deliberations. They continue awhile before Wishart lays down his religious Crosier beside the crucifix major at the Alter of Christ. Wishart turns toward the leaders of the Guardian army, who bow their heads acknowledging Wishart, the master political genius of Scotland.

Bishop Wishart kneels before the crucifix, kisses the body of Jesus, then raises his hands... "My children, we must bow our heads and say prayer to our Lord God and give thanks for his blessed deliverance... let us pray." A silence falls once more in the Pavilion, other than the monologue of prayer delivered by Bishop Wishart, praising almighty God in Latin, but William is praying that MacDougal doesn't say anything else that will make him laugh and get him into trouble with his father, or worse. "Fuckin' religious bastards." whispers MacDougal as he lowers his head discreetly to drink more whisky from his horn during the blessed prayer. "If there's anything worse than a treacherous fuckin' enemy... it's a man o' fuckin' God wanting to fight by yer fuckin' side." With his head still bowed William looks at MacDougal and sniggers, he wants to laugh at this curious form of Godly respect shown by the wild looking Gallóglaigh from Jura. "This is all shite…" says MacDougal "When this is over, ahm getting' tae fuck right out o' here, ahm jumpin' on ma fuckin' horse, then jumpin' on ma fuckin' boat and ahm getting tae fuck back tae Jura." William can hardly contain himself. "Yie seem to curse a lot during the lords prayer MacDougal."

"Ach, fuck their God…" exclaims MacDougal "These religious bastards would make a deaf dumb blind bastard see reason and fuckin' swear at their own fuckin' Maw's for what's bein' said and done here this day…" William laughs out loud just as the prayer ends and everyone cheers; thankful to God that war has been averted.

"I meant to ask yie Wallace," queries MacDougal "What the fuck happened to your face?" Before William can answer, they're all ushered outside the pavilion where they meet up with Bailey, Graham, Moray, Iain Beg and many of the other young Ceannard and Chieftains. The youngblood Ceannard congregate and urgently discuss amongst themselves as to why they have not been called to give witness about the massacres. Alain and Scrymgeour walk over to William. Alain says, "You must leave for home now William. I want you to go back to Glen Afton with the good news, but be sure to keep everyone on a war footing, it's vitally important that you do as I bid, nothing more, for this situation may not be over yet." A confused William enquires "Dá what's going on? I thought we were to report to Wishart about the detail of what we've seen? Listening to the other scouts here, it would appear that there has been the murder of many hundreds in the remote and border lands of Galloway." Alain replies curtly, "Wishart and the Guardians will hear all of your accounts in good time, but not now, not this day, for there are much bigger issues at stake. Any small matter that could ignite us to war cannot be tolerated." Reacting in anger at his fathers words, William states, "The Ceannard are in severe dispute and need answers Dá, many of them had their kinfolk massacred and say it would not have happened had they stayed at home and not came to fight a battle that didn't concern them." William and Bailey look at Alain who appears somewhat shame-faced. Scrymgeour replies, "It's out of our hands young Wallace."

"What?" exclaims William "The Guardians won't hear our witness?" William is Inflamed with a passionate anger, as are many of the youngblood Ceannard, he stands boldly in front of his father, defiantly looking at him eye to eye. "Dá, you had better tell to me why the Guardians think every man, woman, brother, sister, or wains we saw torn to pieces by dogs or those murdered with such despicable brutality or the dead eyes that stared at us seeking justice and revenge... you tell us here that those bastards in the pavilion think it's a small fuckin' matter?" Alain stammers, "William I..." Feeling the ugliness of disgust seethe through his body and mind, William does not wait for his fathers reply as he continues in a rage, "For me and those here, you tell to us that what we witnessed is no more than a small fuckin' matter, Dá you fu…." — "WALLACE…" Commands Scrymgeour brusquely, "hold your tongue still, and be showin' respect to yer father. Though your cause me be just, our hands are tied, you must be accepting the treaty… it's over now." The nearby Ceannard immediately rally round William, thrusting their swords in the air, demanding that they be heard.

Sensing his own anger rising, Alain realises this fragile moment could be one of the sparks that may yet set Scotland aflame, and knowing William and the other Ceannard youngblood are also hot-blooded and reckless, they do deserve an answer. Alain holds his hands in the air to bring attention from all… "Ceannard… we all feel as you do, believe me we do, but this day we have stopped more wives from mourning their husbands, sons and brothers. Had battle been enacted this day, then total war would have followed on the morrow." Scrymgeour speaks "Young Wallace, do not force shame upon your father in your ignorance of youth. You and all of the Ceannard gathered here must trust in the judgment of the Guardians, their decisions are for the greater good of the community." Alain's temperament calms, "Son It's best you get back to Glen Afton now… And take Coinach with you. If by the will of the Aicé, Affric is mending her wounds, and we pray that she is, when she awakes to no family, it may be the worse for her. Coinach should be with her and not be leaving his duty of kinship and care to others." Alain glances at Scrymgeour and MacGilchrist who nod back in approval, confirming Alain's order is for the best, and to get Coinach away to safety beyond any disturbance he may cause during these fragile hours of the new treaty.

Still enflamed and defiant, William searches his fathers face for an answer. "Why do you appear before me Dá as though you are evasive and shamed… why is it the youngblood Ceannard are made to feel we're being sent from this place chastised?" Alain glares at William "I can only tell you that Wishart and the Guardians know and what they must do to save the whole of Scotland from a similar fate to what you have witnessed. You must trust me William, I too do not believe these acts should go unpunished, but for now we must bide our time and retire back home."

"I'm not going fuckin' back," Shouts Coinach "I have no home now… I'll hunt down De Percy and I don't give a fuck what Wishart doesn't want to hear." Alain grabs Coinach firmly by the shoulder, "Your sister needs you Coinach, you'll never find the perpetrators now, all routes are nigh impassable; the snow is deep and more winter storms fast approach." Suddenly Coinach pushes Alain full in the chest. Alain immediately grabs him tightly as Coinach begins to struggle violently, shouting and cursing at the top of his voice about De Percy, Wishart and the Guardians. Coinach breaks loose and begins walking towards the Bishops pavilion ranting…"I'll demand from this Bishop fuckin' Wishart to say to my face that the blood of my family is of little or no account."

"GRAB HIM…" shouts Alain. Bailey and MacDougal grab Coinach from behind. As Bailey puts his arm around Coinach's throat, Sean Ceàrr joins the melee, as he is blood to Coinach. An argumentative affray soon develops with the ruckus growing louder and overheard by the men from Alain's Wolf and wildcat Gallóglaigh. Many of the other hunter scout Chieftains venture over to find out what the commotion is all about, soon they too become involved, tempers flare and everyone becomes embroiled in a fracas. Coinach's remonstrations attract attention from a squadron of passing cavalry. Squire Marmaduke De Percy leads his horsemen past the melee. He exclaims, "Bloody Scotch vermin… They fight like wild animals at the drop of a coin clipping. We show them a tad leniency and they squabble amongst themselves like scurvy rats fighting over a morsel of cheese, what say you Thorpe?" Thorpe replies "Not my business to think my lord. Perhaps we should wait till next spring and let them do our job for us my lord." De Percy glares at Thorpe, "Did I say you could speak?" Thorpe replies, "No my lord." De Percy continues, "Anyhoo's where would the sport be if we left the filthy Scotch to their own devices."

Passing by the quarrelling Scots without incident, De Percy and his troop ride on towards the Pavilions of Robert de Brix. Meanwhile, Bailey grips the fighting Coinach securely and holds him fast with his forearm pressed across his throat, William shouts in Coinach's face... "For Fucks sake Coinach... we understand your anger, but you must stop fightin' us or you'll make it impossible for us to stand by you... don't you understand for fucks sake?" But Coinach doesn't hear a word William has said, or he simply ignores him as he flies into a wild rage, kicking backwards into Bailey and MacDougal, flaying his arms punching and kicking any who comes near him. Bailey and MacDougal grab a hold of Coinach, but they all slip and fall in the thick sloppy mud. William, Sean Ceàrr, Iain Beg and others reach out to catch them when Coinach elbows William with sickening force in the face, instantly the searing pain shoots like a hot knife going through his brain, William immediately falls to the ground in a squat holding a hand over his eyes with blood pouring profusely from his nose. The searing pain relents for just one fleeting second, he immediately springs up, grabs Coinach with both hands, rips him away from Bailey and MacDougal's grasp then he carries the flailing Coinach a few feet away and slams him hard against a wagon while driving his forearm up into his throat...

"COINACH..." screams an exasperated William, "your emotions will be the fuckin' death or injury o' all who stand with you, and that's not what any of us want." The glazed eyes of Coinach seem to react to William's rage. With the two almost nose-to-nose, William can see momentarily that a hint of sanity is returning to the eyes of his crazed friend. Coinach struggles to speak but he can't because of the pressure on his throat. William cautiously releases his steadfast grip. Coinach splutters then raises a hand slowly and points. "What happened to your nose…?" With blood pouring from his nose, William shakes his head in disbelief, he looks into Coinach's eyes, searching for something, anything that will allow him to belt Coinach so feckn hard… just the once… but all William could see is a curious innocence in Coinach's tear stained muddy face. He mutters as he lowers Coinach to the ground. "I don't fuckin' believe this… that's fuckin' twice now." William turns and looks around the gathered Ceannard, then issues commands, "Sean Ceàrr, help us to calm this mad feckr down. If need be, tie him up and throw him in the back of your wagon… and make sure he can't fuckin' escape. Bailey… get the horses ready, we leave for Glen Afton… NOW."

"But…" remonstrates Coinach, "Enough Coinach, I'm fuckin' warnin' yie…" commands William with thunder in his voice. "Secure him in your wagon Sean, sit on him if you must, for he's too bloody volatile to take anywhere but back to Glen Afton. Do it now…" Grabbing Coinach securely and holding him close, Sean enquires, "Where are you goin' Wallace?" William replies, "I'm going back up to Luskie just north of Dunveoch with Bailey and some of the hunters to pyre the remains of old Torquill and his sons, we'll catch up with you just north of the Silver Flowe." William pauses then he looks around at the watching waiting Chieftains, Ceannards and scouts. He commands, "And the rest of you, get back to your fuckin' colours… it's all over with here." Moray, MacDougall, Douglas and Bailey walk over to William where they keep their own council and deliberations while William holds his bloody nose and listens intently. Scrymgeour and MacGilchrist stand quietly nearby, watching the melee with Alain when Lord Hardy Douglas approaches, he says, "I think we have a born leader in your boy there Wallace. He soon nipped that stramash in the bud." Alain smiles then he talks with Hardy, MacGilchrist and Scrymgeour awhile till Hardy and MacGilchrist leave to assemble their own personal household and men at arms for departure with the men of Avoch and loch Sloy.

Alain and Scrymgeour walk over to William who's still trying to stem the flow of blood from his nose by sticking some dry sphagnum moss up each nostril. Scrymgeour says, "Well, you sorted that trouble out quick young Wallace me boy." William glares at Scrymgeour and his father, but he doesn't reply. Alain puts his hand on William's forehead, pushes his head back, then he examines his face, "Ach you'll be fine son... Just get auld Tam to reset your nose when you get back home."

"Are you no' coming with us Dá?" Alain shakes his head, "Naw, the last of the camps will not break till the morn. Scrymgeour and I must travel to Baile na h-Uige with Hardy, we're escorting the Capetians to the boats, then we have a couple of other errands to do for the Guardians before we can return home. I'll scribe you a letter for Mharaidh to take home with you." William, Alain and Scrymgeour talk awhile longer till Bailey, Sean and Coinach bring the horses and wagons forward that will be returning the youngblood to the Black Craig and their homes in Glen Afton.

*   *   *

The men of the Pact are equally thankful as the Guardian army that a bitter civil war battle has been averted. De Brix has used all his political guile to make his Pact confederates and retainers believe a strategic victory has been won, but he knows nothing could be farther from the truth regarding his ambition. De Brix feels bitterly betrayed by Edward Longshanks, someone will pay dearly for the personal shame he feels this day. Before he orders the breaking of his camp, de Brix calls all Pact associates commanders and supporters to his pavilion. He addresses all gathered before him, talking of how he will quickly return to arms if the treaty is broken, but to spare his men to fight in such harsh Scottish winter conditions, it is his decision alone that influenced the Guardians and Baliol to retreat. De Brix tells of how he will escort Comyn back to the border and his son the Earl of Carrick would make sure that the French Capetians return to their base in the southern seaport of Baile na H-Uige.

After he dispatches his captains, de Brix speaks with his close group of Allies and his son Robert. "I plan to winter in my castle near Northampton and our Chelmsford family estates of Uttlesford Hatfield in broad oak Essex. When we leave this place, we shall all initially rest first in my Annan dale fortalice a few days, you Gloucester's shall be under my roof and protection. I have spoken to sir Richard De Burgh of Ulster, he will be taking my grandson young Robert to Ireland for safety should any foul assassin think to strike at my family. All of my grandsons will be dispersed amongst family and friends throughout the five Kingdoms, and when the Crown of Scotland rightfully comes to the Family of Brus, all enmity will end by fealty or by the sword, I don't really have a care which."

Riders are heard arriving outside of the Brix pavilion, "It's Marmaduke de Percy..." exclaims Robert of Carrick. De Percy dismounts and enters the Pavilion as Brix orders his allies to strike camp while he and the Earl of Carrick bid De Percy welcome. De Brix enquires, "Good to see you young Percy, how fair you with the extermination of our woodland vermin?" De Percy replies, "I am flushed with success sir Robert, there are very few Tinklers and Gallóglaigh left within twenty miles your Carrick and Annan dale borders. Some of them have fled into deepest Galloway to the heart of the Wolf and wildcat forest or east to Comyn and Graham lands, but most, which must number several hundreds that once preyed upon your borders my lord, they are now swinging like yuletide ice picks from the trees they so dearly loved, and I must say, they do provide fine fare for the beast so foul that now swell their stomachs on the scavenge gorge."

"Well done young Percy, I am pleased to hear this news indeed," says de Brix "My good friend de Courtney was right to recommend you for the more eh, how shall I say… delicate tasks required that politic cannot be seen to condone. The extermination of base heathens and their brood are no worth of notice to any civilized Christian man, nor will the blessed church be offended by your cleansing the land of their infectious and parasitic blasphemous hides." De Percy smiles, "Why thank you my Lord, I trust you will mention this to our King when next you meet?" De Brix replies, "But of course my young friend. Now, will you be joining us on our ride to the English territory of the Border marches? We won't break camp till the morn, after which, I feel the need to be on my estates in Northampton to be closer to my liege King Edward. I shall return to Carlisle Castle as paladin warden of the marches by end of winter, perhaps I may have some more use for your skills…"

"I am honored by your goodwill Lord Brix," replies De Percy "By your leave, I have one more nest of vermin to seek out not far from here, then I will attend your kind offer of escort." de Brix says, "Then it is settled…", "you must join us in the Annan dale no more than seven days from now, for then we leave on the eighth day for England. Will that be enough time for your fastidious attention to your mission?"

"It most certainly will." replies De Percy. De Brix waves his hand, "Then please be leaving us now Percy, I have much to do here before breaking the camp. I want you to see my taxman and he will furnish you with an extra Yule bonus for you and your men, then take what you require for nourishment and supplies."

"Why sir Robert, you are too kind by far," says De Percy "I shall see you soon then my Lord, for I must bid you a good day sir and you too good Earl of Carrick." De Percy turns and leaves the pavilion. When it's certain Marmaduke De Percy has left the vicinity of the pavilion, Robert of Carrick speaks "He's a despicable coward of a man father, how can you countenance his personage? I would dispatch him damn quick rather than stoop to use his kind of service." De Brix suddenly backhands his son with such force across the face; it knocks the Earl to the ground. He spits his words out in anger, "Do not use such base words with me boy, with your petty air of indignant honor compromised."

Stepping over the prostate body of his son who is wiping the blood from his lips, de Brix snaps, "Honour is simply for the pacification of women, children and feeble minded clerics. You will learn soon enough that all you have in life is power to wield or waste your life in base servitude… Power in Scotland belongs to me boy, learn this well or you will never hold what I and your forbears have ever gained." Robert of Carrick stammers, "I… I'm sorry father," as he wipes the blood from the corner of his mouth. "Get off your knees and follow me you pathetic fool, we have much to do in this infernal place before nightfall."

De Brix storms out of the pavilion, followed meekly by Robert, the earl of Carrick. He stops and looks back to the far corner of the pavilion, there he sees young eyes staring at him, it's his son, young Robert Bruce. The gentle Earl drops his eyes in heart felt shame, then he turns to follow his father. As they walk through the Pact camp, the earl of Carrick enquires, "When do we leave the field of Dalry father?" De Brix looks at his son, "After I have spoken privately with Bishop Wishart."

Fíonn's Fèis

The journey towards Glen Afton for Sean Ceàrr and Coinach is a somber one. It's not till the second day on the road that Bailey and William eventually catch up with them at their Silver Flowe camp. As they sit round a late evening campfire, they discuss all the recent events, it's there that Sean Ceàrr is made fully aware of what befell his kinfolk at the Corserine Gap, and who may be responsible. "Fuck…" exclaims Sean "I saw that bastard pass by when we were trying to calm Coinach, if it's the same De Percy Affric named, then that's the one I saw." William exclaims, "That scrawny wee fucker on the bay horse with the half-bull man's servant? I could have reached out and pulled him off his horse there and then. At least we know now what that particular de Percy looks like, and come end of winter we can hunt him down, even if we have to cross the border marches into England to find him."

"I don't know," ponders Bailey, "we must get this information from Affric to be certain of who she meant and exactly why she called out this name. I've seen too many innocents murdered in a rage or for vengeance because of something someone said, then later it turned out to be mistaken." William enquires, "If it was a de Percy, then which one was it? Did anyone get a close look at the coat of arms?" Bailey replies thoughtfully, "I'm not really quite sure, but I think

I remember that the arms that I saw were like an azure background with maybe five fusils conjoined in a fesse... That's the house of Baron de Percy from Topcliffe manor in Yorkshire ..." William ponders, "A blue background with five yellow stars in a line..." Everyone remains silent for a moment, for none of them could actually confirm the particulars on that de Percy's armorial bearing, William says, "Well if that is the Yorkshire de Percy family for sure, it's given us a start at least." Shaking his head, Coinach speaks, "Fella's ah can't be sorry enough to yie all for ma temper and rage that I put upon yiez back there, for I see now that we might have caught the bastard if my head had been cold for thought and no' se' hot for blood." No one replies verbally, but they intimate their understanding of their feelings to him.

It's late in the third day when the small troop finally makes it back to the safety of Glen Afton. William, Bailey, Sean and Coinach are welcomed with tears of joy upon their safe return. Sean leaves them to stable the horses and kennel his dogs, while the others enter the kitchens with warm fires and hot vittals waiting to greet them after their long arduous sojourn. William passes Mharaidh a message from Alain as Coinach rushes in enquiring urgently, "How's Affric, is she awake yet?" Auld Jean replies while Mharaidh reads the message from Alain, "She's still in a great sleep son, but her bruising is going down which is a good sign." Coinach enquires, "Is she still restin' in the back room crib?" Auld Jean replies, "She is, but please Coinach, be ever so quiet when you enter her room, if you disturb her before she knows where she is, it could cause her terrible pains of both body and mind."

Coinach leaves immediately to visit Affric, while Mharaidh fusses about William and Bailey as they sit to eat. Mharaidh says, "Its good to see you boys home safely, you must tell us what's been happening?" Bailey replies, "Well Mharaidh, de

Brix agreed to take his Pact army away from war and return to his estates in England." William says, "Bishop Wishart, Lord Duncan of Fife and Lord Moray of Avoch led negotiations on behalf of the Guardians of the realm, they managed to broker a treaty that was agreeable to all... "

Mharaidh is visibly relieved to hear this news. "I think I speak on behalf of everyone in saying we are so grateful that war has been averted." William sighs, "Aye, but the nobles are still in great dispute over the Maid o' Norway taking to the throne. It seems as though they've all pretty much agreed that the King of England should mediate, the Norman magnates reckon he will be a fair and independent arbitrator, and this way they reckon we will avoid a civil war. Mharaidh is relieved, "Better debate than war." Bailey scowls and looks away. Mharaidh notices his discomfort, as do the others. She enquires, "What ails you Bailey? I can see you have a troubled heart, are you boys telling me everything?" William and Bailey give each other knowing looks, then Bailey replies "I don't trust any English after what they did to my people in Wales, now I see the same thing is happening here in Scotland with English mercenaries plying the same bloody trade."

"It's for sure an unfinished business," says William, "and the Guardians didn't seem to be interested in what happened to all o' the folk at the Corserine or elsewhere. And from what we heard from the other Ceannard and Chieftains, there were many other clans in Galloway who suffered the same end at the hands of auld de Brix' English mercenaries. We even found auld Torquill Fletcher and his clan had suffered the same fate as Coinachs clan at the Corserine." Mharaidh gasps, "Torquill... No, surely not... this is..." Mharaidh sits down, looking completely drained of thought and energy. She continues "Sometimes it doesn't look like it, but the nobles know what they're doing, you'll see, but I'm worried about your father with all these awful doings and talk of mercenaries. His message said that he'd be home soon, but nothing much else..." she tries to hide her emotions, it's then William realises how traumatic it must be for those who are left behind to wonder and imagine 'what if...' His thoughts are broken when Mharaidh enquires, "Will your father be home soon?"

"Aye," replies William "he's only a few days behind us. And it wasn't just Scots that were at Dalry Mharaidh, there were English, French, Irish and Flemish too. It sure does look like there are many folks who have a keen interest in Scotland's future. The Guardian army broke to marshal the various factions back to their respective borders. Dá went with the Comyn to Baile na h-Uige as an escort for the Capetian soldiers, so he'll be home soon enough." Bailey spoke, "The Lord Comyn brought some fighting force of men with him in support the Baliols. I reckon it would have been some bloody battle if it had taken to the sword. I don't reckon de Brix would have survived had he not backed down..." William hears a noise coming from Affric's room... "How is Affric really doing?" Mharaidh replies, "There's no doubt that she was standing on the edge of the western shores William, but we've tended her well till there was no more we could do but hope and pray that she recovers."

They sit awhile in silence, then Coinach returns from Affric's room, appearing thoroughly drained, William enquires, "How is she?" Coinach replies, "She sleeps deeply, but I've a fear I'll never sleep again till I avenge all that's befallen my sister and my Clan." William enquires "Do yie mind if I go and sit awhile by her side?" Coinach slumps exhausted into a chair, "Wallace, Mharaidh, everyone I am so, so sorry for the state of affairs that I've brought to you and your family… and also by my countenance towards you all. I've been bitter and thoughtless for which I would beg all of your forgiveness." Looking at his friend, William replies, "You've been nothing but a loyal friend to me Coinach ever since I came home, now you're a friend who needs us all to stand by you. And for you to ask forgiveness from us when we could do little to ease the pain you carry, it's been near the breaking of all our hearts." Mharaidh approaches Coinach and embraces him with the love of an understanding mother. "Come Coinach, you should rest awhile. I'll take you to a warm and pleasant crib where you may get some rest; you must be of a stout heart for bonnie Affric when she wakes. I'll have Katriona bring you fresh some vittals and a fine and hot Toddy for when your settled." Mharaidh and Coinach walk away from the kitchens towards the crib chambers. Bailey says, "I think I'll get some sleep too…"

"Aye," agrees William "Ahl see yie later Bailey, I'm going to sit awhile with Affric." As Bailey leaves to billet and get some much-needed rest, William sits alone in the kitchen. He's feeling the power of much needed sleep attacking his senses, but he gets up and walks through to Affric's room to sit by her side. On entering the room he's instantly shocked by her appearance. She's laying naked and shivering, having thrown her covers off in a fever. Her face is still swollen and the colours of bruised black and jaundiced yellow have spread all over from her badly scarred face to her neck, breasts and broken bloodied body. Taking great care not to disturb her, William pulls her covers up gently to keep his dear friend warm and comfortable. He looks intently at Affric; she appears to be at peace and he's glad she's in the deep sleep, it's obvious the pains she would have to endure otherwise may be too much and unbearable to witness had she been conscious, for her body is still in such a terrible injurious condition. Sitting down at her bedside, William clasps her hand gently and looks into the badly beaten and scarred face of his once beautiful friend, a friend who never had ought but a cheeky smile that beamed with the zest of life itself. He smiles thinking of how Affric by her very presence, spread infectious happiness around her with all the joys of life a beautiful, wild woman of the woodland Ceàrdannan brings, who's smile brought a great delight to everyone. While holding her hand, he whispers "Affric, if there is a deity that would grant you once again your beauty and joy of life, then I would sacrifice all of me for it to be so."

For many hours, William sits holding Affric's hand while talking and comforting her till he can barley stay awake himself. He tries to fight against the sleep, hoping his presence will somehow give her the strength she needs to turn away from deaths door, but the Gods of sleep easily overpower William as he lays his head to rest on the crib beside her.

After a while he hears the door opening behind him, he turns to see a tall gangly stranger enter the room. Through his tiredness and the dim light from the flickering candles, he couldn't clearly distinguish who it is. When he realises the stranger is not one born of glen Afton, "Who are you?" The stranger replies, "I don't mean to be disturbing yie young Wallace, my name is Sir Thomas Learmont of Ercildoune, some folks do call me Thomas the Rhymer or True Tam." Looking curiously at True Tam, William enquires "Was it you that I saw last year back at the Ach na Feàrna, gatehouse when the Guardians came to tell my uncle of our Artur's death?" True Tam ignores the question as he walks past William, as though he isn't there. Slightly disturbed by the odd characters presence, William reluctantly moves his chair aside as True Tam sits on the bed and puts his hand on Affric's forehead, clearly offering a great care for her. "What are you doing here?" Enquires William. True Tam rummages about in a little bag by his side and pulls out various herbs, liniments and tiny pottery phials. He replies, "I'm here to care of my niece, the bonnie Affric." True Tam begins applying the various potions to her wounds and bruising; then he lifts her head gently and pours a tiny amount of potion from a phial onto her lips as William watches curiously.

True Tam tends Affric awhile longer then sits back and looks at his niece "I have an old medicinal phial here Wallace, I'll it leave behind that will help to heal her mind when she wakes. Show it to her, she will know how to apply it, but I fear though that I may not be able to heal the scars of her heart." He pours more of the elixir into a tiny horn cup and slowly feeds it to Affric.Almost finished with his application of care to Affric, True Tam smiles at William… "And you young William Wallace, I have heard much about you from both your dear grandmother and bonnie Affric."

"Aye," replies William "I recognise you now, it was you at Ach na Feàrna with the guardians wasn't it?" True Tam replies, "I was there." William continues, "Has Affric been tellin tall tales about me then?" True Tam smiles, then he replies, "Some tales… You two are quite infamous." William gazes at this strange looking figure tending so gently to Affric, then he smiles to himself thinking of what may have been said about his reputation with Affric and their lusty woodland Fèis adventures. True Tam packs away his little bags and walks towards the door. "I will be back for you another time young Wallace." True Tam leaves the room, quietly closing the door behind him. William settles back down to comfort Affric, though he is still curious at the appearance of the odd character True Tam. '*then he said he will be back for me another time?*' William ponders awhile longer the he rests his head on his arms and closes his eyes. After a few moments he thinks he can hear faint cries of someone calling out his name, he looks about the darkened room, but he can't see where the voice calling him has came from, again he hears his name called, but he cannot fathom from where… One more time he hears his name called, but this time he recognises Affric's voice, he thinks *'But where is she?'* "Wallace…" calls the voice aloud. William opens his eyes… Affric is staring at him from the crib… "Affric…" he exclaims, "I thought… I thought I must have been dreaming?" Cupping her hand joyously, William stammers, "You're awake? Oh ma bonnie darlin' you're back with us… Wait, wait… ah must be getting Jean and Mharaidh, ah have to be fetchin' Coinach to be seeing yie too, oh wee darlin…"

"Wallace," pleads Affric "I've been awake awhile now… please be telling to me it's a nightmare that I wake from… I feel deep pains in my heart. I know my body is broken… yet I find you by my side in this strange dwelling, tell me Wallace, tell me it's not true… tell me that it's just me and that I have gone mad with some malady." William can't reply, he doesn't know how to, he can't find the words to even begin to describe to Affric the circumstance that he, Bailey and Coinach had found her in at the Corserine. Stoically, through tear filled eyes, she continues, "My sisters are dead, and my Clan, it did happen didn't it?"

William can only look on as tears begin to fill his own eyes. Affric stammers, "It is true…" She turns her face away and looks out the small window in silence. William could see tears flowing down her cheeks, he lifts up the hand he still clasps and kisses her gently… "Dear Affric, I'll go and fetch the others, your wounds are bleeding again and they will know what comfort and healing they may address upon you. Oh Affric your back with us…" Before he leaves the room to fetch Mharaidh, Auld Jean and Coinach, he stops at the door and looks back. He sees that Affric has not taken her gaze away from the small window; then he sees the tears are still flowing down her cheeks. He's so relieved, so sorry, but he is also so elated. He thinks *'Affric lives...'*

The kitchen of Wallace Castle is very busy with everyone in for morning vittals when William burst through the door, "She's awake..." he calls out, "Affric has been talking to me, and she's awake..." Mharaidh drops a platter with the excitement. "Wee Graham, go and fetch Coinach, he sorely needs some light and joy in his soul." William exclaims, "She was so badly beaten, her bruises and wounds made me want to look away when I first saw her awful condition, but Affric... she's awake and I've spoken with her, she's sitting up and she's talking..." Mharaidh insists that William sits down as she issues more orders then turns to speak with him. "Now calm down William, tell me how Affric fares before I go in to see her, how is her wits?" William exclaims "I almost felt I should not leave or come out of the room Mharaidh, seeing her awake and not believing my eyes. Mharaidh, she's back with us..." Mharaidh weeps with unreserved joy upon hearing the news. William gently wipes her eyes as they fill with tears of relief and joy. Mharaidh says, "It was not thought we would share another day in her company again, the angels have answered all of our prayers." Auld Jean comes rushing into the kitchen then goes straight through into Affric's room with Mharaidh. William turns to see auld Tam and Bailey clinking two whisky jars, smiling broadly and saying a wee prayer of thanks for Affric's return. William joins his kin at the table, "Here, ah need some o' that..."

Suddenly the door crashes open with Coinach half dressed running straight for the room where Affric lay. Wee Graham happily wanders into the kitchen from the whisky cellar then stops beside the table where William, Auld Tam and Bailey are seated. With an enormous grin he says, "Ah thought ah could smell the celebratory craitur on the go." Then he joins his Kin's toast to the bonnie Affric. The relief and joy amongst the erstwhile friends is palpable and almost beyond words as they rejoice in Affrics return to the world. "Oh…" exclaims William remembering something important, "Where's sir Thomas…? Whatever he gave Affric has made all the difference, I must tell him…"

"Tell who what?" Enquires Bailey. Everyone at the table looks at each other with blank expressions. William is emphatic, "Thomas the Rhymer, True Tam, Sir Thomas of Ercildoune or whatever his name is, Affric's uncle… where is he?" Wee Graham ponders, "True Tam?" Again everyone looks at each other slightly bemused, William continues, "Aye the big tall skinny fella who came in to see Affric then left only a wee while ago. He said that Affric is his niece?"

"Thomas the Rhymer?" queries auld Tam, "He's a fella no' tae be messed with young Wallace, but for sure he's no' here, and we've been sittin' here for hours."

"The Knight wie the sight?" enquires Wee Graham as he sups his nectar. "Aye him," replies William. Wee Graham sighs, "Naw, ah'v no' seen him, and there has been none entered the glen in over a week ceptin' you fella's."Bailey shakes his head,"Nope… nobody been here but us all night." William is adamant, "But he was here just a wee while ago, then he said he was coming back for me?" For a moment there's a curious silence, William looks completely baffled, then auld Tam says, "Son, we've been sittin' here most o' the night and you were alone all night in that room with wee Affric, I think yie must have been dreamin." William appears perplexed, "Feck that's strange… I could have sworn it was real… I must o' been dreamin' right enough? But ahm certain he was here..." A grinning Wee Graham enquires, "So William, is the bonnie wee lass back with us, sound in soul and hearty then?"

"Aye, that she is," replies William, "and looking so bright and keen in the eyes as well, despite her body being in such a perilous condition." Bailey says, "I hope this good news brings Coinach back to us too, for he's been like a man demented. Though maybe he's contained his madness better than any of us here ever could, but Christ he's been one crazy fucker hell bent on a mission that none of us could fault."

"No' half," agrees William "ah don't know how anyone could handle having their family murdered, I don't know what I would do if that happened to me?" Then William remembers the same fate had befallen Bailey's family, William is humbled as he sees how Bailey appears to be in complete control of his thoughts and emotions regarding such a heinous and barbarous memory. "I don't know how you've managed Bailey? If you were my elder brother, my heart couldn't be any fuller with pride and respect for you." Bailey nods, then with a faint smile he looks down at the table thoughtfully. William feels a tap on his shoulder... he turns to see Wee Graham, "Come with me over to the fireside Wallace me boy, and grab some of ma craitur too, for yer goin' tae feckn need it." Auld Tam calls out, "I'll need to be fixing your nose again son, or you'll be lookin' like you're meant to be sniffing things around corners. What the Feck have you been up to anyway?" William walks over toward the fireside and laughs, then he replies, "Ach nuthin..."

The house of Wallace thrives with joy this cold winters morning. Affric is back with them and they know that in her own time, she may tell them of what really happened to her Clan at the Corserine Gap, more importantly, who is responsible. As everyone relaxes that morning, Auld Jean and Katriona set to making morning vittals. William thinks back on his dream, it is still puzzling him… it felt so real. He remembers that it's not the first time he has seen True Tam and feeling very 'strange' in his presence. He recalls that it was definitely True Tam he'd seen at the gates of Ach na Feàrna. He also remembers how the strange looking knight left him feeling cold when he kept pointing at him before the mysterious character left on his horse at a gallop; then he kept glancing back till he was out of sight. William shudders as though a cold wind has blown through his bones.

*   *   *

Alain Wallace and the Gallóglaigh of Glen Afton finally return after almost eight days driving through the harshest of winter conditions. They meander towards the stables at the Craig Darrach on the last morning of the old year, when the day of the wrens and Fionn's Fèis begin the Hagmonaidh (New morning of the new year) Fèis celebrations in the Glen of Afton. Reaching the corrals, Alain dismounts and drags his tired body up the steps and through the door of Wallace "castle" where he's instantly greeted by his adoring wife Mharaidh, she runs over and throws her arms lovingly around her husband's neck and kisses him passionately, so grateful for his safe return. "Oh Alain, we have all missed you so, and there is so much to be telling you, oh my love, I'm so glad you are back with us whole and hearty." A relieved Alain replies, "And I. It could have been all so different if de Brix and his Pact had not backed away from war… it was a close run thing Mharaidh. There were many thousands who had gathered to confront him and his Pact forces, then the strangest thing happened, he simply backed off from conflict." Mharaidh holds Alain close, "Oh Alain my love, we can talk of these things later, I'm just so glad you are all home safely my love."

Shivering with the bitter cold, Alain painstakingly begins to remove his heavy sodden winter clothing. As Mharaidh assists him, he enquires, "And what of young Affric, William told me that he had brought her here, how does she fare?"

Mharaidh replies while busily unclasping Alan's armour and fussing about him, , "Affric had been so badly beaten and abused Alain, we thought she may not live, but she's recovering slowly now. Her wounds are deep but she's healing well, thankfully it looks as though she may recover much of her health, for she opened her eyes for the first time only the other morn." Helping Alain off with his cold wet heavy brat, Mharaidh continues to inform Alain of Affric's condition... "When the boy's came home she seems to have came back too, now she's making fine progress. We've settled her in a wee obhainn at the foot of the kailyards, close to the King's stables. She's found her health, but she can't be walking about unaided yet. The wee soul is on the right side of recovery though." Wearily stripping away the last of his sodden layers of clothing, Alain enquires, "Did she tell you what happened at the Corserine?" Mharaidh replies, "No, she said she doesn't remember anything. William Coinach and Bailey have told her of their accounts as gently worded as such a terrible thing could be, they've also told us in great detail of all they witnessed, but Affric says she doesn't have any memories of what happened nor who it was who carried out the atrocities."

"Perhaps that's for the best," Says Alain "but then we still don't have any insight as to the perpetrators of this evil deed. Is there anything at all she remembers that would help us find or identify the murderers of her people?" Mharaidh replies "None." Alain continues, "Then we may never know who was responsible." Mharaidh sighs, "I hope they're caught someday Alain."

Pausing a moment, Mharaidh says, "One name being talked about is De Percy. A name she often calls out in her nightmares, but that doesn't mean anything to us." Alain ponders as he brushes his cold body down with a warm blanket, "The only De Percy I'm aware off is a Henry De Percy down in England, Baron Percy of Alnwick. But he's a respected knight of King Edward's council and he would be in France I believe with his King, or at his family estates in Yorkshire in the North-east of England. I couldn't see him being in the Galloway forest so far from his royal luxuries nor perpetrating such base deeds. I think Affric must have other reasons for calling out his name?"

"We shall talk of this later my love," says Mharaidh, "you look so tired, and you must be ravenous for a warm meal… I'll prepare a hot tub then you can bathe awhile. I'll get Jean to fix you some fine food for you then we shall go and see Affric before we celebrate the Oidhche Samhna Hagmonaidh and Sainin Fèis. (Household ritual festival.) later on this eve." Still vigorously rubbing his body down, Alain says, "It should've been William's birthing day celebrations a few days ago Mharaidh, ah wish I'd been here, I wanted to give him something special to celebrate his coming of age. Certainly I wouldn't have given him what he has seen these last few weeks."

"Alain…" says Mharaidh softly, "we did no celebrating of any kind, for none here were in much of a mind to celebrate. We only had prayers and thoughts for wee Affric, your safety and the men of your command. All we could think off was for everyone to be returned to us safe and well." Alain says nothing as he steps forward and wraps his arms around his beautiful wife. He pulls her close and they kiss passionately with the intensity of true lovers reunited from a long fraught separation. After many moments of loving bliss, Alain retires to hot bathe and force the winters chill out of his weary bones, Mharaidh goes to the kitchens to ready him nourishment and refreshment. Jean and Katriona prepare a handsome meal for everyone, including Auld Jean baking her famous goat butter Hagmonaidh Black-cake.

All are busy cooking and baking or going about their chores when Bailey and William come rushing in through the door. "Is ma Dá back?" enquires William, visibly excited at the prospect of seeing his father "Aye," replies Mharaidh, "he is, but he's bathing now, though he told me that he'll be glad to be seeing you in a wee while." Slightly deflated, William lifts a hot black cake but gets smacked across the fingers by a wooden spoon handle from Auld Jean. Mharaidh says, "Oh William... your father said he has something very special for you, but he'll give you whatever it is later."

"Somethin special, for me?" exclaims William. Mharaidh goes about her chores smiling; then she replies, "Aye something special, just for you."

"What is it Mharaidh?" enquires William, "and what's it for?" Mharaidh looks at him with a twinkle in her eye, "Awe naw... I recognize that look Mharaidh, have yie been takin' scoldin' lessons from Wee Maw?"

"Aye that I have William Wallace," laughs Mharaidh, "do you really want to be testing my resolve and finding out?" Mharaidh thumps a wooden flour-rolling baton in her hand, "you'll be finding out what your father has for you at the Hagmonaidh celebrations later this night, now you and Bailey, away and be doing somethin useful like getting some kinlin' and dry peat for Affric's obhainn, or I'll be giving you both needy chores to do in the kitchens here helping Jean and I." In jest, both William and Bailey rush towards the kitchen door, Bailey grabs a pile of Auld Jean's hot black cakes on the way out. William calls back cheerily, "See yie later Mharaidh."

Leaving the kitchens behind, they stand in the main hall of Wallace Keep. Bailey hands William a couple of the hot black cakes he liberated from Auld Jean, "Here boyo, while you were busy with Mharaidh, I found some more of these." William laughs while accepting the hot roasted black cakes. "Tá Bailey." They both quickly scoff Auld Jean's delicacies then William says, "Feck Bailey, Mharaidh really does take after Wee Maw. We'll have to watch our step with her or we'll be in trouble right enough." Bailey laughs, "I see the education of the warrior woman in her, that's a certainty. Anyway Wallace, what's Hagmonaidh? What's that all about?" William looks at Bailey curiously, "Don't yiez celebrate it in Cymru?" Bailey replies, "I don't know look you Scotchman, not if you don't tell me what it is." William retorts, "How don't you know... for fuck's sake Bailey." A bewildered Bailey replies, "You haven't told me what it is yet, that's why I don't fucking know."

Grinning, William replies, "Well then my primitive Cymran cousin, prepare to be educated." Putting his hand on his forehead Bailey moans, "No please, not another bloody history lesson." William glares at Bailey humerously, "Well its got to be better than your feckn Devil cat of Carlisle story..." Bailey enquires, "This wont take long will it?" Ignoring the obvious disdain, William commences... "Hagmonaidh, along with the Sainin' is a special time o' the year for swallowin' as much craitur as you can, plenty of the dancin' singin' and playin' o' music for as long as you're able to stand, and of course, much squeezing o' the maids... Do yie know Bailey, sometimes Hagmonaidh lasts for weeks, its even been known to carry on for months."

"Months" queries Baillie. "Aye," replies William, "or so Wee Graham says, and HE is the Hagmonaidh expert." Both laugh at Wee Graham's experienced and learned advice. William continues with authority, "Aye, it was Wee Graham himself who recalled the immortal words o' Lilith when she spoke to God for the first time outside the Garden of Eden… *'if we're all havin such a great feckn Hagmonaidh, then why the feck would yie ever be wantin' to be stoppin on a Sunday…'* it just doesn't make any sense." Bailey laughs and nods in bemused agreement with Wee Grahams philosophical logic. William continues, "Most folks here try an' last as long as Lá Fhèill Brìghde Fèis." Bailey mutters, "Awe for fucks sake…" William enquires, "What was that yie said?" An agitated Bailey replies, "Nothing…"

William looks curiously at Bailey… "Anyway, the Sainin is natures way of blessing us all and is usually inaugurated by someone special from Affric's Clan, someone who can invoke the initial rite of blessing for the spiritual protection of all the folk o the household, the beasts in the fields and the livestock. THEN…" says William mimicking a scholarly mentor with a thick-brained student, "On the morn of the new year, everyone in the house of celebrations starts drinking the craitur once more. After that ritual, anyone still capable of standing goes around the other dwellings in the glen, blessing all the kinfolks and all of their livestock too, including the ferrets, chickens, hunting hounds. Then the folk sprinkle the magical water taken from a dead and life burn on anything and everything else that moves, feeds yie or can keep yie warm." A very bored looking Bailey enquires, "Wait… what's a dead or life burn?" Taking no notice of Bailey's surly attitude, William continues "A dead and life Burn refers to a small flow of running water that's crossed by both the living and the dead… obviously." Bailey enquires, "What the fuck are you talking about Wallace?"

"Our culture," replies William. "Then… after sprinkling of the magical water in every room and all the inhabitants, the Obhainn, castle or whatever you dwell in, it gets sealed up with everybody inside. Then… previously made bound clutches o' dried juniper, hemp, sages or blue grasses are lit and allowed to smolder, after that, they are carried to wherever has been sprinkled with the magical cleansing water."

"I wish I'd never fucking asked," mutters Bailey as William continues undeterred… "The scented smoke is allowed to fill the house till its near impossible for anyone to breath and your clothes are so full o' the sweet-essence that they quickly discard all unwanted tenants that bite yie and makes yer skin itch at night. And come the time when it's too difficult to breathe, anyone that's still conscious, opens all the doors and windows to be lettin' in the freezin fresh air of the New Year…" Bailey enquires, "Then What?" William grins, "Well if the house hasn't burnt down which happens quite often, the Lady o' the house administers more medicinal treatment from a flagon o' magical craitur as the Clan sits down for their New Year break fast, and maybe a tune and a song if they are of a mind to do so, then yie start the whole celebrating ceremony all over again the next day and so on and so forth…" Just then, Wee Graham and Auld tam enters the hall. Wee Graham enquires, "Did ah hear yiez talking about the Sainin and Hagmonaidh?"

"Don't ask," replies Bailey. Wee Graham rubs his hands and wipes his lips in anticipation "Naw its fine Bailey, ah already know. What ah really want to find out is, when do we start?" Auld Tam walks in through the doors and enquires, "Ho… Wee Graham, Ah thought we were goin up to the fishin at the deep pool?"

"We are," states Wee Graham emphatically while looking at Tam as if he's stupid, "but we don't want to be freezin our auld bones by the spey-side, when we could fish wit' some fine hot Hagmonaidh blood runnin' freely through us now would we Tam?" Bailey snorts, "Right that's it, I've had enough. I'm going to fetch the kinlin' and peat for Affric's obhainn, you Scots can deliberate about whisky and Hagmonaidh all day long as far as I am concerned." Bailey storms off to do his chores. "Hmm… it really worked," says William to himself with smug satisfaction. Auld Tam enquires, "What worked?" William gleefully replies, "Nuthin…' just talking to ma'self Tam." Wee Graham enquires with a knowing smile, "Was that the tell some mug the auld Hagmonaidh story rather than do the feckn chores yourself that yie just caught Bailey out with there young Wallace?"

"Aye It was." replies a chuffed William, rather pleased with himself. "Ha-ha," laughs Wee Graham. "Ah told yie it would work," William laughs, "It did." Then he says, "Right, I'm away to see bonnie Affric, so you fella's have a good days fishing and I'll see yiez ready for the Hagmonaidh?" William walks back into the kitchens, picks up some hot porridge and more black cake and walks off toward Affric's obhainn. "Strange boy…" says Auld Tam, "Now Wee Graham, away and be getting the spillage craitur casks, we don't want tae be freezin do we?" Wee Graham replies, "Right yie are Tam." then immediately makes like a bow legged winter sprite towards the storehouse next to Affrics Obhainn, where he knows his heavenly nourishment awaits him.

At the same time, William enters the little obhainn where Affric sleeps and sits down beside his slumbering friend and watches her in the hope that each and very day that passes, will bring the old Affric nearer to him. He knows it will be a long time before she may fully recover, and he's determined to be by her side whenever she needs him, then he notices the little phial he thought True Tam had used… curiously he picks it up and looks at it, he sniffs the scent of the contents, shakes his head and places the phial back where he found it. *If True Tam wasn't here, then where did this phial come from?'* Suddenly Affric groans as though she is in great pain, distracting him from his thoughts. William spends most of the day talking with Affric and looking to her needs, when he hears horses and many voices outside her Obhainn. A voice calls out… "William Wallace…" Affric enquires curiously, "Who's that shoutin' after you Wallace?"

"Ahm no' sure," replies William with a smile… "but ah think ah recognise that voice?" The voice calls again, "William WALLACE, GET YOURSELF OUT HERE… RIGHT NOW." This time the voice has an authority that he recognises immediately. William exclaims, "It's Wee Maw right enough…". He jumps up and moves quickly to the door, calling out to Affric, "Wee darlin, ah'll be back soon, it's Wee Maw Wallace from Ach na Feàrna." He opens the door and rushes out of the Obhainn, to his astonishment and delight, he sees Wee Maw sitting on the driving seat of a large bow wagon, sitting beside his milk mother Margret and his uncle Malcolm. He also sees Uliann and Aunia are there too, then another wagon arrives with Sandy, gentle Andrew and Malcolm óg aboard, and there too is Wee John and Ròsinn who have travelled from Connaught in Ireland. The whole family from Ach na Feàrna have made their way down to the Glen Afton for Hagmonaidh, William is overjoyed to see his entire family, when he is slapped forcefully on the shoulder from behind…

"Well me foin friend, is it not me'self you'll be a' welcomin' back to your foin humble abode then?" William spins on his heels to be met with a cheery grinning face. He exclaims "Stephen ua… What th…" William and Stephen warmly embrace. "For feck's sake Stephen, how did you get here?" Stephen laughs and nods towards the bow-wagon. "William WALLACE…" grouches Wee Maw… "Help me down and get me a pee churn before ah make a puddle here."

William replies "Aye Granny right away." He turns to go back into Affric's obhainn for a churn, then he stops in his tracks… with a little trepidation and fearing the worst, he looks back and enquires, "Eh Granny, did you just ask for me to help you down and fetch you a pee churn before you make a puddle here…?" Wee Maw tucks her tiny fists into her waist and gives him the dreaded 'Look…' she replies, "Naw yie deaf, daft big dumplin', I said help me down and give me a wee hug and a cuddle dear." Wee Maw appears very stern, giving William the infamous and deadly Look once more… then she breaks into her cute wee wrinkly Granny smile. She beckons him with outstretched arms.

Everyone laughs except William, who goes red in the face, for just a moment… then he laughs too, realising she was funning him. In one giant step he bounds over to the wagon and lifts the Aicé matriarch of the Clan Wallace off the wagon to embrace and squeeze her with great affection. Wee Maw, with her legs dangling far off the ground, taps William gently on the nose with her finger and enquires quietly of her loving Grandson, "What happened to the nose then son?" William replies, "Ach nuthin' Granny, just a wee accident." Fondly she looks at her grandson; then with a knowing smile, she says "You'd better be puttin' me down son or ah'll really will be havin a wee accident." Smiling and lowering Wee Maw to the ground, she takes him by the hand, "Now William, ah'v brought some o' my special medicine for wee Affric." She turns waves and calls out, "Uliann, Aunia, Ròsinn… come on girls, we're going to see our bonnie Affric to see how she's keepin'. We need to be givin' her some time away from these big hairy beasts o' men that fill this wonderful Glen." William laughs, "She is a lot better o' health now I'm pleased to be tellin' yie Granny." Wee Maw replies, "Right William. You go tell Mharaidh and your father we're here and I'll be up to the big house after I tend to Affric. Then I want you, Stephen, Malcolm óg and wee John to help Sandy get the wagons up to the house and unloaded." As Wee Maw arrives at the door of Affric's obhainn, she turns and calls out one last order, "And be telling Wee Graham there is no any leakage's in any o' the casks we brought down for the Fèis, so he's not to be wastin' his time lookin… though ah know he will anyway." Wee Maw mutters to herself as she Uliann and Aunia enter Affric's obhainn. William and Stephen jump on the bow-wagon with Malcolm and Sandy then the happy clan drive their horses and wagons up towards the Darroch corrals. William says, "Stephen ma friend, ah reckon this is going to be one Hagmonaidh to remember…" Stephen grins, "It sure is."

As the day wears on, more surprise guests arrive at the Black Craig, Andra Mac an Taoiseach, and Seamus MacTavish with their giant Tibby drums, Grant the piper, William's uncle Ranald Crauford, his uncles and cousins from Galloway, David Joahny Seoras, Bryan and their families, this is turning out to be the biggest Hagmonaidh gathering the Wallace family spent together in living memory. They all spend much of the late afternoon together gathered at the foot of the Wallace Keep, where William tells Stephen all about the Pact, the Lords rebellion and the massacres at Corserine and Dunveoch. He also talks eagerly about the Gallóbhan and his experiences at the camp of Saint John of Dalry.

As the afternoon light begins to fade and the dark night creeps over the glen of Afton, William and Stephen are nearing the front door of Wallace Keep when Mharaidh comes out, "William, get all the young men gathered together, your Granny is needing you all to be getting ready to start the festivities. She wants you all to be knowing what to do, when to do it, to be doing it right and no mistakes."

William replies, "Aye Mharaidh, we'll do that now." Wee Maw exits the door behind Mharaidh, "You boy's, listen up now, I want you to tell everyone to be gatherin' around the great Shinin' fire near the Craig o' Darroch, Wee Graham and auld Tam have had it lit for many hours now, so it's a' glowin' fine with much warmth there for everyone." Wee Maw pauses, then she says "And you boyz, I want you to be bringing Affric carefully from her obhainn to sit beside me at the time o' the Shinin' fire. And mind to be wrapping her up well, for she is an honoured part o' this sharin' o' Hagmonaidh happiness, the Winter Wanderers would no' be the same if there wasn't a Summer Walker with us to make our spirits complete this night." Wee Maw continues talking a little while longer, till everyone is absolutely certain of their duties.

Later that night, the Fionn's Fèis and Hagmonaidh festivities are about to get underway, many are in the billets at S'taigh am Rígh mòr, the obhainn's and bothies around the Darroch of Glen Afton, as the proud but small Wallace Castle could not accommodate such a large gathering of people. Others are lodged in the retainers obhainn's and bothies of the single men, quickly adapted to accommodate a less than sedate gathering of Scots who believe fervently in the joy of bringing Fionn's eve and the new year season in with verve. Eventually all the good folk of the glen gather at the Darroch crag, waiting for the moment when the clan matriarch Wee Maw, with the Fae Aicé of the Fèis, Affric, will launch the Hagmonaidh night into its wonderfull festivities and celebrations. William and Coinach have carried Affric from her obhainn where she sits beside Wee Maw for the inauguration of the Fèis. Wee Maw steps up onto the centre steps of a large bow wagon to address the gathering…

"As yie all know…" says Wee Maw aloud, "Hagmonaidh begins on the shortest day and longest night of the year, the Solstice, and concludes with the moon birthin' o' a new sun. We need everyone without exception, to be playin music, hoppin' or singin'," she pauses to make sure all are listening, then she continues, "Wee Graham, Auld Tam and all the younger boys and girls will be winter-walkin' to the Southern-most part of the glen to the tip o' Black Craig itself, and coming back swinging fiery pitch balls on twine ropes in great big circles all around their heads. And you all have to be encouraging them to be getting the newborn sun to be thinkin' kindly on us for this next year a' coming. Remember this you wains… if the young sun sees how much we celebrate and enjoy the thought of his company, he'll be happy to come out and smile upon us often in the coming new year."

"No' often enough." comments a thoughtful Wee Graham, but he expresses himself a bit too loud, everyone smiles and laughs on hearing his remark. "What are yiez all laughin' for?" enquires Wee Maw. Silence falls upon the gathering as Wee Maw gives everyone the Look. A few moments stony silence passes then Alain shouts out loudly… "Because we're all happy…" A grinning Wee Maw clasps her hands together with glee, "That's right ma' boy," she continues with a big smile, "And that's the kind o' noise that will bring sunshine and happiness to our wee humble gatherins' this incoming year." Everyone laughs heartily and cheers in merriment as Wee Maw calls for hush… "This night, the moon goddess will give birth to a baby Sun for the coming of the new year, born specially for the benefit o' Magda Mòr, now don't yiez be worrying if ye don't see the new boy sun in the morn, even if its rainin' or snowin', so long as yiez keep the fires lit and the candles burnin' then at some time he'll appear." Wee Maw sups some craitur as Alain exclaims humorously, "Eventually." then he slaps Wee Graham on the back. Wee

Maw points at Alain, "Ah… don't you be funnin' too much Alain Wallace, for yie know we need the sunshine in our lives, talk like that will maybe frighten the young sun away, and he may no' come out to see us for days, maybe even months… and it'll be all your fault." She turns to look at all the Children gathered, "What dyie think of uncle Alain now then wains?"

All the children boo and hiss Alain, who mocks great shame, till they all eventually quieten down. Wee Maw continues, "Now, does everyone have a gift to be encouragin' the sun to be comin up and out early in the morn wains?" Everyone including the adults call out at the top of their voices "Aye…" Wee Maw smiles then enquires, "And what's that gift?" everyone responds as one "A BIG SMILE…" Wee Maw raises her finger for silence, "Now I want yiez all to be takin' your precious gifts for Magda mòr away up the braes to place them at the foot o' the great Yew, Oaks and Hawthorns. You harvesters place your apples biscuits and berries next to the fruitin' trees if yie be wanting a successful harvest next year." Wee Maw looks at the young single men and women then grins, "And all o' you un-betrothed bonnie darlins with yer love charms at the ready, yie must tie them to the Trystin' trees for the bringin' to yiez o' a good man, and likewise you young fella's who would wish a bonnie wife to bear yiez strong daughters… and the odd son."

Everyone laughs again as Wee Maw continues, "And of course no' forgetting you traders…" she pauses then smiles, "Coins may bring you wealth, so be sticking them in all the cracks and crannies of the bog myrtle and hawthorn trees." With a big smile, Wee Maw looks at the gathering of excited children "And next, this is especially for you bonnie wains, I want yiez all to get your spookin' and wren masks yiez have all made up and put them on yer bonnie wee heads, so that any bad spirits that might just wonder over here this night by mistake are scared away from the glen, then I want yiez to take a piece o' cloth, tie it to the oak, birch and ash trees and make a wish, but be sure you be telling no-one what yie wish for... And last but no' least... we cannae be forgettin' you wedded young bucks o' the glen, and some o you hopeful auld ones too, yiez should all be layin' your winter nuts at the foot o' the yew trees for fertility... and ahm speaking to you in particular Wee Graham..." Great roars of laughter erupt from the gathering; Wee Graham appears mortified, as does his ever-suffering wife Auld Jean. But there's only happiness abroad as Wee Maw continues with her guide of the Fèis. A great feeling of kinship emanates from the gathering at the 'Shining' fire of Craig Darroch in Glen Afton.

After a few moments, Wee Maw raises her hands to gain everyone's attention, then she calls out her last orders, "When you wains want to leave here for the north and south roads, I want yiez to look out for Wee Graham and auld Tam, these two auld worthies will be leadin' yiez through the old sacred groves o' the Darroch and up the S'taigh am Rígh hill. Your all to be leaving your blessing's along the way, while all the married folk will be crossing over the Afton flow to walk the long way up the Black Craig, us auld yin's will get everything ready for the feastin' and libations. The rest o' yiez that ah mis-mentioned, uze follow Wee Graham, Auld Tam and the wains throughout the Glen spreadin' the suns light wie fireballs, torches and much merriment as yiez go, then we'll see yiez awe back here for the midnight Hagmonaidh Shining fire." This is the last 'command' of Wee Maw. Affric pulls at William's léine, "She's a great wee wumman yer Granny," William replies, "Aye, she sure is."

To signal the beginning of the Hagmonaidh Fèis, Grant and Seoras start up the bagpipes and march forward, all others attending the great clan gathering now move to the paths that lead to the gifting trees. William glances at Affric as she watches the clan and his kinfolks begin their celebration walks. It's the first time he has seen her smile since before the Corserine massacre.Affric is warmly wrapped in plaid and a large fox fur pelt brat, she watches the boys and girls with their fireballs swinging like meteors as they make their way through the glen. William enquires, "Do yie want me to put anything on the Clootie trees for yie Affric?" She sits motionless; then replies, "I'm too ill to move Wallace, I couldn't do it, not without feeling great pain." He enquires, "I'll carry you up there wee darlin' if you would like me too?" Affric appears extremely uncomfortable "No Wallace, the pain would be too much, but tá anyways. Ahm feelin a bit tired now, will yie carry me back to ma obhainn, ah think ah'll rest awhile." Dutifully, William lifts Affric up gently in his arms and carries her to her obhainn and lays her on the crib beside the centre hearth peat fire. He begins to stoke the fire, and heats some hot wort soup for her.

Sitting contentedly by the fire, William says, "Bailey brought you some thick kinlin' logs and he's stocked up the peat wall, and ah'v left some block pile kinlin' near the hearth if you want a flame fire?" Affric replies, "Ahm fine Wallace, but ah want yie to do somethin for me." William replies, "Anything wee darlin, what is it you want me to do?" She continues, "Will yie tear two strips off my breacan-feil (tartan wrap/plaid) and hand them to me?" William picks up her plaid and tears two long strips from it, then he enquires, "What dyie want me to do with them?" Affric replies, "Ah want yie to take them to the Clootie trees and pick the finest growin' oak, then tie them both high up on the branches. They are to be in memory of my people who have passed to a better place." William enquires, "Would you want me to do anything else?"

"Aye I would…" replies Affric "I want you to get Coinach

when these festivities are all long past and tell to him that when I'm fit to travel, we'll go back to the Corserine and have the same Fèis there, for it was here and at the Corserine where my mother's hands picked the plants, moss and gathered the wool to make this plaid." She looks longingly at the two tartan strips of cloth in William's hand then she reaches out and holds the two strips gently for a moment, then leans her head forward bringing the "ties" to her cheeks, closes her eyes and caresses them as though she were a child resting on the safety of her mothers bosom, tears gently fall to be lost in the weave of the ties. After a few moments, Affric releases them to William and lies back down in her crib. "Will you leave me now Wallace, for ah must sleep?" William kneels beside her crib and kisses her gently on the cheek, but she shows neither emotion nor reaction. As he walks away to fulfill his duty, he opens the door, turns towards her "Ahl be back in a wee while ma darlin'"

"Naw Wallace…" says Affric, "give me till late, then maybe look-see in on me." She turns and stares unflinchingly at the blue-reddish glow of the warm peat fire. William walks outside her obhainn, stops and stands awhile, thinking. He knows there is something very wrong in Affrics heart, she is not the vibrant young woman he once knew, part he could understand, but there is more that he can't understand. Emotions well up inside of him then he feels tears in is eyes, he knows she is in such great pain from her wounds, but he's seen in her eyes that her pain is even greater in her heart and thoughts, but something else about Affric's demeanor is disturbing him greatly, he knows something is different about her…

As Affric lay alone in her obhainn, she grips her mantle with such angst; her knuckles turn white. Suddenly tears begin to flood down her cheeks, uncontrollably. She heaves great sobs and struggles to breath, despite all that she has told others, she's not forgotten any of the terrors nor any part of her ordeal in the Corserine gap at the hands of the murderers of her people. She has told none of her detailed memories, not even Coinach, for Affric wants vengeance herself. She knows who is responsible and remembers every single detail of the assault placed upon her and her Clan. She also knows that William, his family, Coinach and any that would assist her, would be at great risk if they were to find out what she knew. She also knows in her heart that she can say nothing about her vivid memories, for almost certainly, the only folk left in this world she cares about would be killed or murdered if they recklessly sought out vengeance on her behalf. She alone wants those responsible to pay, she alone will do what is required… the commander of the beasts will suffer greatly for his heinous crimes placed upon her family, she will do this by her own hands, for Affric is a true Aicé of the Gallóbhan. She whispers quietly… "Marmaduke De Percy… I will soon have my vengeance upon you and yours…"

THE GIFTS

oinach is on his way to see his sister Affric, when he meets William sitting at her obhainn door. "How's she faring Wallace?" William replies, "I don't think Affric really needs me Coinach… she's making such an effort, but I reckon the pain in her heart ails her much more than any pains in her body. She's asked me to hang the wishin' ties o' your family colours on the great oak near the crest o' the Craig, she's also asked if we will all do the same some time down at the Corserine when she's fit and well enough to travel." Coinach looks at William and can see in his eyes how much everything has affected his friend, he also senses William is far from his usual humour, it's the first time he's ever seen him like this. The realisation of how much William has been troubled by the scenes at the Corserine, strikes Coinach hard. "And you Wallace, are you feelin all right… for yie don't look se' good?" William finds it near impossible to reply, such is his heightened state of emotion. Coinach sees him struggle, but he says nothing as he steps forward and embraces his loyal friend, a gesture that almost tips William over the edge emotionally, then a familiar voice calls out, "William Wallace, will yie be coming with us to the crest o' the Craig?"

Coinach and William look at each other, more understanding passes between them in the momentary glance than could have been said in a lifetime. Coinach smiles as William looks towards the voice that hails him, it's his father Alain calling. He sees that Wee Maw and the rest of the family is there too. Alain calls out... "C'moan son...". Coinach senses William's pain and troubled heart, he reaches out his hand and places it on William's shoulder, "Away yie go Wallace, ah'll go and see to Affric." The two friends part at the door of Affric's obhainn. William walks over and joins Wee Maw and the family for the long walk across the Afton River and on up towards the rest near the crest of the Black Craig. They soon saunter along on their journey, talking under the mild cloudless night sky, with the moon goddess shining brightly upon their path, bathing their journey in a cool white luminescent glow.

Wee Maw holds William's arm as they walk a little way back from the rest of the family. She enquires knowingly, "Do yie love her William?" He looks at Wee Maw curiously; though not surprised at her ken, but feels he can't reply. Wee Maw speaks as if she can read his thoughts. "Ah can see there is much affection that's a very powerful bond between you and the bonnie Affric." William tries to explain, "Ah don't love her granny..." Then he hesitates, "Well... I do love her, but not in the way you may think... ach Granny, I wish we were in love, as does Affric who feels the same as I do, then surely life would be so much easier for us both." Wee Maw enquires in a tender voice, "What else ails yie then son?" William looks into the steely blue eyes of this wise old woman, "Ah love another Granny, and Affric is heart soul in love with the Ceàrdannan prince, Páidín ua Bruan o' Galloway." Wee Maw queries, "And who is it that has your heart cradled in her hands then son?" William sighs, "A young maid from near Lanark... but I don't think she loves me, but then I've got this feeling in my bones that she does." With her uncanny way of simply knowing, Wee Maw enquires, "Is it the bonnie

maid o' Lammington?" William is surprised, "Aye, Marion…
Sir Hugh Braidfuite's daughter." Wee Maw squeezes his hand,
"She's no' his daughter son."

"What?" exclaims William. "Oh, It's no' a secret," says Wee
Maw. "Marion and her sister Brannah were made orphans in
the Kings city of Rosbroch when the burgess there had her
parents burned alive at the stake for witchery or something
or another." Taken aback at the horrific thought, William
exclaims, "Naw, that can't be true?" Wee Maw shakes her head,
"Aye it's true enough son, it was a terrible thing to behold and
very strange in the reasoning." Wee Maw continues, "Marion
and Brannah's mother and father were Ceàrdannan who lived
in the woodlands just outside Rosbroch town walls, when
Marion and her sister Brannah were but wains. Her parents
were what we call wise or good folk,who lived by nurture
and they had the gift of healing folk's ills by using nature's
magic potions. Then there came a time of much pestilence
and bad harvests thereabouts, so the religious townspeople
of Rosbroch accused her parents of being to blame for all
their woes, and all because they were outsiders. The priests
and the burgess had them cruelly tortured for so long, that
they admitted to dancing and fornicating with the Devil.
All the Breitheamh Rígh and even the Garda Céile Aicé tried
to save them, but the priests threatened their families with
the same fate if they continued to object. Then the priests
had the bonnie lassies dear folks burned alive after that,
for the practise of witchcraft."

"What craft?" enquires William with anger evident in his
voice. "Witchcraft," repeats Wee Maw with much chagrin.
"Son… though ah don't know what that really is myself, it's
something religious people seem to know a lot about, but
nobody else does. And yie can believe this me boy, there have
been no nobles, Bishops nor any of their own kind made

to suffer the fate they apply to their poor victims... or are likely too either." William is perplexed, "I don't understand Granny, why do religious people burn and kill the wee folks, yet nobody does anything about it."

"I don't know," replies Wee Maw, "These religious madmen are worse than any Roman or Norse warrior... at least with them you can fight back, but you have no defence against religious zealots son, you mind these words." William enquires, "Then how did Marion and Brannah become the foundlin' daughters o' sir Hugh? And from them being Ceàrdannan orphans to being ladies in waiting to the Aicé Yolande herself in the court of France?" Wee Maw replies as she recalls fond memories, "Marion's mother and father were fine folks indeed William, they stayed north o' Rosbroch in the lower forest between the foot of the Braiden and Lamington hills. I mind meeting them with your grandfather Billy many years ago. Marion's father was a master hammerer and he could fair change metals from one kind to another, oh, and her mother was such a beautiful soul too, so gifted with the power to heal. Sir Hugh knew her folks and loved them dearly as friends, but when they were murdered by the townies of the burgh, sir Hugh took the two girls in as his own... at some risk to himself. I may add. " William replies thoughtfully, "Ah didn't know..."

As they meander along, Wee Maw sees the expression on William's face. "So it's the bonnie Maid Marion o' Lammington is it, she's the one who has your heart all a' beatin' then son?" William replies, "Aye granny, she does." Wee Maw smiles, "And does she feel the same about you?" William sighs, "Ah think so, I think she does, but ahm no' se' sure." Wee Maw stops and holds his hands, "Then what of bonnie Affric and yourself, what goes on there with you two?" William replies, "We're the greatest and closest o' friends Granny, and we talk often about our true loves that seems to be kept away from us for whatever reason. It's in that state we find great comfort in each other that we seem to find with no other, but we also know that some day, one or maybe both of us will find our one true love." William pauses and looks at Wee Maw, "Does that make sense granny?" Wee Maw replies with a curious smile. "More than yie will ever know son. Now me fine boy, we should be catchin' up wie' the family for they'll all be back down the Black Craig before we get to the top."

Eventually, William and Wee Maw stand near the rest of the Black Craig not far from the gathered Clan, where they are standing watching the fire processions winding their way up the nearby S'taigh am Rígh slopes. William takes out the ties from Affric he had placed inside his léine, "Granny I've to hang these ties on the oak tree for Affric, I'll tie one for my own wishes, dyu want me to hang any up for you?"

"Naw son, yer fine," says Wee Maw, "ahl do it me'self." William reaches up high into the branches, pulls one close, attaches the two pieces of cloth that carries Affrics tears and makes a wish of good things to come for both Affric and Coinach. Next, he ties his own colours to a branch and wishes in the hope the fae will hear his thoughts for good things to come for all his kinfolk. "Here, lift me up son," says Wee Maw, "I want to tie my own piece to the tree… you're never to old tae make a wish." William smiles and lifts Wee Maw high to affix her wish. After a few moments, he lowers her to the ground, where they stand a little while longer in solemn thought, then Wee Maw points high into the trees, "Do yie see away up there near to the top o' the great oak William, there are two very old ties that are still tied and fly together."

"I do." says William. Wee Maw continues, "Many years ago that's where me and your grandfather Billy tied the knot on our wedding day." Wee Maw stands still for a few moments, gazing at the top of the old oak. William could see that in her heart, she appears to be right back to the wedding day of her youth. "Right William' says Wee Maw, "Stop dreamin' and let's be having yie now, walk me to the family standing over there and stop gawkin' like the good grandson yie are."

They walk a short distance, then they turn to look back at the Clootie trees of wishes and see how impressively they're adorned, with hundreds of ties fluttering in the gentle moonlight breeze. For a magical moment in time, they can 'see' that hundreds of folk must have tied many things for as many reasons to the trees of this sacred land for over a millennium. The lowest branches are all festooned with this years ties, and many still hang in its highest limbs going back to the time when the trees were no more than healthy saplings, strong enough of bough to hold their first wishing ties.

A particular old oak is adorned almost from antiquity, with ties from the many generations of Wallace who have lived, died or visited the bonnie Glen Afton. Wee Maw chuckles to herself. William is curious, "What are yie laughin' at Granny?" Wee Maw laughs, "Witches bloomers…" (Knickers)"Witches Bloomers?" repeats William. Wee Maw laughs, "Aye, The religious folks think that witches can fly and these tree branches rip the bloomers off ther' bonnie bums when the witches skirts blows up as they pass by too close to the trees, they think the ties are witches bloomers."

Both William and Wee Maw chuckle at the thought. They turn to watch the long fire procession passing every Bothy, obhainn, sheilin and anywhere that people dwell in Glen Afton. Importantly, none could be missed by the procession as it passes each dwelling where candles or fires are lit in the doorways and windows. As the procession passes by, the youths of each particular dwelling would come out and join in the procession, making the newborn sun of the coming new-year feel honoured and wanted by that particular household. Curious, William enquires, "What's the real meanin' o' the Shinin' fire Granny?" Wee Maw smiles as she replies. "Son, these Shinin' fire festivities are to encourage the new sun in its thoughts of rising with vigour early in the morn and to be greeted by the awaiting Clan and country folks of auld Scotland. The activities this night in the Glen of Afton are to be lighting up all the homes on Magda mòr, as though the fairy folks themselves had brought the most beautiful twinkling stars to earth to join in with the country folk to be greeting the new morn sun." Wee Maw and William continue talking as they make their way to where Alain and the family stand on the rest of the Black Craig. Stephen, accompanied by a blushing Katriona, soon catch up with them.

The family all turn to look at the two young lovers in a critical silence. Katriona appears flushed and giggles nervously; then she hides her face partly behind Stephen, who is also looking very sheepish and more than a little bit nervous.A moment of silent tension passes before Stephen thinks to react, he points at the Clootie trees and says with absolutely no conviction in his voice, "Eh, lovely Clootie trees yiez have there to be sure Lady Wallace." Another moment's silence passes by, with the family's stern focus upon Stephen and Katriona. Wee Maw is excelling in giving them 'the look.'

Everyone laughs then welcomes the two obvious young lovers to the family midst... William throws his arm around a relieved Stephens shoulders and hugs him close. With his fist, he scours the hair on the top of Stephen's head, fun-burning his scalp. "Got yie there my fine Irish friend." A much-relieved Stephen replies while rubbing his sore head. "Yie did there right enough, ya big feckr yie." Everyone huddles close in the mild winter eve as a loving family, watching the bustling fiery lights of torches and bonfire celebrations in their glen, giving off a wonderfull glow all around the hilltops that can be seen for miles around. In the distance, a feint thumping sound could be heard from Andra's boys on the Tibby drums, the pulsing thump travels around the glen and likens to the imaginary sound of mother natures beating heart. Then the bagpipes start playing to signal for the processions to make their way down the Glenside. They all begin to move forward and down each hill like a myriad of slivery-gold lava trails, all flowing toward the great Shining fire from the heights and crags surrounding glen Afton.

Tugging at William's léine sleeve, Wee Maw says, "C'moan son, lets be seeing in the Hagmonaidh together." They walk arm in arm away back down the hill following the children, single men and girls, all with their flaming cycling torches and buckets of fire, swinging them wildly as they march down the drovers roads and paths from all the surrounding hills, proudly marshalled by the old warriors of times past, Auld Tam and Wee Graham, and on towards the great Shining fire at the head of the glen at Craig Darrach, till all the Wallace kith and kin eventually reach the central Shining fire with only moments to go before the magical moment of Hagmonaidh. Wee Maw turns to William, "Will you Coinach go and fetch bonnie Affric? We'll soon be reaching that special moment when the old year dies away and the new sun for the new year readies to rise." The two friends rush off to fetch Affric, when William enquires, "Dyie think she's fit for this Coinach?"

"Ah think so," replies Coinach, "when ah left her earlier, she asked to see if Uliann would go back down and help her, the two of them have clicked well as friends." William exclaims, "Uliann? I didn't know they knew each other that well?" Coinach replies, "How dyie think that Affric knew se' much about yie big fella?" William grins at his friend's remark, "Awe, ha… so it's Uliann who's been tellin' her all those stories about me. I knew it must o' been someone close, either that or Affric really is a mind reader." Coinach laughs, "Aye Wallace, Affric's all o' that and more." It's not lost on William seeing Coinach smiling again, maybe there really is great healing to be had at a time of celebrations such as this.

As they approach the little obhainn, Uliann comes to the door, with Affric by her side holding on tightly to her arm. William and Coinach are amazed to see her upright and attempting to walk. The two young men quickly rush over to help Uliann to bring Affric outside. "You shouldn't be trying to walk yet wee darlin," says William, "you've plenty o' time to be healing your broken bones, this might be a wee bit too soon for yie." A frustrated Affric replies tersely, "Ach Wallace, shut it big fella, it's too late now… can yie no' see I'm already walking." Coinach holds out a hand of support, "Can we carry you over in the rocker Affric? For you're to be the Aicé Bahn Rígh of the Hagmonaidh Fèis this night." Smiling faintly, Affric agrees to be carried. They gently set her carefully into a deep-seated wicker chair, with William at the back and Coinach at the front, prepared to carry their Aicé. Uliann quickly throws pelts of winter fox over Affric's legs and wraps a thick fleece and triple wolfskin pelt around her shoulders to keep her warm.

"Can I be your lady in waiting?" Enquires Uliann smiling at Affric. Before Affric could answer, Uliann says, "Wait a moment everyone." She rushes back into Affric's obhainn; then comes back with dried flowers she had bound earlier into a beautiful posy head garland, "A crown for our Aicé Ban Rígh Sídhe?" Uliann places the beautiful cluster ring of flowers on Affric's head then they all walk towards the gathering. When the "Royal" cortege approaches the great

Shining fire, all in the glen are gathered to greet the Ban Rígh Sídhe, the fairy Queen. Everyone cheers and shouts heartily as William and Coinach help Affric up onto the bow wagon to sit between Wee Maw and Mharaidh, to great approval and applause from everyone, for the gathered clan folk are proud that Affric, a noble Ceàrdannan princess, is to be their Aicé of the Hagmonaidh Fèis. Wee Maw reaches out and holds Affric's hand.

Mharaidh and Affric look at each other; then Mharaidh reaches out and gently holds her other hand. Uliann and Aunia stand behind Affric and wrap their arms lovingly around her. Wee Maw smiles, "Will you be reciting our blessing bonnie Affric? The clan o' the Wallace and all our kinfolks would be so honoured if a real Fionn Ban Rígh Sídhe, namely your bonnie self, would commence and take us into the Hagmonaidh Fèis." Stoically, Affric slowly stands up with the help of Wee Maw and Mharaidh, then she waits awhile in silence, looking around at all the gathered folk of Glen Afton, as though she is searching for the faces of her own clan… just one face from her own clan, but she searches in vain. Another few poignant moments pass in silence, everyone begins to wonder if Affric will say anything at all, another few tense filled moments pass by, when suddenly, as though she is now in another place, Affric slowly raises her palms facing up towards the night sky, she looks to the moon and begins to deliver the Fionn's Aicé blessing and incantation to the silent gathering…

> *"Sun and moon gie' hear ma plea,*
> *ther's non se' blin' wit canne see*
> *black blood frae hame's will rivers run,*
> *frae wains o' bears, who hails the sun…*
> *Feel ma pain an' hear ma cry*
> *Only yee will ken for why…*

Why se' sair tae me moon mother,
Yie make tae tak' ma wain,s, ma Maw,
ma sisters, faither and ma brother...
Fae folk o' the wheat n' barley corn
wie blessed sight our love was born,
then warm oor hearts and light the morn.
or oor wains ne'er see the dawn...
But freedom comes frae men of wood
they'll keep us safe frae evils brood...
tak' the God sic' black o' heart
tae cause the wilder geese tae part...
tae fatten wolves on slaughters glee
that eat the flesh o' you and me,
while Corbies gorge on hero's ee'n,
as yee and me hae never been...
Tae Tír Na n'Óg our fall birds flee
our tears frae bones will feed the tree...
Blood drowns the earth from west to east
but Dragons soul ne'er fear the beast
till Broom is gone and cannae feast.
our lives we give to yee...
Sun and moon gie' hear ma plea
though lookin' back is all we see,
though may pass a thousand years
though every yin is grief and tears
though I love and honour thee
for all to live... and all go free,
I gift tae you... all o' me..."

Affric gazes wide-eyed at all the faces in the gathering while everyone looks back in stunned silence... Not a single sound can be heard in the glen, not even the crackling of the Shining-fire. Wee Maw, slightly shaken by Affric's incantation, swallows hard and quickly composes herself to break the mesmeric moment, "We will all be thanking you bonnie Affric, for that was such a beautiful blessing upon our Fèis." Everyone remains silent; most still with their mouths open, staring at Affric. Wee Maw breaks the silence as she calls out… "WHERE'S WEE GRAHAM?" Then she sees him sitting with auld Tam at the Shining fireside, each of them with a craitur flagon in each hand, their mouths gaping open in complete consternation upon hearing Affric's fae blessing.Suddenly, Wee Graham responds, "Oh aye right yie are ma'am…" He stands up and calls aloud the honours… "LET THE HAGMONAIDH BEGIN… Grant, Seoras, if yie wouldn't mind?"

The glen Afton pipers start up the tunes of joy as auld Tam signals everyone to walk a distance away from the Shining-fire, then everyone and anyone who holds anything aflame, from a simple fire-stick to a fiery pitch ball awaits the command to launch their flaming missiles into the air with all their might. Affric raises her hands skyward then she smiles. The many fire-carriers upon seeing the approval of their Aicé Ban Rígh Sídhe, hurl their fiery messengers high into the night sky to arc, peak, then fall towards the centre of the Shining-fire as a wonderous heavenly waterfall of living star lave, cascading from the heavens above. A great roar of approval goes up from all at the clan gathering… the Hagmonaidh Fèis has now begun in the bonnie glen of Afton.

Stephen enquires curiously, "Jaezuz feckn Christ fella's, what the feck was that bein' all about comin' from Affric?" Coinach and William watch the Shining fire billow flames high into the night sky. William, himself is still slightly bewildered, "Ah really don't know…" Coinach shrugs his shoulders; then they walk over to ask Affric. Uliann says, "She's tired and feeling much pain." Wee Maw comes over and wraps a shawl around Affrics shoulders, "Aye, Affric wants to go back to her obhainn, will you boys help us?" Stephen replies, "Sure ma'am, that's what we're here for." Mharaidh speaks, "William, you wait here with me and your Granny a moment," William calls out to Uliann, Stephen and Coinach, now aiding Affric back to her obhainn, "I'll catch up with yiez in a wee while."

The Solstice festival is now in full swing with much merriment, dancing and singing at the northern gateway to the sinister Wolf and wildcat forest. Standing by the Shining-fire, Wee Graham shouts, "Listen up every one… All you wains who would like to hear the story aboot the mighty fightin' Giants Fionn McCool and Ben an Donner… yiez are all to be goin' away up tae the big hoose right in a wee while, for Wee Maw has a great story tae be telling yiez very soon." Wee Graham sits back down again beside auld Tam and his flagons of craitur. Alain joins William as Mharaidh speaks to him, "William, your father and I require your presence up at the Keep for a little while." He replies curiously, "What is it you want me for?" smiling, Alain replies, "Wait and see…"

As they meander through the festivities, Mharaidh walks between Alain and William by linking arms. Alain says, "We're sorry we didn't have a feast for your birthin' day son, but despite the circumstance, it's no' been overlooked, just a wee bitty late, that's all." Stopping for a moment, Mharaidh clasps William's hand. "Your father and I have some gifts for you that are precious to both us." William appears surprised. With a teasing smile, Mharaidh continues, "Meet us at the keep when you've settled Affric, that'll give us time to prepare… but don't be too long."

It takes William awhile to sort out his vittals with Affric before he makes his way back up to Wallace Keep, when he opens the oak doors and walks into the main hall, he sees his father Alain, Malcolm, Mharaidh, Wee Maw and all his nearest kith and kin standing by the great fire warming themselves and chatting, then everyone turns to welcomes him with a rousing cheer... He glances at the great feasting table to see that the gifts he'd received just before he left with the regiment of the Black Craig Wolf and wildcat Gallóglaigh to protect the peace of Scotland with the Guardian army.

On the table are his father's bull-leather battle-jack, his grandfather "Big" Billy's Dragon helm, broadsword, chainmail haubergeon and coif, are all meticulously polished and placed at the head of the table. Alain reaches out and puts his arm round his son's shoulders, Wee Maw stands beside him as the family gather around. Alain speaks, "Son... as your coming of the twenty first year, we all have little gifts we would want you to have to mark this special time in your life." Then Ranald offers the first gift... "William, I've a personal gift of Saint Jerome's Vulgate codex Amiatinus for you. As you know, this was the first book of your early Latin learning." Ranald looks at the codex. "It's the book that you and I will always remember as our bond of teaching and learning. I would wish you to have it as a token of my respect for you." Ranald lays the Codex of testaments on the table before William, who can see it truly is the book of his childhood learning in Latin scripture.

Uliann and Aunia unfold a beautiful stitched léine of dark green, with gold thread needlework and inlaid ornate Cruathnie knotwork embroidery, displaying the symbolic totemic history of the Wallace, The artwork includes the mighty Caledonian bear, flighted Morríaghan, the forest wolf, mountain wildcat and silver unicorns. He's amazed upon seeing the exquisite stitching of deep blacks and ochre shades of the flighted Morríghan sewn so intricately and with such detail into the panels of the léine. Centred on the chest is the stunning representation of a golden veined and turquoise spread winged Dragon, clutching five golden arrows. Uliann and Aunia both declare, "This is for you dear cousin, by our own hands we did spin and weave the cloth, then sewed it with all the family emblems and totems taken from the legends of Wallace history that represents us as a family, in both nature and in kinship, to you our brother, so dearly loved." Before he could respond, his cousins Malcolm, gentle Andrew, his brother wee John and Rosinn, present him with a large heart shield of great proportion, made of layers of boiled bull-neck leather, with a wheaten white frontage embossed in more delicate knotwork. On its outer edges and centered with the same stunning embossing, is the two clawed spread-winged Dragon of the Glen Afton Wallace coat of Arms.

William looks on in awe as they place it on the table beside the other family gifts. Gentle Andrew says, "We made this especially for you." William is amazed; all he can say is, "Tá wee brother." Wee Maw, Alain and Malcolm finally step forward. Alain speaks first, "We have something here for yie too William, this gift once belonged to your grandfather Billy." Alain hands a linen wrapped object to Malcolm, who hands it to Wee Maw, she says with a tear in her eye, "Your grandfather passed this gift to your uncle Malcolm, and we are all agreed that the time is now for you to be having all that was your grandfathers, as you are both so alike in looks and by your very nature."

Wee Maw pulls up her apron and blows her nose, displaying a rare moment of public emotion when speaking of her late husband, William's grandfather, then she presents a particular gift wrapped in a silk saffron cloth and contains something so precious, that he takes great care unwrapping the object, then he sees exactly what it is... "Naw...this is just incredible..." he exclaims, "I... I just don't now what to say..." Malcolm speaks, "This was made by Leckie mòr Lynn, when in his prime as master sword maker to Alexander. The metal comes from two ancient leaf blades that belonged to the Aicés Morríaghan and Devorguilla, broken at the battle of Alt Cluid Goram. Leckie made one for our late King Alexander, who was so impressed by the workman'ship, he had another made for your Grandfather, and as your brother Alan is in the priest-hood he has no need for its qualities, it falls it should be passed to you."

William gazes at the gift in his hands then he holds it high for all to see, revealing a beautiful ornate Dirk Sídhe, (spiritual knife) approximately fifteen inches long, with the Dragon of the Artur Àrd Rígh intricately carved into a handle made from bleach-white narwhal ivory, held fast with golden thread wire and silver rivets. Inlaid are small precious sapphire and cairn Goram gems, the blade is forge pleated over a thousand times while the many fine layers of metals were still white hot, then beat-welded together on the master hammerers forge. Finally tempered in live blood till the metal is the colour of the autumn sun, causing the blade to appear naturally inlaid with glorious knot-work patterns throughout the blades length. William has only ever heard of this dirk of antiquated legend, few have ever seen it.

Studying the exquisite detail of the dirk, William notices engraved writing in Latin just below the shoulder of the blade running down the full length of the blade, he flips it over and the other side face is inscribed with ancient script of Oghamic text. Wee Maw says, "Read out the inscription son." William pauses, then begins to speak fluently in Latin, reading the inscription upon the magnificent blade… "Dico tibi verum libertas optimum rerum, nunquam servili sub nexu vivito fili." Glancing around at his family, William is near overwhelmed by these gifts of blood and kinship. He composes himself, then translates the Oghamic script on the nether side of the exquisite blade… "I tell you this truth my son, the best of all things is freedom, never live under the bonds of slavery." William is stunned into silence, he has often heard his uncle in Dunipace say these words to him from his earliest childhood, but never in his wildest dreams could he believe that it would have such a profound strike on his senses on this night of nights with all his family and Clan present. Wee Maw puts her arms around him and kisses him gently on the cheek, she says with a passion in her voice… "Now you take care William, and may the forged steel and armour of our ancestors always protect you from harm and the bite from a snake." Wee Maw continues, "We'll look after these gifts for yie son, now away yie go and be seeing tae bonnie Affric, she wanted so much to be here with us but she asked to see you on your own when we had honoured your coming of age."

William stammers, "I don't know what to say…" Wee Maw replies with a smile, "Well here, afore yie go, there is one last gift for you that I wove myself for your Grandfather." She pulls from behind her back an old thick coarse-wool belt, about two yards long and four inches in width, with pastel colours of ocher red, blue, white and yellow. She deftly wraps the belt around William's waist and ties it together with a special slip-knot, then she pulls the hanging fringed excesses to his side, so that it drops down the outside of his leg. Standing back a little to look at him, Wee Maw says, "This was your grand-fathers Anam Crios (Spirit belt), It's a revered symbol that marks someone who is highly respected and loved by the members of the Clan Wallace, and in our hearts, it is for you William, so very much loved by us all."

A tearful Wee Maw steps forward and hugs her beloved grandson once more. Before he can react, Wee Maw sniffs and becomes emotional, "Now you be away and see to the bonnie lass son, for we celebrate this comin' year like no other… After all, we want the new young sun to shine bright n' warm for us the morrow don't we?"

Leaving the gathering, William makes his way from Wallace Keep totally lost in his thoughts, when he's confronted with Bailey, Coinach and Stephen blocking his path. Stephen says unceremoniously, "Wallace me boy, we've got something special here for yie too." He hands William a thick leather battle-jack, then says proudly. "Oi made it me'self." William looks at the battle-jack and could scarcely believe the quality of workman'ship and the long hours it must have taken Stephen to make it, he stammers "But…" Coinach hands William a crossbow, "This was my fathers, few men have the strength to pull and cock it, and my father loved you like a son Wallace, as I do like a brother. I know he would have wanted you to have this." William looks at them both, now he is totally lost for words. Coinach steps back a pace, whereupon Bailey walks forward and hands William the most stunning Longbow of full height, strength and draw.

Bailey looks proudly at William… "This is the finest bow I have ever made boyo, and I would wish you to have it, for I have never met a finer bowyer, here nor in my homeland of Cymru, apart from me that is…" William does not know what to say. Stephen says, "Right good sirs, if yie please… Shall we be going to the Fèis for some fresh libations? For young Katriona awaits her gift from the Gods, and if that's not my foin company this foin night… then the sweetest of dreams are not for her."

The three friends cheerily begin to make their way towards the shining fire to get their night started the way they mean it to continue. Coinach hesitates; he turns to look at William. He could still see the hidden pain beneath the happiness he exuded. "It's you she needs now Wallace." Still humbled by such loving thoughts and precious gifts, William nods in unspoken agreement with Coinach. For a second time this night, the young men look at each other; there are no words that can fill the moment between them as much as the great understanding and immeasurable trust each has for each other in their friendship. The young men part and William returns to his thoughts of this evening's amazing events. He walks onward deep in thought, until he finds himself at the door of Affric's obhainn. For some reason, he feels nervous about seeing her, he doesn't know why, then realises that he must wait a few moments to compose himself, then he opens the door, but he can barely see inside, the only light comes from the dull glow around the peat fire and the small tallow candles flickering their dance of light on the obhainn walls. He notices Affric lying on a deep pile crib of rug and woolskins beside the peat fire. He enters quietly, sensing an almost pungent aroma of heavily scented herbs and spice filling the air.

"Is that you Wallace?" enquires Affric as she painfully tries raising herself up to greet her visitor. "It is." replies William. He rushes over to her side and speaks with concern in his voice, "Wee darlin' don't try to get up, you should no' be moving so or you'll no' heal as well as yie should." Affric lies back down again, but she screams in pain. William tries to help but he doesn't know what's wrong. Finally she manages to lay down, then she speaks with great pain evident in her voice, "I'm bleeding bad Wallace, I think it's where my ribs broke through the skin." She puts an arm over her eyes as if to shield away the pain. Tears run from the corner of her eyes as she lay tortured by the pain from her injuries. With a care in mind, William lifts the warming mantle that covers her, revealing her naked broken body. He looks all over to hopefully reveal the source of pain. Though familiar with her body, the overwhelming mass of yellowish-blue bruising cannot hide or mask her natural beauty. Affric speaks with a little humour in her voice… "I see yie looking Wallace."

"Oh… ahm sorry Affric," exclaims William, "I was just trying to find the source o' your pain to see if I could help." Despite the excruciating pain, Affric leans over on her side, revealing a broken rib that has punctured through her skin. William sees the bleeding wound, "Thankfully it's only the wound that's broken; the rib has remained inside your body." Affric says, "There's eels soaking in uisge bheatha (Ooshga-beth - healing Whisky) over by the corner." She points to a wide mouthed silver Tinkler pot in the corner of the room. "There's some smithy water just over there too… The eel-skins are as fine as silk Wallace, soak them in that warm hot whisky pot a wee while then put it over the wound, then pour some fiongeur and smithy water over the poultice." Finding the large pot, William half fills it with smithy water then he puts a much smaller pot in the centre, fills it with whisky and hangs them both on a chain beside the peat fire. He lifts six long river eels from a bowl, skins them and puts the eel meat and skins back in the pot as it comes to a low boil. "It sure is the water of life Affric." exclaims William, referring to the many uses for whisky. He lifts the inner pot out, soaks the calfskins then wrings out the excess of whisky and begins to cleanse the wound in Affric's side.

"Wallace… break some of those duck eggs and separate the whites and put them on the wound next, that'll clot the blood in the wound." He dutifully separates the egg whites then repeats the same gentle actions of cleaning her wounds by applying the whites into the wounds. As he tends to her, he hasn't noticed Affric is looking deeply into his eyes while he concentrates on his task of putting egg whites and fiongeur on her wounds. He sits upright and looks at her, "Right wee darlin, do you want me to put the moss on the wound and seal it with the veal skins, fiongeur and smithy water?" Affric replies, "Naw, before you do that, go round the rafters of the obhainn and collect all the blanket-web from the spiders and lay that on the wound too." For the next few moments, William goes about a task that requires the finest touch to collect the gossamer blanket-web. It isn't long before he has more than enough web to lay on top of her wounds. Affric says, "Yie know the medicines of the woodland folks so well, don't yie Wallace?" Without looking up, he continues his medicinal preparations, "Aye well Affric, I've had some fine tutors for the learning ah reckon." William looks at her and winks, for much of what he has learned about healing has come from Affric herself. He painstakingly lays the web on the wound, then pastes a sfaggy moss and may butter poultice on top, sealing in the medicinal compounds, next he covers the wound with veal skins that have been soaking in hot whisky. "I'll need to slip the eel-skins under your body next to bind the veal skins and poultice tight, feck Affric, I'll try not to hurt you." William pauses, "Are yie ready?"

Affric nods while looking deep into his eyes as he cares for her. She is amazed and heart warmed to see such a tender caring side of William, she feels her heart beat stronger in her bosom at her thoughts. She's never seen or perhaps even had a cause to ever notice William being so gentle, caring and thoughtful before. She watches intently as he takes off his léine, revealing his smooth athletic muscular chest and torso. The heat in the little obhainn is so immense, combined with his exertions around the hot glowing peat fire, that William is soon sweating profusely as he diligently applies the medicinal elixirs and healing packs on Affric's broken body, completely unaware of Affrics growing arousal and passions rising.

Moving the pots to the side of the hearth, William takes out the supple eel-skins, pinning each one to another with hawthorn needles, giving him three long strips. He begins to slip them under her body, wrapping them around her torso to hold the poultice tight to her wound, then he leans closer to pull the eel skins around her back and under her breasts, suddenly, he stops and looks at her, he can feel her sweet hot breath on his neck, again she looks into his eyes with his face mere inches from hers, their eyes catch a glance, for a brief moment. The urge to passionately kiss his beautiful woodland lover is almost overwhelming, but he resists and continues with his nursing till he's bound the ends of the eel-skins tight, then he soaks it all in fiongeur and smithy water. Nothing is said as they both take in the time for the pain to ease from her body. Affric looks up at him once more, curiously… "Wallace…" she says while looking into his eyes. He picks her hand up gently and clasps it warmly. "Aye, what is it you ask o' me darlin'?"

Affric queries him, "Do you still find me beautiful? Am I still beautiful in your eyes?" William looks into Affric's dark brown almond eyes, "Affric me bonnie darlin' your beauty is soul deep and only matched by your beautiful smile." Suddenly she pulls away from him and holds both her hands over her face, then she rolls over, burying her face deep into the soft fleece of the winter crib and begins sobbing, wracking her body and causing her great pain. William is bewildered; he sits back up from the crib, feeling hurt and helpless by her display of emotions. He's at a loss and doesn't know what to do? Is it something he did or is it something he has said? Confused and concerned, William exclaims "Affric… Affric darlin' what is it that ails you? I don't know what to do?" He enquires again with urgency and confusion in his voice "Is it your wounds… tell me, what is it?" Affric stops sobbing after a while, much to his relief, but he's still deeply concerned and still quite unnerved. "It's my heart that pains me so Wallace, I fear you and all men will turn away from my marked face and body for all time." She looks at him with piercing eyes, "I may never know the love or passion of an honest lover ever again." Tears roll down Affric's cheeks as she begins sobbing uncontrollably, wracking her body with pain once more. "Awe bonnie Affric." says William with honest sympathy in his voice. He lay down beside her, "Affric ma darlin… we will always be the wildest o' lovers from the Wolf and wildcats."

A moment passes in silence, then she enquires with an emotional tremble in her voice, "Do you mean what you say Wallace? Tell me the truth… for I will surely know." William replies, "Did yie no' see the look on my face as I tended your wounds darlin'? That look must tell yie more than words could ever say." Affric's demeanor solemnly changes as she begins to speak to him with utter contempt and almost hatred apparent in her voice… "Do not lie to me Wallace… you're supposed to be my guardian… I needed you to protect me from harm, where were you? How can I ever trust you when you twist your knife in my heart and lie to my face… Wallace, it is a worse pain you cause me now, you with your false words of love that hurts and pains me more than I ever suffered when I was raped…"

This accusation strikes William deep into his heart as he involuntarily recoils… he can't believe what Affric has just said to him. His head spins, almost nauseous at such a heinous accusation of his supposed betrayal of their loving friendship. The thought is utterly confusing him that she would use such venomous words with such a conviction, how could his intentions so caring have made her say something that any man of honour would be heart and soul crushed by.

Affric glares at him, but he says nothing, he couldn't be certain of how to settle her demeanor and he's finding it impossible to understand how he could ever now bring her to peace. Sitting up slowly, he strokes Affric's long black hair with affection, comforting her, but she shrugs him away.

Eventually Affric appears to calm down as her pains ebb, then a tapping sound is heard coming from the door. William turns and sees Uliann's head peak inside the obhainn. He raises a finger to his lips, signaling for Uliann to enter quietly. She enters and carefully closes the door behind her then comes over and sits beside William on Affric's crib. "Uliann is that you?" enquires sleepy voice from the crib, "Aye it's me," replies Uliann. "I've come to sit with you for I thought yie might like some company." Affric looks up, "I would like that." William and Uliann glance at each other, as kin they both know something is badly amiss, Uliann frowns and signals for William to leave, Affric looks up at him with a strange hostile look in her eyes. "Wallace, you have your family out there celebrating this night... I will be fine in Uliann's company. Please... just go, go now and leave me alone." Affric sullenly turns her face away. William knows that he cannot find any way to break Affric away from her dark thoughts of what she appears to believe of him.

"Are yie sure you want me to leave?" Affric will not look at him; she speaks curtly, "Go Wallace, just leave me alone I say..." William is struck by a deep hurt he's never known before, he knows he has hurt Affric, but he doesn't know the how or why. Not quite knowing what he should do, he leans over Affric and kisses her gently on the forehead, but she makes it obvious his touch is unwanted by looking away from him. Still confused, William quietly gathers his clothes together, pulls on his breeks, (trousers) grabs the rest of his clothing into a bundle then looks at Affric. He is about to lay a hand of comfort upon her, but feels that it may only inflame her. Putting on his brogan, William walks with Uliann to the door; then he stops and looks back, "She'll be fine." whispers Uliann with a faint smile. He looks at Uliann and cups his hand to her cheek; then they embrace. He speaks quietly, "I dearly hope so sister." Uliann quietly closes the door behind him as he leaves the obhainn.

William is confused and feeling utterly devastated. His heart is in great pain caused by Affric's words, for in her mind, he is somehow at fault. He wanders over to a large ancient standing stone while pulling on his winter brat to fend off the extreme cold after being in the warm atmosphere of the obhainn. Looking around the glen, he can see the varied states of celebration being enjoyed by his kith and kin, but his thoughts return once more to Affric. Perhaps her emotional turmoil is because she knows he loves the maid Marion, but that truth has always been open and apparent since ever he knew he had those feelings himself, as has Affric's love for the Ceàrdannan prince of Galloway has always been apparent. But her outburst haunts him, her venom and almost hatred… then he thinks… *'Perhaps there is no Ceàrdannan prince… Could it be that Affric loves me as deeply as I love another?'*

İ∏VERGARVA∏E

Winter turns to spring, then into a glorious summer as the people of Scotland nervously await the arrival of the maid of Norway to ascend the throne. An uneasy peace settles in Scotland between the antagonistic Lords Baliol, Comyn and de Brix.

Meanwhile, an early season harvesting is at its height in the old Kingdom of Galloway and everyone in Glen Afton celebrates the wedding of Katriona Graham to Stephen ua H'Alpine of Connaught. Almost fifty miles away, a meeting is being held between Bishop Wishart and True Tam in the Bishops Palace near Glasgow... "I'm telling yie Robert," says True Tam, "There's a great evil stalking this realm, it will enslave us all and spill the blood for generations to come if we don't prepare." Wishart broods over True Tams words, "But what can we do? De Brix has shown us his hand, other competitors have sworn to civil war if any claimant again tries to usurp the throne from the Maid. It may be we must look to the youngblood Tam, young nobles that want to change the world, not old men who wish to own it." True Tam says, "There's one youngblood in I notice in particular, he's not a noble by any means Robert, but he's from fine Céile Aicé stock. I often see signs that he will be a deciding cohesive force for Scotland when the time comes, and there surely will come the time when he will bring all of

Scotland together as one, even the nobles, of that I am certain. Whenever I see him, I see surrounding him the colours of blood, death and utter destruction, yet I know he's never the instigator. I fear his life may be short and many will die because of him, but many more will live as free men because of him. Often times I dream strange dreams and I see him or the Blue Dragon uniting the otherworld to protect us from this imminent evil." Intrigued, Wishart enquires "And who is this archangel you speak of Tam, who will be our saviour?"

"Young William Wallace…" replies Tam. Wishart raises his eyebrows in surprise, "Young Wallace… from ach na Feàrna? Surely you jest with me Tam, he's the son of a lowly knight, Alain Wallace of Glen Afton. We both know the nobles will never be led by a youth such as he on the morrow, for we already know they cannot agree amongst themselves this very day. It would be beneath their dignity to follow some untested shallow youth. They'd far rather go to war and destroy this realm on a misguided sense of personal injustice first. I think your visions are confused with hallucinations in your fae kingdom Tam." Undaunted, True Tam continues, "I tell yie Robert, all of my troubled life I have read the signs and you have listened, and these seeings have always proved to have been true. Well, I tell you now, I emerge from a time of my deepest troubles, and young Wallace's spirit is surely now entwined with my own. If I was born to serve this realm as a seer, then I believe I must now hone my lifelong skills to serve this youth when the calling comes… and Robert, the calling is a' coming, and it will be a slave's life and death for us all if we don't prepare."

True Tam pauses, his eyes pleading for Wisharts understanding. "I speak to you Robert as a fellow Céile Aicé and Breitheamh Rígh, as well yourself being the religious leader in our realm of this Christian faith. Your love of our realm's independence will only be slaited sweet if you at least consider the voices of the Fae and the Anam Alain (Beautiful spirit) of this land." Wishart says, "Any other who spoke these words to me Tam would be deemed a witless fool, or worse, a heretic. But a lifetime of understanding you as not only a loyal friend, but as a brother Céile Aicé and Breathaim Rígh, this alone makes me heed your words, perhaps now more than ever. These times are something none of us could ever have dreamt of before Alexander's death." True Tam sighs, "Aye and that's another conundrum that still remains as unfinished business…" Wishart knows to consider in earnest the prophecies from the Old Tongue and seeing of True Tam. Wishart says "Should I lay aside the cloth of the church that you may speak more freely Tam… do I really want to know what you see?"

"Robert, there's a dark side to the moon, we know we will never see it, yet we all know it's there. The dark side of what I have seen is fast approaching this land and I see it. I should have shared this with you before and with all the other Guardians freely; you know this also to be true. I should tell all who would listen of what I see." Wishart sups from his goblet then enquires, "Tell me then Tam, what is it you see?"

True Tam gazes intensely through the magnificent stained-glass windows at the loch-moat that surrounds the opulent palace of the Bishop, then he replies, "I will tell to you Robert that this young Wallace and I will ne'er live to see this land free from the oncoming scourge of the Black Dragon." Surprised by this comment, Wishart exclaims, "What say you, about a visitation of the Black Dragon?" True Tam continues, "Should you choose to see with your ears the words of the Neachneohain (NicKnevin) I'll surely tell to you of what words I heard when Aros Séran spoke to me when last in ma' otherworld home in Huntley bank." Wishart sees an expression on his friend's face he has never seen in a lifetime of friendship. "You would tell me what the daughter of the divine sister has foretold old friend?" True Tam holds is head as though an excruciating headache is taking control of his entire body, then just as quickly, he calmly looks at Wishart and says…

"Neath the hollows o' the Eildon tree,
When sight ne' mair shall speak tae me
There bides ma wife the Aicé o' Sídhe
When ears ne'er hear o' all I see,
By men o'broom ahl be took away…
Upon the fifth return o' Lamass day…"

Wishart sits back and exclaims, "You'll lose the gift of the sight?" True Tam laughs, "No my friend, I shall be murdered." Wishart splutters, "Murdered…?" Tam smiles "Aye Robert, they will come to me five years hence, men o' the broom will take my life, but it will be too late for them with their vile and evil ambitions, for all that I have said to you, will be as our David faces their Goliath of Gath… IF you heed my words about young Wallace of Ach na Feàrna. I tell you this now Robert, that my life must be dedicated to his very nurture and offer to him many choices that he may not have otherwise had in this life."

"You say men of Broom, isn't that the house of the Angevin Plantagenet's… the King of England…" Wishart gasps "Longshanks will have you murdered?" Tam nods, "Aye it would seem so Robert, but it's awhile away yet…" Displaying no obvious reaction to Tams words, Wishart solemnly enquires, "Then what does the Aicé Aros Séran say, your Queen of the Fae, what does she predict for me then Tam?" True Tam replies curiously, "Do you really want to know what the dark side has seen for you?" Wishart smiles, for he has no fear of the sight, but in these dramatic times… "Aye Tam, tell to me what your wife the Aicé o' otherworld does say about me, and of that which would protect our realm… and hers." True Tam reveals to Wishart Aros Séran Neachneohain's prophecy…

"A sea o' blood shall blanche this land,
The dragon black, yie'll kiss his hand…
Yet he yie fight yie'll join his band,
then damn yie be as a man of war,
buried deep in a sudron torr…
But come the year, that yie'll ne'er see,
The Dragon blue will set yie free
For then yie'll hear th' raven sing,
Where fish can't swim who hold the ring.
Neath' a flaming hazel oak that ne'er shall grow,
Your life shall free this realm from woe…."

"The Black dragon… Longshanks again." exclaims Wishart. "Aye," says Tam "And you know it will mean no quarter given when he unfurls the Black Dragon banner upon this land." Scratching his chin, Wishart continues to ponder over the prophecy. "And you say that one day I'll welcome him as my lord, yet I'll be imprisoned by him?" True Tam sighs, "Aye, for many long years too ma auld friend." Wisharts hazel eyes are pinpoint focused as he looks at True Tam, "And I'll return to walk these lands of the fair green place as a blind man, and you will die by another's hand…" True Tam smiles, "Death comes to us all ma' friend, but I'll be residing in the Eildon Hollow with my Aicé bahn Sídhe Aros Séran, that's where I truly belong." True Tam grins "And naw… ahl no' be dead Robert, I'll simply be free from all these earthly woes.

And you ma auld friend, where might you be… sitting in the lap of your Christian God?" Wishart smiles, "Ha, never mind about me Tam, but tell me more about the youngblood of your dreams. I know young Wallace well, but I've not seen him in awhile, not since he left the calling for life with Alain down in Glen Afton. Tell me what you know of him first."

"He's from the blood of the Blue Dragon Robert, this you already know. I've observed this young fella awhile now. The Ettrick, Wolf and Wildcat forest hunter packs grow stronger each day under his leadership. And with all the Gallóbhet youngblood coming of age, Wallace is now firmly established as a chieftain Ceannard of these hunters, as well as his own clan. Old hunters have blessed his following by naming them the Wolf and Wildcat hunters, calling upon the spirit of those noble beast to attend them in great measure and character, gleaning the same stealth and bond pride as a band of brothers and sisters. The Wolf and Wildcat hunters who follow young Wallace have established themselves as the most efficient and effective hunter group in the southwestern forests of Scotland. Young Wallace instills a similar command structure on his hunters as the Gallóbhet war bands, running the hunter packs on the Sparr system. He has three Ceannard who help him train all the youngblood Ceitherne. I tell yie this Wishart, Wallace prepares and hones his natural skills unwittingly for a war that will one day defeat the guile of any invading army."

Looking at True Tam thoughtfully, Wishart enquires, "You say these youngblood Gallóbhet may be the saving of Scotland Tam, and who else is with young Wallace that I should be aware off, who else may flock to the banner of his Blue Dragon?" Looking deeply into Wisharts eyes, True Tam says, "I see the friendship of many powerfull youngblood who will stand by his side, the likes of young Moray of Avoch,

Stewart of Bonkill, Graham of Dundaff, the Comyns of Lochaber and Badenoch, Fraser of Neidpath, young Robert Bruce of Carrick and the Douglas, they are but a few, and all of them but the Bruce are first degree Ceannard of the Garda Céile Aicé. I will tell you this too, dwelling right under your nose there are supremely intelligent clerical minds who will see in Wallace great leadership… Baldred Bisset, Duns Scottus, John Blair, Bernard of Kilwinning, William Lambertoun… all of them and more who would wish to change this world before the heavens falls upon us and we're lost forever. Though they know not yet of this path, I do know they sense it may be coming. And one day soon, you too will flock to his banner Robert."

Wishart contemplates this revelation as True Tam continues, "Young Wallace is honing skills you will most certainly need with his Gallóbhet o' Galloway." Wishart replies with disdain, "A dangerous profession to ply with those wild and savage animals o' Carrick and Galloway Tam."

True Tam smiles, "Aye, that may be so Robert, but they were the backbone of the guardian army when we had to thwart the Pact of de Brix, and with their warring prowess, they have rightly earned the honour to fight in front of our Kings since time began. Lift your mockery of them Robert, for you and Scotland will surely need those wild savage animals of Carrick and Galloway as you call them, and this need will come much sooner than you think, for without the courage and tenacity of the Gallóbhet, we may as well forget any notion of remaining a free and sovereign realm, now and forever."

"And you say the key to all of this is young Wallace of Glen Afton? Despite our realm having such great nobles who would think us witless at the thought?" True Tam shakes his head, "Many of these great nobles you cherish will fade away before your eyes for gold, silver or even perhaps simply the fear of losing their English lands to Longshanks, but hear me well Robert, one day all young men and women of Scotland will follow Wallace's leadership without question, it can already be seen by the mettle of the Gallóglaigh resolve in Carrick and Galloway. The Gallóbhet system of warfare and their selfless sacrifice will buy Scotland the valuable time it needs."

"And what is this system you say may be our redemption led by this young saviour our army and nobles will follow Tam, incredible as all this sounds to me, I want to know of the impossible…" True Tam replies, "The Gallóbhet battle structures are each run by three Ceannard who have in turn three Ceithernach, which makes the numbers of each hunter pack generally twelve hunter stalkers and thirty-six scout trackers at any one time, depending on the hunt. Multiply that throughout the entirety of all the hunter packs in Galloway and this will number fifteen thousand experienced Gallóbhet or more, this is how they will fight in war Robert, not as soldiers of battle, but as hunters of prey…" Wishart enquires "And what of Wallace's brothers, what part may they take in this supposed play?" True Tam replies, "There has been the return to Scotland of his elder brother Alan from France."

"Aye" says Wishart, "He has completed his studies in our Cathedral of Cluny and now tutors at the Augustinian Priory of Cambuskenneth as the head of languages. Young Alan often resides on the priory estate near Dunipace between Glasgow and Stirling, a second home to the Wallace boys and known well from their youth." True Tam says, "One day their detailed knowledge of that land in particular will be pivotal in the saving of Scotland from this coming evil. Young Alan will also be of use in the future with International diplomacy and links with your Holy Father, if we can bring young Alan under the wing of Bernard of Kilwinning, Duns Scotus and Baldred Bisset… then these are the youth who will take up your cause when your fingers no longer feel the reigns and your eyes no longer see the road ahead…"

*   *   *

A peaceful Life in Glen Afton continues with the folk there having no earthly knowledge of True Tam and Eros Séran's predictions; nor the drama that is about to unfold. The clan of William and his friends nesting in the ancient fastness of Glen Afton is growing rapidly with both new friends and old joining them, including William's old friend, the roguish chaplain John Blair. Despite his token resistance, he had finally succumbed to the temptations of the young French sisters of sensual mercy, which is the main reason he has been expelled from his studies in France, under pain of being severely flayed by the monks for his disrespect in the ways of the church. The other reason for his expulsion is for his inability and not growing a little wiser before he thought to put many young French nuns to condition of birth.

Affric has greatly recovered from her ordeal and has found a welcoming home in the fastness of glen Afton. Her health and demeanor has benefitted immensely from the love and affection she receives from the Clan folk of the glen. But unknown to William, she has fallen deeply in love with him, though she does not dare tell him, nor dare show her feelings, her fear is that it may bring her catastrophe and a broken heart which she is not yet ready to deal with should he reject her love.

Most expected is the love between Stephen and Wee Graham's daughter young Katriona. They've married with the blessing of her father and mother Auld Jean, who were more than happy to consent to the union, Stephen proving to be astute, intelligent and so very devoted to Katriona, and of course he is of fine Irish stock as wee John had found in his wife Ròsinn, Stephen's sister.

The wedding banns have been read and the mid-summer wedding day hand-fast celebrated, the bride and groom have both successfully peed in the bucket of love and will soon be going to Ireland to celebrate the union with Stephens family, accompanied by Wee John and Rosinn. The celebrations of the wedding in Glen Afton, has lasted for many days, with most attendee's now sleeping off terrible hangovers due to their affection for the Craitur. William, Coinach and other members of the Wolf and Wildcat hunters are sleeping off their excess in a hay barn when Bailey wakes with a start upon hearing many raised voices outside the barn. Pulling himself together despite a thundering hangover, Bailey sits upright and pushes his wild unkempt long hair behind him and listens intently, he looks to see where his friends are to make them aware of this noisy disturbance outside. Focusing in the dim barn, he sees William and Affric sleeping nearby. Some of the others he could vaguely distinguish in the gloomy light, looking dead to the world. Others he couldn't see, but can easily guess where they are, guided by the snoring and coughing coming from darkened areas of the barn.

Bailey looks around the gloomy interior while listening to the raised voices outside. Sleeping beside him is the beautiful Gallóbhan, Lihd, who has been visiting Bailey on many occasions since they first met at Saint John's. They too have found that love has blessed their hearts and they've now become virtually inseparable. Bailey whispers, "Ho Wallace, wake up…" but there's no response. He leans over and pushes William to wake him up. "Fuck off Bailey…" groans a groggy William as an equally dazed Lihd stirs. Bailey insists,

"Wallace, get up… quickly, there's something going on outside the barn." then he calls for everyone to wake and rise. Eventually they all begin to stir, Coinach, Andra, Seamus and Tam óg fall out of a hay stack as one tangled drunken heap, revealing they're in the company of a few of the more liberated glen maids who have also been enjoying an eve of wedding craitur excesses, and somehow found their way to the barn with the leaders of the Wildcats. Rubbing the sleep from his eyes, William enquires, "What's happenin'?" Bailey, now on his feet, quickly tries to gain everyone's attention… "Fella's get up quickly, I'm tellin you boyo's… I've heard voices that are sure not blessed with any peace just outside the barn a moment ago." Pulling on his léine, William mumbles, "Its likely Auld Jean beatin' Wee Graham with a big stick or somethin." Suddenly the doors of the barn are flung open and Alain calls out… "William, Bailey, get up… everyone get up quickly, we need yiez now, there's has been a terrible trouble."

"What the Fuck?" Exclaims Bailey. Alain calls out, "Bailey quick… get everyone up and then meet us at the kailyards as soon as yiez can." Bailey kicks at his friends to emphasize the urgency of the moment, "Lihd, William, Affric Coinach… get up, we're needed urgently." The Wildcat hunters slowly pull themselves together… for the craitur shows no mercy on heads that invites excess. They all attempt to get dressed of a fashion, then they stagger towards the confused noises they hear outside the barn. Finally they make their way through the barn doors to see what's going on. William and Coinach exclaim almost in unison, "Fuckin' hell…" Coinach cries out, "I'm Blinded, too much light in me eyes." William cringes, "Jaezuz… if drinkin' the craitur and settin' yerself on fire during a wedding Fèis brings the sun out happy to see us, I don't think it'll rain for another feckn year." Shielding his eyes and trying to focus, William sees that Lihd and Affric both trying to wake themselves up with the shock of the cold water, by burying their heads in a water trough between two drinking horses. Andra and Seamus sit leaning against the barn doors, basking in the mid-morning sun, covering their heads and trying to return to sleep, for they're still very drunk. William, Bailey and Coinach haul them to their feet then they follow the rest of the Wildcats wandering up to the kailyard where Auld Tam greets them,

"You lot are to meet up with yer father right away Wallace, he's up in the big house with the Chieftains, the Ceannard o' the Clan and some knights from the council of the Guardians." William's fuzzy head clears hearing the earnest tone in Tam's voice. "What is it Tam… what's been happenin'?" Auld Tam replies, "Yie had better get the news from the man himself son." Auld Tam continues, "Bailey, Lihd, you two go with him. Andra, Tam óg and the rest o' yiez had better wash up and get some vittals in yie and be prepared for a long campaign, then I need yiez to get up the S'taigh am Rígh and draw your weaponry and armour, yiez will be leaving as soon as yiez are ready." Upon hearing this information, William, Bailey and Lihd rush up the steps leading to the Keep and are about to enter, when the outer doors burst open and everyone comes flooding out, all dressed in war armour, battle dress, Haubergeon and leather battle-jacks, and all are armed to the teeth with a fortitude grim.

"Feckn' whoa…" exclaims William as he's knocked sideways by a giant of a man who comes rushing through the door like a charging bull, hardly noticing his contact with William. Alain and Malcolm come out the door to greet them. "We need you all to get up to the S'taigh armoury fast and get your fighting gear on, we need every Gallóbhet we can muster." William is concerned at the urgency in Alain's voice. Malcolm briefly acknowledges William as he brushes past making his way towards the Ach na Feàrna Gallóglaigh squadron resting down by the Afton water. The serious countenance on everyone's face confuses the Wolf and Wildcat leaders.

"What is it Dá, what's goin on?" enquires William. "It's the Brix and Baliol," replies Alain "they've fuckin' attacked each other again, but this time its no' any false bravado, it's open civil war… and it's spreading throughout the whole of south west o' Scotland like a wildfire, and there's many Irish and English mercenaries fighting on each side." Alain notices Lihd as he pulls on his gauntlets, "Lihd, you may leave us now and join the Gallóbhan down in Galloway if you wish, but I reckon it would be too dangerous to move on your own, and they're about a fifty odd miles away. I'd prefer it if yie stay with us till we meet up with Faolán and the main body of the Gallóbhan. You're more than welcome to join with us till you meet your people." Lihd has no hesitation in her reply, "I will stay with Bailey and William." At that moment, Affric arrives, Alain says, "Affric, I need you to go to Mharaidh, down at the stables to be helping to get my horses and tack ready for the journey, will you go there now?"

"I will." replies Affric. Though she is well recovered from her injuries, she is still too weak for any great exertions, and has difficulty walking from the slow painful healing of her broken leg. Affric dutifully turns and makes her way slowly down towards the stables to help, while Alain speaks to William, Bailey and Lihd… "I will tell you of all we know at the moment. De Brix and Baliol have sent many bands of soldiers and cutthroats into each other's lands and now they're killing everyone in the Balloch's, shielin's… and any strangers they can find in each others territories." William looks at Alain, "This is terrible news Dá. What do yie want us to do?" Alain replies, "It's a time that we must go to War son.

The fighting is spread over the whole of Galloway and into Annandale, and it's not just as two armies, there are many smaller units hunting down and killing everyone they can find, we are tasked by the Guardians to contain this disaster, or eliminate any who would resist this command. Should we fail in our task, the fighting factions will quickly spread this malice throughout the entire realm. We know the entire houses of the Comyn's army has already gathered and on their way down from the Highlands in support of Baliol, we also know many more Irish pressed levies under the command of the Red earl of Ulster are coming across to support de Brix, as well as his own English levies and allies flowing across the border. We must do everything in our power to stop this."

"What will we do Dá?" enquires William. Alain replies "Get the Wolf and Wildcat hunter scouts together, then get all your packhorse loaded with a week's supply of vittals. We need you to scout the northwestern Carrick and Galloway borders between here and Invergarvane... I need you to keep us informed by relay and messenger pigeon of all you see." Alain pauses seeing the eagerness on William's face. "I want you to heed these words son, under no circumstance are you to get into any fights or skirmishes, that's not your remit. You're to avoid any contact with hostile troops. All we require is your eyes and ears, not heroics, is that clearly understood?" William replies emphatically, "Understood..." Alain continues, "Now go and make ready..."

William notices four armoured knights approach them as he prepares to carry out Alain's orders. He watches as they make introduction with his father. "William, hold a moment," Says Alain "this is Sir John Stewart and sir Colin Campbell, lately of the Brix Pact, and these other men are Sir Simon Fraser of Oliver and sir John de Graham from the guardian army." The knights acknowledge William, Coinach,

Bailey and Lihd then turn to talk with Alain. A voice beside William says, "I see that you've warmed up a little since we last met Wallace." Recognising the knight instantly, William exclaims... "Feck me Graham, I thought it was you..." The two friends embrace then they talk about the crisis. A renewed friendship is developing between these two young men of similar age and striking physique. They discuss what has happened since Saint John's and what they are about to venture, when they notice a lone knight galloping up the drove road. Eventually the rider pulls his warhorse to a halt beside Alain then dismounts. William recognises the strange looking knight as the man he saw at the gates of Ach na Feàrna; True Tam, then he remembers that he thought he had seen him at Affric's bedside, or he had dreamt it? But he'd definitely found the phial he had left behind...? Sir Malcolm returns as True Tam and speaks urgently with Alain and the other knights, Alain turns and calls out, "William... Graham, over here... now."

They quickly attend Alain who informs them, "There are many deserting the Brix Pact, the Lords Stewart and Campbell here have came over to the Guardians and inform us that they have been duped. They tell us de Brix had simply feigned his last uprising to gain detailed knowledge of who would resist his desire for the throne of Scotland. De Brix has stepped into the background and is firmly behind his son, Robert Brus the Earl of Carrick, who now leads the new Pact." Lord John Stewart speaks, "The ambition of de Brix is not in the interest nor for the benefit to the community of Scotland. He serves only his own ambition and firmly rejects the Maid of Norway as our next regent. Now Brus of Carrick makes his own claim while disregarding the treaty, this we cannot condone, nor can we stand at his side in this heinous rebellion." Alain says "We have also found out from other sources that Brus and his father have made another pact with forces outside Scotland." Stewart says "Aye. De Brix has made a deal with the Dutch magnate Count Floris. In exchange for supporting the Brus with monies, ships and mercenaries, De Brix will grant Floris and another claimant from England, sir John de Hastings, an English Baron who rules the Welsh gateway of Abergavenny, one third of Scotland each if they swear fealty to him as their liege lord, which they have already foresworn and ratified by attaching their seals to the Turnberry Pact charter. De Brus has also agreed with De Burgh of Ulster that should he wish to elevate as the King of all Ireland, de Brix will support him in full." Alain exclaims, "I cannot believe what I'm hearing, but believe it I must." Lord Stewart says, "De Brus has attacked Baliol, Douglas and Comyn's lands during the summer harvest Fèis, he knew that everyone would be at their most vulnerable at this time of harvest to gain total advantage by surprise. His English, Irish and Dutch allies bolster his forces and are now wreaking death and destruction into Galloway, if we don't stop Brus now, Scotland will soon be at total war with itself. De Brix has set his path on the destruction of houses of Baliol, Douglas and the Comyn."

True Tam says, "Brus has Baliol's mother Devorguilla trapped in Dalswinton, castle in the southwest, Comyn has responded by putting another two large armies in the field as Brus has already attacked Comyn's strongholds of Dun Fries, Cruggletoun and Bedrule. Baliol in retaliation has brought in his northern English levies in to fight his way through Galloway from the east, but Brus has surrounded Baliol's castles with English mercenaries, Norsemen of the isles and Irish mercenaries coming from the Earl of Ulster. Baliol's fierce Gallóbhet are now moving fast to break them out of the trap by attacking the Brus' Pact from the west."

Exasperated, Malcolm says, "Brus may try and kill Devorguilla, for she is next in line to the throne should the maid for whatever reason not be crowned."

Appearing deeply concerned, Alain says, "We may yet save her and contain this war in the southwest if we make speed, but this will be extremely difficult, for the fighting is now spread over hundreds of square miles." True Tam speaks, "Messengers have been sent out for the northern Guardian army to regroup and make haste. They will meet with Comyn's forces driving south towards the Annan dale and plead with the antagonists to desist, though I fear that gesture will be futile as we are likely too late." For a moment, the silence of thought is deafening amongst the gathered warriors as they consider the catastrophic situation, then Colin Campbell speaks, "If war breaks out in the eastern borders between the Comyn Clan and count Floris' mercenaries coming in from Newcastle, Scotland will surely tear itself apart, or perhaps even risk a war with England if Floris' mercenaries are halted in the English side of the border marches. We must contain this outbreak in Galloway at all costs for we fear de Brix will not stop Until he wrests the throne of Scotland for his son, or die in the attempt."

"It is time my Lords," says Malcolm "We must make haste to Rosbroch then onwards to Dun Fries and get between the factions, every minute we delay bleeds our realm with a fatal wounding." The Guardian council quickly disperse to make ready to leave. Alain turns to William, "I want you to proceed with your orders and leave for the Carrick and Galloway border marches. Bailey, go and make sure everything is ready, I'll talk with William and give him exact orders that you are all to follow." Bailey acknowledges his orders and leaves with Lihd to carry out his duties and prepare to leave Glen Afton. Alain speaks to William, "You've heard as I have heard son, now understand this, your orders are as important to me, for our very lives may depend on you carrying them out, no more no less. Do not get involved in any battles or fights, I can't stress this enough, we need all the information you may send to us, is that clear?" William replies, "I understand." Stephen of Ireland comes rushing over with his chainmail, armour and sword in his arms. Alain demands sharply… "Where do yie think you're going?" Stephen replies, "Oi'm comin' wit yiez wherever that may be." Alain shakes his head "You're newly wed Stephen, you're staying here with Katriona. We have enough men going with us and I would not be responsible for your safety to young Katriona or your father should anything happen to you. It's not your fight Stephen, and today you will leave for Ireland with Katriona." Stephen splutters "But…" Alain is adamant, "That's a command, do not disobey me." Stephen dumps his kit on the ground then sits down on top of it, totally dismayed. Graham speaks to William, "We need your hunters and trackers to do exactly as your father bids you Wallace; there is only you and your men who know these glens, hills and mountains like no others." William replies earnestly, "You have them."

As Alain and Graham prepare to leave, they pass by a demoralised Stephen, Alain pauses a moment then puts his hand on his shoulder, "I am sorry Stephen, but it's not your fight." Stephen shakes his head then looks away. Alain, his face relenting from that of a stern commander to that of a father, walks over to William, reaches out and clasps him by the hand. Looking proudly at his son. He says, "Take care William. Do as I have ordered and you'll be safe, I need you, Scotland needs you… do you understand me?" William replies, "Aye Dá, I understand you." Alain continues, "Be cautious and report everything back to me by a relay to our forward positions, and I mean report everything."

William nods his head, "I will Dá." Graham, who is standing nearby, speaks to William with a wry smile, "In this life or the next?" William laughs, "This life…?" Graham then leaves with Alain to muster the Guardian troops and all Wolf and wildcat Gallóbhet gathered in Glen Afton. William glances at Stephen, "Ma friend, I wish you were coming with us, but if it's too dangerous for you to head west to catch your ship to Ireland, why not bide here till we return? Then we'll see if me Dá will change his mind if this madness is still aflame." Standing up, Stephen shakes William by the hand, "Away yie go Wallace. Sure now, wont you be needing a man of the finest caliber making it so that this glen is as you would wish it to be by your return? And wit yiez all been and gone, oi can hone me lovemaking skills wit me bonnie new wife without disturbance…" William and Stephen both laugh out loud, "C'mon Stephen, yie can help us get ready."

The two friends make their way down to the corral to meet with all the young men of the Wolf and Wildcat hunters, who are stunned when they hear of the news in detail from William. Hundreds of mounted men from the Guardians, Black Craig, Cumno and the Wolf and wildcat hills speed past them on horseback towards the southern gateway of the Glen Afton, prepared to confront the Brus Pact their allies and levies, this time as major detachments with forces to be spread out to search for the warring factions and to bring them to peace… or eliminate them. William says, "Galloway is an ill and desperate land to do battle Stephen with its great thick forests and deep ravine gullies, craggy glens, marshlands and moors." Stephen replies, "Feck Wallace, oi'm only here a little while so it is, but even I have seen that the territory of Galloway is a treacherous place for the unwary, and it's sure not a place fit to feckn fight a bleedin' bloody war." William nods forlorn at the thought.

The Wolf and Wildcat hunter scouts are preparing to leave when William speaks once more with Stephen, "I really am sorry you're not coming..." Stephen replies, "Wallace, I'm not leaving you this day, and I won't be leaving here till you're back here safe and this tragedy is over and done with." William grins as Stephen continues, "And you're right there Wallace, it wouldn't be safe to travel with Katriona by me side, and all of that to be worrying about is somethin' that I will be avoiding. So, if this war is true to be sure, then who would be protectin' everyone here while you lot are all away gallavantin' around those there bleedin' hills?" William mounts the horse that Bailey has brought, then he smiles at Stephen, "Thanks to yie brother."

Stephen looks on as Bailey, Coinach, Lihd and the youngblood scouts all mount their horses, armed and dressed in their léine, Haubergeon and leather battle armour. The youngblood proudly hold their fluttering pennants of house and clan high. A despondent Stephen calls out, "You lot take extra bleedin' care without me'self being there to look after yiez, will ya?" Affric and Katriona come over and link arms with Stephen as they watch their young friends prepare to depart. Rushing forward, Affric reaches up to William with something in her hand, "Take this charm with you Wallace... and you bring it back home to me, safe and sound." William reaches down where she can place a little piece of dried white heather in is hand. He looks at the lucky heather, then leans over and kisses Affric on the brow, for a moment, the love between them is profound. William places the white heather between his heart and battle-jack, pulls is horse around and begins to canter along the drove road. Stephen, Katriona and Affric wave farewell to their Wolf and Wildcat friends as they watch them canter away and along the northern drove road that leads out of the glen Afton fastness and across to the west coast once more, in defense of the realm. An exhilarating feeling flows through William's body and mind, but this time it is tempered by the experience and witness of the Corserine Gap and Dunveoch. He makes a silent vow that the same will not happen here in Glen Afton, for the world would not be ready for the vengeance he would wreak upon the perpetrators. Meanwhile, Malcolm, Sir John Stewart, Sir Colin Campbell, Sir Simon Fraser of Oliver, John de Graham and True Tam sit on their horses beside Alain, watching the forces of the western Guardian army leaving Glen Afton. True Tam moves his horse close to Alain…

"I fear the worst for our realm Alain. De Brix has firm designs set upon the Crown of Scotland going to the house of Brus. Eric of Norway seeks the crown through his granddaughter and both Comyn and Baliol prepare to make a legitimate claim for Devorguilla. Wishart told me that the Bishops delegation they sent to Longshanks has brought back news that should this civil war engulf Scotland, then he will arbitrate. But Longshanks insists that all our armies be stood down and disbanded, including the Garda Ban Rígh. He will then bring English peacekeeping forces into the realm, and only then will he support whoever has the legitimate right to the throne. But first, the nobles of Scotland must recognize him as their liege and legitimate Lord."

Shaking his head in disbelief, Alain says, "It will be a day of reckoning if that day should come to pass." True Tam replies, "I fear that the day of reckoning is nigh upon us Alain, for I know Longshanks will not stop at arbitration, he will try and seize this realm." Colin Campbell overhears True Tam, "Unless someone more powerful than us can stop this madness, then I fear Scotland could be lost forever." Alain's concentration is broken when he sees the Wolf and Wildcat Hunter scout detachment thundering towards him.

William notices True Tam staring at him, but this time he is smiling at him. He sees Tam raise a finger, tap his helmet, nod his head; then point directly at him. Shaking off this strange gesture from his thoughts, William salutes his father as he passes by to fulfill his mission… "He's a fine young man," says True Tam upon seeing the expression of concern on Alain's face, Tam continues, "He'll come back to you Alain, the deity of the Aicé has a future of merit marked out for your son." Alain looks at True Tam, who gazes back at him as though he had said nothing. Malcolm then speaks to pacifying the concern in Alain's breast. "The fighting is all in the south and south-west Alain, he'll be fine, he goes only to observe the Northwestern gateway, there he'll find no ill in the mission required of him." Alain watches William and the hunter scouts disappear over the hill towards Am Magh Baoghail (Maybole) then onward with thier mission towards Invergarvane. Alain says, "I pray that you are right Malcolm." He watches the Wolf and Wildcat hunter scouts travel away from glen Afton towards the west coast.

*   *   *

For the next few days, William and the Hunter scouts spend their time scouring the west coast then working their way lower and returning east again. With every sweep of the land, William sends occasional outriders forward to pick up any signs of martial movement. Many places of habitation are desolate or completely destroyed, with the inhabitants having fled the marauding groups of mercenaries and warlords… or dead. Those innocents caught by a warring faction are now but bloated bodies, rotting and decaying where they had fallen, or are half-eaten by scavengers. Soon the hunter scouts come upon a Balloch with similar scenes to the ones William, Bailey and Coinach had witnessed at Corserine and Dunveoch. On entering the Balloch, William can see the inhabitants have met a similar brutal fate. The stench from rotting corpses is almost unbearable and the scouts are forced to hold wet cloth over their faces, preventing the smell of rotting human and animal carcass making them ill or sick. Bodies and parts of men, women and children are scattered all around this village. A particularly gruesome scene greets them where it appears a great pile if severed heads has been covered in pitch and set on fire, where burning the flesh off the skulls gives a perception the killings have been ritualistic. Some bodies are limbless, most had been decapitated, except for the few poor inhabitants who are still hanging from trees, some by the neck, others by one leg, but all without exception, have had their stomachs opened and have been gutted like fish, with much of their faces, eyes and soft areas of their bodies eaten away by rats, crows and other vermin, providing easy access to the inner bodies for other smaller scavenger creatures to feast and gorge. "I'm glad our Youngblood are scouting the perimeters of this village," says Bailey, "This is not a sight for their senses and young eyes." William replies "And you think that my eyes are accepting this so easily Bailey?"

They sit still awhile on their horses observing the carnage, then William speaks, "I can't understand what's happening Bailey, these are not soldiers nor warriors, they're simple farmers and families of this village... They were no threat to anyone, I don't understand?" Bailey replies, "There never seems any rhyme or reason for this butchery of innocent people, it's a bad business." William shakes his head in despair as they walk their horses slowly forward through the remains of the tiny Balloch.He says, "If this war spreads throughout Scotland, then the future this madness may bring upon us is unimaginable." Grimacing as he looks around at the desperate carnage, Bailey says, "What's happening in Scotland right now is what happened in my Cymru, but that was by the English invading our realm, not us doing this to ourselves like what appears to be happening here now." William looks at Bailey, "De Brus and his Father fought with Edward against the Cymrans didn't they?"

"They did," replies Bailey, "De Brix in particular was as merciless and ruthless then as he appears to be now... But I cannot understand why he attacks his own countrymen." William says, "Brus is not a Scot. My father told me told me he's Norman-English and their true homeland is Whittle in some place called Essex." Bailey sighs, "We are all mixed blood William... at what point do you start being petty over birth and belonging?" William replies, "At what point do you stand against tyranny and those who foster it? This and everything past is because of Norman nobles fuckin' greed, and de Brix is at the heart of it all." Lihd speaks, "I'm all too familiar with these scenes too. The first time I experienced this carnage was when the English visited the same wretchedness upon my Clan on the borderlands of Annan and Ettrick, where my entire family had been cruelly murdered in such a way..." Suddenly, messenger scouts come thundering into the Balloch behind them, bringing news of the fighting to William. After a brief discussion with the scouts, he turns to his men...

"Brus has split his main army into two large units with his largest force laying siege to Dumfries Castle, the second force still lays siege to Dalswinton Castle where Baliol's mother Devorguilla is trapped. The Comyn's force from the north are about to attack Brus there. The orders are for all the guardian forces to meet at the mouth of Loch Ken." Bailey enquires, "What's our orders?" William replies, "We're to take the Wolf and Wildcats west to Invergarvane and make camp near the Duibh Hill overlooking the sea-landing there." Coinach enquires, "Wallace, are yie talking about the old Cruathnie fort at the top of the Duibh?" William replies, "Aye, we can see from that vantage as far south as the Galloway point, as far north and west to the Mull of Ceanntyre and all the way across to Rathlan off the Irish coast. Its from there we're to look out for any of the Red Earls sea marauders coming in." Turning to the scouts, William enquires, "What is it my father requires of us once we're there?" The lead scout replies, "We know Longships of Aslikkør Ranald and Angus Óg's fleet are bringing more reinforcements in to support de Brus and his English allies. The isle men of Angus óg need little excuse to fight against the Scots, for they still wrankle over their defeat at Largs. We need to know if they land any men on the coast North of Galloway. If they do, you're to send riders to inform us, telling of what size the force is and also which direction they take and where they may gather or camp."

While the youngblood patrol talk amongst themselves, William enquires, "Do we make contact with any we meet or see?" the lead scout replies, "On no account are you to have any contact with those who would make a landing, just watch and report. You do only as Alain commands, in that, you observe and follow them discreetly, sending riders out periodically and keep us informed of any progress at all times."

"Wallace…" says the second scout, "You're to rendevous at the old ruined fortalice of Balquhan on route; the Crauford's and Boyd scouts will meet with you there." Bailey says, "At least we'll be joined by trusted kinfolk." The scout continues, "There will also be hunter scouts coming from the Stewart's o' Dundonald, they're sending their young trackers for you to command. Now make haste Wallace, every moment we delay this conflict grows unstoppable, remember your orders, do not under any circumstance or provocation make contact. Avoid any possibility for affray to be introduced, for we cannot have this situation flare up behind us." William replies, "I understand, we'll leave here after we've cremated these people."

"No time," Commands the lead scout, "get your hunter scouts together and make haste, we need you overlooking Invergarvane with utmost urgency. If the detachment you're to meet at Balquhan aren't there, then leave a couple of your men behind to wait for them with orders to follow you on to Invergarvane." The orders from Alain have been delivered and agreed, both parties set a course on their respective missions. Half a day passes before the youngblood arrive at their first rendezvous; having been delayed due to finding another massacre of the nomadic Ceàrdannan. They slowly and cautiously walk their horses along the last part of the drove road leading into the tiny Balloch of Balquhan, where they find the place is deserted. Coinach points to the ground, stating that many riders had not long passed by. "This is not good." says William, "There's hearth smoke coming through the roofs, yet there's none here to greet us." He issues orders for everyone to search the small Obhainn's, barns and outhouses "Andra, Tam, Seamus... take our youngblood to the Balloch perimeters and look out for the detachments we're supposed to meet, they should have been here by now waiting for us, not the other way about."

Dismounting with swords drawn, William and Coinach walk towards the drinking well at the centre of the small Balloch while his scouts search for any living souls nearby. William says, "Maybe they're in hiding for fear of us being hostile." Closing on the old well, Coinach notices the ground is sticky underfoot. As they reach the well, he looks into the depths while William scans the horizon, then he ponders,

"I wonder where the other detachments are, they should have been here by now?" Coinach exclaims "Fuck naw…" William turns gripping his sword, "What is it?" Coinach points into the well, his face turning ashen grey. William rushes towards the well and notices his feet too are sticking and sliding in the thick wet blood coloured mud. He leans against the well wall and looks down into its depths… "Awe naw…"

"WALLACE!" a voice calls out, William looks over to see Andra waving frantically from the top of a hillock at the far side of the Balloch. Coinach shakes his head in dismay, "I'll wait here Wallace." William runs over to Andra as everyone rushes across to the hillock where Andra and Tam óg are staring wide-eyed into a deep hollow. As William reaches the hillock, the scene before him is absolute bloody carnage. He sees the butchered remains of men and boys, brutally tortured before being slain, limbs have been hacked off and most of the wretches disemboweled, with their intestines strung out as the most basest slaughterhouse offal. The unfortunate victims heads had been piled pyramidal in the centre of the carnage, covered in pitch oil and set on fire as the last village had suffered.

A shaken Andra says, "It looks to be about fifty or sixty men and boys in there." Looking around the outskirts of the Balloch, William issues orders, "Search everywhere thoroughly; see if there are any left alive in this Balloch." Andra, Tam and the younger men go into the ghastly hollow to search for any survivors, William halts Bailey by pulling him back by his arm "What is it?" enquires Bailey. William says, "It's the Balloch drinking well Bailey, It's all but packed to the top with the headless bodies and torsos of women and children." The two kinsmen look at each other, no words can express their feelings, Seamus, who is kneeling and looking on the ground a short distance away calls out,

"Wallace, I've found the tracks of many horses..." William calls out orders as he makes his way over to Seamus. "Andra, Tam, get the Ceitherne to rip off all the thatching from the roofs of the Bothies and Obhain's, then pile them on top of the bodies in the hollow, we'll burn them, there's no time for anything else." William soon arrives beside Seamus who's still kneeling and checking the ground around the mouth of the drove road. William enquires, "What have you found?" Seamus points at the fresh prints, "It wasn't hard to find, whoever perpetrated this massacre doesn't have a care, or they want us to follow them. Another odd thing about these impressions is that they're not coming from any working horses, they're shod military style and heavy in weight... see, from the depth of imprint..." William queries, "Knights? About how many do yie reckon?"

"I don't know about Knights," replies Seamus, "but definitely a martial household. And it looks to be a fairly large force too, maybe about fifty or so." William looks along the west road. Seamus nods, "Aye, and there are more that's been corralled over there by those trees too, I count maybe a hundred or so in total I reckon." William ponders, "It can't be the detachments marks we were supposed to meet, is it?" Seamus replies, "Naw, they'll be using Garron, Cob, Nag and Hablars, much like our own horses with broad hooves, these are from a different breed o' horse, and I reckon I've seen this imprint somewhere before, but ahm not sure where..." While Seamus studies the imprints, William looks up and scans the horizon, "They've came from the east and appear to be heading west, the same as us... Fuck, we have to make west on this same route. Walk with me Seamus, we need to talk with Bailey and Coinach." They hastily walk back into the small Balloch where the Ceitherne have torn most of the thatch from the roofs and are preparing a large funeral pyre on top of the dead. Bailey and Coinach have pushed the well side-walls in and are now bringing heavy boulders over and throwing them on top, making a macabre stone Cairn. Bailey and Coinach see William approach. William enquires, "Who do you think did this?" Bailey shakes his head "I don't know." Coinach punches the oak post beside the well "It has the same bloody mark as at the Corserine, Dunveoch and all those other villages we passed earlier." Seamus, who is still pondering as to where he had seen that particular print from the horseshoes, "It's a mark of a smithy... But not of this land, I've seen this mark once before when I served apprentice time with a travelling blacksmith working for the lords of Cumbria in the North of England. I recognise the sizes of shoe and hammer marks that leaves those particular impressions."

Coinach exclaims, "Wallace... yie don't think..." Just then, Andra and Tam come rushing over. Tam says, "Wallace, you have to be looking to the youngblood with us, they're in a state o' terror and shock." Tam points over to the prepared funeral pyre of the villagers where all the younger hunters are gathered, some of the youngblood are being physically sick, others are shaking visibly. "Look at the state o' them." says Tam óg. William exclaims, "Fuck, I never noticed... I was too taken by necessity. Have we become so hardened to these scenes already?" Bailey speaks, "Seamus, Andra, go and gather the youngblood and take them to the edge of the village... but don't be lighting the pyre just yet." William agrees, "I was starting to think that too Bailey, I don't want whoever did this to know we're following behind. It's likely they're expecting that any decency from the finders of such evil that they would light funeral pyres." A wry smile escapes Bailey, responding to William's wise observation. William calls out, "Everyone, come to me and form a circle, I've vital information for you all to hear."

All quickly gather shoulder to shoulder and form a circle, as is the way of the parley. William speaks, "This village is on Clan Crauford land, where we were supposed to meet with detachments from the Crauford's, Stewarts and Boyd's, instead, we find this scene of massacre. Many of our youngblood here are shaken and disturbed by what they've seen, so I'll be sending some of them home with news of this for the Guardians." Looking at the distress in his younger Ceitherne, William commands what is to happen. He points at a young Ceithernach; "I want you to pick three o' the most affected by these scenes and return to Glen Afton with the news of what we've found. It's to be sent on directly to Alain. Get going… now." He points at another Ceithernach, "I want you to wait here, pick your best three riders, then I want you to wait here on the re-enforcements, give them instruction to follow us west, then you're to leave for Afton with that news update. Each news group will overlap and return back to us on duty, I want to keep the numbers of the Wolf and Wildcat contingent stable in the event o' us runnin' into any trouble."

As the first riders set out for Glen Afton, William sees Coinach kneeling beside Seamus. Coinach says, "Wallace, there's a number of tracks making north towards Kilmaurs, some o' those horseshoe imprints are noble stock and not that of an ordinary horse-soldier, I'll follow them and find out if it's a de Percy commanding…" William speaks with authority, "Naw Coinach…we've got to make speed for Invergarvane; we need everybody present. If the other scouts who we're supposed to meet arrive later, then they must follow on. I'm leaving some of the young Ceitherne here, so we'll need everyone else with us… ahm sorry Coinach, but that's ma orders." William knows Coinach is seething inside, desperately seeking revenge for the Corserine, but none could know yet for sure who has perpetrated this slaughter on the folk of Balquhan. He also understands the urgency of fulfilling his father's command. He orders everyone to mount up, then, with the remainder of the Wolf and Wildcat hunters, they speed out of the Balloch toward to their destination on the west coast to overlook the great Minch seaboard above Invergarvane.

By the time the Wolf and Wildcat hunter scouts reach the heights above Invergarvane, it's a clear, warm evening. They quickly settle in amongst the remains of the old fort that had once protected the Northern gateway to the ancient Kingdom of Galloway. So well placed in the terrain is the ancient fortress, it dominates the country for many miles around. The breathtaking and vast panorama that lay before them means that strategically, anything that moves can easily be seen from its commanding heights, be it on land or sea. The Wolf and Wildcat hunter scouts soon settle into their makeshift bivouac, making shelter, sleep and rest areas in the nooks and crannies of the ancient fort.

William stands on an old battlement wall, gazing at the magnificent vista before him, studying the land below and observing the small fishing Balloch of Invergarvane. Bailey and Lihd join him. "What do you think Wallace?" enquires Bailey as he hands William a bowl of hot thick nettle wort soup, William replies, "I'm thinkin' about the Balquhan massacre Bailey, It's been creeping up on me seeing such cruel senseless murder brought upon those innocents... who could be doing these deeds and have no fear of retribution? That's what I can't get my wits round." Bailey replies, "I don't know... but I do know when the English did this in Cymru, the purpose was to strike fear into the local population and eliminate any thought of resisting their new English masters, or fall themselves to this imposition of terror and barbarity. But you don't have the English here trying to subdue your kingdom, this is what perplexes me." Bailey pauses as he too observes the beauty of the sunset seaboard panorama. Lihd brings Bailey another bowl of hot refreshment then the three friends watch the majestic sun setting cross the mighty Minch where the west Highland peninsular sweeps down to meet the sea. Their eyeline follows the horizon southward, where the sea cliffs of Ireland seemingly rise infinitely into the darkening sky.

Feeling an ominous foreboding with the sun setting before them, William's attention is momentarily focussed toward the centre of this great seascape. He observes in wonderment the magnificent cone shaped island of Creag Ealasaid, situated in the middle of the sea between Scotland and Ireland as if it were a giant sleeping sentinal, almost what he thought in his minds eye what Tir Nan Og may look like. Bailey enquires, "That's a curious looking island over there, do you know what it's called?" William replies, "Aye, its the Creag Ealasaid, ach sorry Bailey, in the English it would be known as the Ailsa Craig. Supposedly it's a rock thrown by the giant of Ireland Finn McCuil at the Scots giant Ben an Donner, when it landed halfway, they both agreed to use it as a stepping stone when one is to visit the other.

Gazing at the island and surrounding vista, Bailey says, "This is some advantageous position to see any that may travel about these lands and seas." William as he points seawards "It sure is. Over there to your right is the Ceanntyre highlands, to your front and left is Ireland, and down there southwest is the lands of Galloway, below us is Invergarvan, the western gateway to all you see. And where we are now, this is the best place of all to observe what is going on for about twenty land miles. North of us is Turnberry Castle, home of Brus the earl of Carrick." Letting his guard down for a moment while savouring the absolute beauty of the seascape between Scotland and Ireland, Bailey says, "I can understand why you Scots and Irish feel that when you pass from this world to the next, your spirit takes flight and heads out west, this is one of the most beautiful sights you could see in this life." Lihd holds on to Baileys arm and exclaims, "It's so beautiful...." Finishing his food, William streches out his weary muscles "Come you two, we'll set a guard perimiter with lookouts for the night, we must be prepared for whatever may be our destiny." The three friends walk to the centre of the camp. Bailey reflects on how William has kept growing in stature since he had first met him. He remembers meeting a young man coming of age, but from the Corserine and Dunveoch and the slaughters he had witnessed, William has shown to Bailey that his young giant kinsman has natural leadership qualities. If William has the same clinical approach in actual battle, then this young man before him will be a most formidable charismatic leader and chief. At that moment, Coinach and Seamus come back from scouting the area and make report.

Seamus speaks first, "We found those same horse tracks on the old drove road leading down into the Invergarvane landings. The marks we saw are the same as those at Balquhan." Coinach speaks, "Do we send men down to scout to see if they are camped nearby." Thinking a moment William replies, "Naw, if we're discovered we'll have destroyed our mission's intent looking for someone we know little off or who may not have anything to do with our orders, a mistake I'll not make." For a moment, Coinach simply glares as William enquires aggressively, "DO I MAKE MYSELF UNDERSTOOD?" Coinach spits the words out tersely in a sullen reply, "Aye... ah hear yie Wallace." Then he turns his back on William and sullenly walks away. "Bailey, Seamus," commands William "Make sure the camp perimeters are set and guards are on watch all night. Select the guard, I'll stay here for the first watch." The Wildcat hunter scouts settle for the night in the old ruins of the ancient frontier fort of the Kings of Galloway. "Wallace..." whispers a voice, "Wallace wake up..." Bailey forcefully nudges William. Startled, he wakes quickly to see Bailey and Lihd lying beside him, discreetly pointing over the ridge down towards Invergarvane.

William crawls up to the ridge to see what they're pointing at, then he sees the object of their focus down at the beachhead. Lihd says, "Two Hebridean Longships have beached on the foreshore, they must have come in before sunrise on the high tide, it looks as though whoever it is that's landed has dispersed and set up a camp." William exclaims, "Where are our fuckin' guards?" Replying in a whisper, Bailey replies, "I don't know, Coinach was last on last guard with Andra and Tam óg? They must have fallen asleep." William curses, "Fuck... How many do you reckon have landed?" Lihd replies, "There would be at least fifty in each boat, so there must be at least hundred down there." Bailey says, "And that's not counting the horse troops we followed, and whoever's meeting them." They continue observing for anything that will help them understand what could be happening down at the beached Longships, but all they can make out is a few men tending small fires. William nudges Bailey and points "Fuck Bailey... look over there..."

Bailey looks down the hill and sees what appears to be about a hundred and fifty men stretched out in a line starting to appear through a low lying sea-mist coming straight up the hill towards them, accompanied by about forty well armed horsemen with dropped lances, all winding their way up the steep slope towards their position. Tam óg and Andra join William, Bailey and Lihd, as the rest of the Wildcat scouts move cautiously toward the parapet edge to look at the scene unfolding below them. William enquires, "I thought you fella's were on guard with Coinach?" Andra replies, "We were, but he said he was going to scout out the Longships on your orders?" William exclaims "Fuck…" when he notices Lihd putting on her Gallóbhan war helm and reaching for her short bow, knocking one arrow and clutching three arrows in her draw hand, signalling power and speed archery is her thoughts. Andra enquires, "Who do you think that is Wallace? I recognize the isle men with the flags of Angus óg's people." Tam óg replies "Aye, and that's men o' that dirty big bastard Aslikkør Ranald beside them too. But who is it that's leading them with the horse troops."

Screwing up his eyes to focus, Bailey suddenly exclaims, "Fuck, I know who that is…" Suddenly Coinach comes running at speed over the back of the old fort wall, shouting, "Quickly get up… we're in a trap." William tries to understand where Coinach has been, but his instinct makes him issue immediate orders, "Tam, Andra… get everyone armed with their bows." Bailey, still continually scans the hillside, he shouts out, "CAVALRY…" and points away to their right flank. Appearing from a hidden gulley less than five hundred yards to their right flank and riding directly at them, is a large body of cavalry and mounted soldiers following the old drove road directly in front of the fort that passes the Wildcat secreted bivouac.

It's now too late for William to disperse his men and it's obvious the cavalry could not fail to see them. William urgently enquires, "Who is it?" as he observes the armoured riders getting ever closer to their position. Bailey replies, "They have blue flags with five diamonds running through the centre… That's the colours of the English knight sir Henry De Percy…" Nearby, Coinach overhears Bailey and freezes hearing the name De Percy, he quickly composes himself and makes his way over to the rest of the Wildcats to pick up his bow to get armed and prepared. William quickly places his grandfathers war-helm on his head, then he speaks to Bailey quietly, "We're fuckin' trapped here Bailey... if we move we'll be seen, if we stay they'll be upon us, yet we don't know if they're friend or foe." Both scrutinise the scene unfolding before them. Bailey says, "There's only twenty-five of us... And more than a hundred and fifty of them that I can see..."

Turning to check if all are prepared for the unknown, William sees Coinach leading Andra, Tam Seamus and the other Ceannard, each followed by two Ceitherne. The practice of the woodland bowmen, like the Gallóglaigh, is when the lead bowman selects a target, his two apprentice hunters fix on the same target, ensuring a heart shot at any prey is accompanied by another two close shots on either side of the heart, making certain of a quick and definite kill with three flights of the grey goose wing arrows striking with deadly accuracy. Three more arrows hanging in the draw hand supports the deadly fusillade with astonishing speed of loose to follow on. While trying desperately to assess the situation, William senses fear. He isn't sure what may happen next. He is vexed by his own indecision—his father had warned him to make no contact—and it appears it's now too late to send out any riders for help. Whatever happens next will be as a result of his own decision.

Bailey enquires, "What do you want us to do?" William replies, "I'll stand up and declare our presence Bailey, that should suffice... I'll tell them we're hunters that have simply got lost, that's all I can think of... What do yie reckon?" Pulling on his war helmet, Bailey replies sardonically, "I reckon we are fucked." William enquires "What should we do?" Before Bailey can reply, William sees Coinach stand above the parapet pulling full on his longbow, following his example is Andra, Seamus, Tam óg, all the Ceannards and their Ceitherne, the Wildcats stand proud pulling full-strength on their longbows… "NO…" shouts William… But it's too late. Coinach lets loose his first arrow directly toward his target, Sir Henry de Percy, followed simultaneously by two more arrows loosed from his Ceitherne, three arrows strike home, but they strike a rider crossing in front of De Percy. Coinach's arrow hits the unfortunate rider full in the face which offers little resistance as the arrow speeds through the back of the riders head, with a slight deflection it buries itself deep into the neck of Henry De Percy's horse, causing it rear and topple, throwing De Percy to the ground.

Thinking it's by William's command, all of the scouts follow Coinach's example. With all their Ceitherne, they collectively let loose a deadly tracer arrow fusillade at the approaching danger, striking the lead riders with at least two arrows buried deep into each target, some passing through the men and striking riders following behind, bringing many of them all down. William tries to stop his young Wildcats, but all twenty-two of them let loose another lethal torrent of arrows at their prey. The screams of wounded, dying men and horses on the slopes of the hill and drove road is horrific, and increasing as every one or two seconds, volley after deadly volley from the barbed and vicious tracer arrows loosed from the Wolf and Wildcats find their mark. Even a hundred men could not withstand such a ferocious and relentless onslaught from such deadly pinpoint accurate destruction.

Another volley strikes the men coming at them up the hillside; soon, more than a third of the men coming at the Wolf and Wildcats now lay badly wounded, dying or dead. The killer accuracy of the William's Ceitherne is relentlessly destroying the oncoming soldiers and horsemen. After a few moments and many more volleys, only a few of the attackers are left as they desperately seek shelter behind their dead and dying comrades. William tries to think of what should be done next, but at that same moment, he sees Coinach pull his sword from his belt and charge down toward the enemy below, quickly followed by his loyal Ceannard and Ceitherne.

Everyone else charges down the hill behind Coinach, yelling their war cries and scattering the surviving riders and soldiers. Just then, William sees another line of about a hundred of Óg's Islemen who had been hidden from view, appear from a sloping bank behind the first attackers and launch themselves uphill straight at the Wildcats. Bailey shouts "Over there…" He and Lihd pull with all their strength on their bow's, but William sees they are about to fire another direction, he turns quickly to see that it's a trap being sprung as more riders charge over the top of the hill behind them, this new force rides fast over the rough hill ground towards them with lances pointed directly at William. Bailey screams "MOVE…" he and Lihd both loose arrow's simultaneously to skim past William's face, striking the lead rider only yards away with such kinetic energy, both arrow's pass easily through the riders head and stick deep into the chest of a following rider, bringing both men down and causing the oncoming riders to evade their fallen comrades. William starts loosing his arrows beside Bailey and Lihd, collectively they bring fifteen riders down in as many seconds, causing the remaining riders to divert away and lose their vantage.

"Bailey, Lihd…" shouts William "Grab your weapons, the youngblood Ceitherne are in trouble." They grab their weapons and prepare to run over the crest and downward into the melee when William is struck hard in the shoulder from behind by a crossbow bolt, knocking him over the edge of the parapet. Bailey spins round to see they are now being attacked on four sides now, a force of Aslikkør Ranald's

Isle-men come rushing over the back of the old fort, when another crossbow bolt glances Bailey on the jaw, knocking him over the edge to land beside William. Lihd quickly pulls on her Bow as she bravely jumps over the parapet and stands guard over William and Bailey. She instantly looses an arrow that strikes a horseman dead riding directly at them, she looses another arrow and sticks a horse deep in the eye, driving the barbed iron tip straight into its brain. The horse falls screaming and kicking, throwing the rider at Lihd's feet. She quickly pulls out both her gutting blades and stabs the rider rapid in the throat and neck from both sides, pulling the vicious blades backwards to sending a spray of blood from the dying man outward to cover the three of them in a bloody mist. Bailey quickly helps William to his feet…

"Look out…" shouts William. Another horseman charges down on them and drives a fearsome lance point at Baileys head. Bailey ducks under the tip of the lance as William drives his sword high into the rider's stomach with such force; the sword is pulled out of his hand. The knight drops his lance as his horse carries the dying rider away with William's sword stuck in his stomach. William picks up the fallen lance, instinctively he knows the only chance they have is to run directly into the melee and fight, to run anywhere else is not an option. William pauses, trying to make sense of what's happening. They cannot fight uphill as the isle-men are coming at them from the back, horsemen are coming at them from the right and left flanks, which means their only chance to survive is to impact the skirmish below and try and break out the back of the fight with his men. Lihd notices a crossbowman raise to shoot at William, she looses an arrow which hits the man in the wrist, the arrow driving under his skin with the point ripping out at his elbow, as he drops his weapon another arrow from Lihd catches him full in the throat. The impetuous action of Coinach has turned a trap into a possible victory; the ferocious fighting of the Wolf and Wildcats has caught the attackers by surprise. Although outnumbered and green to the way of battle, it seems as though the fighting instinct of Wallace's Wolf and wildcat scouts are driving the attackers back and falling over their own dead and dying comrades trying to flee from the onslaught. William raises his arm to signal Tam óg, but the searing pain of the crossbow bolt stuck in the back of his shoulder causes him to almost pass out. Bailey sees this, grabs William then they both run head long into the fight.

Lihd looses tracer arrows deep into the bodies of five soldiers approaching William and her lover, bringing them down. She runs to join them when suddenly an arrow glances of her helmet, another strikes deep in her thigh, then another buries itself deep in the side of her neck, as she stumbles forward another arrow strikes her high in the chest, knocking her to the ground behind Bailey. Lihd tries desperately to get up but falls back against a large boulder. She pulls off her Gallóbhan war-helm, her long brown hair tumbles and flows freely in the light sea breeze as it falls from it's constraint of the helm.

Fighting backwards to protect Lihd, Bailey swings his great claymore, decapitating an isleman, in the same instant Bailey is struck in the chest by two arrows and falls back, tripping over Lihd's feet. He sees her condition and freezes, Lihd looks into his eyes and attempts to speak, but only a trickle of blood flows from the corner of her mouth. Bailey screams like a man demented as Lihd raises her hand and smiles, he snaps the arrow shafts sticking out of his chest and stands above Lihd in a blood rage. William takes off his war helm and throws it into the face of an oncoming foe and moves forward to protect Lihd too, but a large armoured English yeoman in De Percy colours appears in front of him, the two adversaries stop for a second. Instinctively William drives the lance point into the man's foot, bringing the Englishman's head forward, as the man screams in pain, William drives the lance upwards and strikes the yeoman deep in the throat then lunges forward with all his might, driving the lance upwards and deep through the man's throat and into his skull. Only William's knuckles stops the lance point going through any further. He keeps pushing the yeoman hard and backwards into other soldiers bunching behind the Englishman. William pulls the lance free and skewers another yeoman in the chest; then he swings left, slicing another attacker deep through the face. Bailey crosses in front of William with a ferocious slicing move with his sword, chopping clean through an arm wielding an axe intended to strike William, who quickly ducks under Bailey's swinging arms and shoves his lance upward into another attackers face about to strike Bailey, with a sickening wet sounding crunch, the lance tip plunges through the man's skull...

The fighting is utterly chaotic as men fight desperately to survive; yet despite the odds, the Wolf and Wildcats are maniacally destroying the enemy with a precision and skill they never knew they had. William sees Coinach and his Ceitherne are hacking limbs and stabbing blades deep into bodies, he can also see the remaining Wolf and Wildcats are picking up discarded spears when the blood and gore on their swords has made them too slippery to wield proficiently. With spear, axe and lance in their hands the Wildcats are causing devastation amongst opposing forces. William thinks *'Maybe... Maybe we may win this day...'*

The skirmish has now turned into a brutal no-mercy bloody affray. With such a small group as they are, the Wolf and Wildcats have two unexpected advantages because they seized the initiative and attacked, the initial surprise has given them vantage and are savagely dispatching and diminishing the numbers of the enemy swiftly, also, the numbers ranged against them means only the men at the front of their opposition could strike at them, causing their supporting fighters to stumble over their comrades bodies.

Looking to his left, William sees Seamus decimating many with a large spartaxe; then he sees a knight raise his sword and plunge it into Seamus from the back. Seamus roars in pain then turns and strikes his foe with the mighty two handed spartaxe, splitting him from collarbone to the lower part of his ribcage. William sees another soldier running at Andra. William raises his lance and throws it for all he is worth, striking the warrior in the chest, the lance ripping almost fully through his body. Andra turns and splits the warrior's head in two with his sword, but then, several arrows strike both Andra and Tam óg simultaneously, they show no pain and keep on fighting to drive De Percy's men back.

"NO…" shouts Bailey as he sees Lihd slump over behind him, William turns to see what Bailey is shouting at when a giant of an isle-man who has been skulking in the background, sees that William is unarmed. He launches himself from behind and hits William with such force on the shoulder with a war mallet. He strikes the back notch of the crossbow bolt, driving the bolt-tip through William's body causing the point of the bolt to burst through the front of William's chainmail haubergeon. The isle-man quickly raises his heavy mallet again and strikes William with all his might between the shoulder blades, knocking him to the ground breathless between two large boulders. A fantastic pain like a lightning bolt shocks William's brain as he is struck on the head by another glancing blow that would have killed him had it not been deflected by one of the boulders that he now lay between. Bailey spins around to see his charge lying wedged between the two long boulders, the large isle-man raises his war mallet to obliterate William's skull with another strike while William is partially dazed and winded. Looking up through his haze, William sees the badly wounded Lihd pull on her bow and loose upwards, burying the arrow deep under his opponents chin, stalling the blow. Bailey swings his sword with such force the giant isleman's head separates from his body and spins high into the air then falls downwards, striking William on the head with a dead weight, almost knocking him out.

Fortunately, the Isleman's great beard cushions the heavy weight of his skull as it strikes William. The Isleman's head rolls next to William's face, the eyes in the Isleman's head stare at him in disbelief, with the bloody mouth gawping like a fish out of water but making no sound. Suddenly the Isleman's body slumps on top of William, crushing him with the weight and force of the fall and squeezing the breath out of him. Still dazed, William struggles vainly to be free of the crushing weight just to breathe, through the mist of pain he hears Bailey shout … "A WALLACE…A WALLACE!"

Unable to move and fast losing consciousness, William's face is pressed into the bloody mud by the dead weight now crushing him. He's in danger of drowning in hot blood pooling below him from his own wounds and the mass of blood still pumping out from the Isleman's opened neck arteries. Through the fog that's clouding his brain while trying to free himself, William senses Bailey is standing over him, protecting him from further harm. Lihd, who is leaning against the boulder close by, looks into William's eyes, she smiles weakly and reaches out to him with a blood soaked hand, she grips and holds on to his hand firmly, then smiles again, so serenely. Amidst the carnage William sees in Lihd's blood spattered face, expressing a look of peace and reassur-ance that all may not be as bad as it seems, strangely, a bond of eternal love with Lihd slowly sweeps over him, taking away his pain as though Lihd is really an angel in disguise. He feels safe as she holds his hand. William closes his eyes as a warm feeling of peace overwhelms him amid the bloody carnage, while the warm blood from the body of the dead isle-man still pours copiously over his head and face.

Opening his eyes, William doesn't know how long he has lain there, he can barely see with blood now sticking his eyelids shut. Time passes by like an eternity for William when he suddenly remembers where he is. He panics, but cannot move underneath the deadweight crushing down on him, with his mind reeling and spinning. He eventually opens his eyes enough to see through a gap in the boulders, he sees Tam óg ferociously fighting his way towards him. William also sees Andra and Seamus getting separated from the surviving Wolf and Wildcats, both are fighting like demons possessed, hacking and slashing wildly as they too try to fight their way over towards where he lay. A sense of peace and sleep is overwhelming William amidst of the madness, blood and butchery.

Slowly, he reaches into his léine and pulls out the pressed white heather gifted him by Affric. He looks at the innocence of the bloodstained heather, suddenly he feels Lihd's grip ease, he looks up and their eyes meet, her dark beautiful almost mysterious eyes and her serene smile again reassures him till he can resist the need to close his eyes no more. He gives way to the overwhelming urge to sleep, he knows in his dazed serene world with his friends around him, everything would be right and he would be safe...

THE BICKERING BUSH

William wakes suddenly with a thundering headache, he groans and thinks the pain is about to make his head explode. He tries to open his eyes, but he can't, there's a heavy wet dead weight covering his face. He tries raising his hand to remove the obstruction, but the pain and weakness in his body leaves him helpless. "Wallace can you hear me?" says a voice in the distance. The excruciating aching in his head only brings a groan from his lips in response, he wants to answer but an overwhelming feeling of nausea makes him wretch, but nothing other than acidic water comes to his mouth, choking him, burning hot, dry and sticking his palette together as if a red hot knife has been passed down his throat. "Wallace, are you awake? Can you hear me?" He thinks it must be an angel speaking to him, so peaceful and reassuring is the voice, he thinks, '*Am I in Tír nan óg?*' then he feels himself drift away into the realm of sleep once more, escaping the unbearable headache and pain.

Feeling the sense of awakening return, William can still feel the heavy weight on his eyes, but he notices that the awful headache has ebbed slightly, he tries to lift himself, but he has no strength to even lift his arm. "Wallace are you with us?" enquires the angelic voice once more. He can feel hands on his body, he mumbles desperately in a croaking voice. A feeling of panic starts to overwhelm his mind and he begins to struggle. Exhaustion and weakness in his muscles are overwhelming. "Take this thing from my face!" he cries. "Shhhhhhh… easy Wallace… try not to move." William knows this is the voice of a woman. He forces a whisper, "Marion, is that you… is that your voice I hear?" But there is no reply; then he feels hands gently alleviating the weight from his eyes. After a few moments he feels relief, whatever has been compressing his eyes has now been removed, replaced by caring hands softly moistening his eyelids with a warm wet cloth. Slowly his eyelids part, he tries to see but can't focus, his mind begins to swirl; then his severe headache returns, followed by nausea. In the midst of his pain he hears more voices, he thinks he recognises them, he's confused, he can't understand where he is. He closes his eyes once more and the headache abates slightly, the strain is becoming too much for his senses, the safety and peace gained from the sanctuary of sleep proves to be a place his mind would rather be as he loses consciousness.

William opens his eyes… this time he feels no ache in his head and there's nothing compressing his eyes. He blinks; then blinks again… yet all is black around him. He lifts his head and looks about in this strange dark place, he moves his fingers slightly, touching and feeling his surrounds, he realises he is in a soft crib. '*Has he been dreaming? Where is everyone? Where's Bailey, Lihd the Wildcats?*' He lay awhile longer trying to get familiar with his surroundings, but he's still weak and very confused. He beings to realise that he's looking into the dark surrounds of a night-time bedchamber, he can make out the old oak rafters and Cruk beams of a roof. He stares at the ceiling—then he hears a crackling sound nearby. Slowly and very cautiously, he turns his head and sees a log fire glowing at the far end of the room. There he sees two people sitting hunched and immobile on the floor in front of the fire, though he can't make out who they are, he watches awhile longer, then one of them stands up, he thinks he recognises the body shape, but he says nothing, he just lies there trying to gather his strength. Whoever these people are, or wherever he is, now that he's awake and should it be a place he did not wish to be, he knows he needs whatever strength he can muster to escape or to fight. As he lay motionless, he thinks he recognises the feminine shape standing in front of the fire... "Marion..." he says in a low broken voice, "Is that you my love?" The female instantly turns to face him, a man still seated beside the fire quickly rises up too, but with the fire blazing behind them, it causes their features to remain dark and unrecognisable, then he hears a female voice... "Wallace, are you awake?"

The woman rushes over to his bedside and is quickly joined by the man who stands by her side, "Wallace it's me... it's Affric, and Stephen's here with me." She starts to cry with excitement upon seeing her sweetheart awake. Stephen enquires, "Wallace are yie all right me boy?" Recognising the Irish lilt, William reaches out to hold the hand of Affric, who collapses to her knees beside his crib as tears of joy roll down her face. "Stephen," cries Affric "Go and fetch Ranald, tell him Wallace is back with us." But Stephen is already on his way to the door, he stops and calls back joyously, "Sure now me darlin' I am on me way already.'" William is still very confused, he enquires, "Affric, what are you doing here, where am I, where's Marion?" He looks about him but he doesn't recognise where he is, "What am I doing in this place? Where..." Affric places her hand gently behind his head and raises him up slightly..."Here Wallace, take this, it's a wee honey toddy with some special hot smithy water, we need to be bringing your strength back." William needs to know many things as his mind races. Affric raises the cup to his lips and he takes a sip of the medicinal craitur, then he lies back down in his crib, feeling relieved. A peaceful sleep begins pulling at his senses. Stephen and Ranald rush into the room. "Is he awake?" enquires Ranald, with a mixture of deep concern and relief in his voice. Ranald enquires urgently, "How is he?" This is all William hears as he drifts off to sleep once more.

Waking with a start, William is almost blinded by an early morning sunlight breaking through a small window in this unfamiliar room. He looks around and sees someone, fast asleep on the floor wrapped in large sheepskin beside the fire. Pulling the mantle from his body, he sees that his wounds have been wrapped tight with eel-skins, sphagnum moss and a may-butter poultice around his chest and shoulder. Trying to gain some sense of what's happening, he pulls some of the bed clothing around him and slides himself off the crib to stand barefoot on a cold stone floor. He looks around this strange but familiar place, only moments ago in his mind he was fighting for his life on the side of Duibh Hill, now he's leaning against a crib in a luxurious chamber. He studies the surroundings that's now becoming more familiar, but he still can't rationalise what he knows and what he could see around him, even with the early morning sunlight beginning to illuminate the room, he thinks, *'Is this a castle?'*

He finds himself wandering over to the window when he notices a door ajar, he makes his way slowly across the room, through the door, down a spiral stairwell then out through a large oak doorway to be met by a fresh morning sea breeze. His eyes hurt adjusting to the light and he's feeling extremely weak. He sits down outside the building. Moments pass as he breathes in the crisp morning air into his lungs. *'What's happened…?'* He's bewildered, there's not a soul to be seen as he looks around at the buildings and surrounding landscape.

His confusion is quickly followed by a sense of realisation, now he knows where he is, the familiar location is his Uncle Ranald's fortified house of Crosbie, though he is still trying to make sense of what makes no sense. As he sits on a large stone horse trough, his uncle Ranald comes out through a door and sits down beside him. "Good to see you're with us William, you had us worried awhile there." William shivers in the cold morning air "Uncle, tell me, what's happened, for I cannot fathom what is and what was… I only remember being in a fight for my life on the Duibh Hill, now I find myself walking about your home in Crosbie, and I see that the leaves are dropping from the trees and the wind blows like it's the fall… Am I dreaming?"

"No William," replies Ranald, "I dearly wish it so that you have been dreaming." William looks curiously at Ranald, "What dyie mean?" Ranald shakes his head, "You were out scouting for the Guardians at Duibh Hill, but when you didn't return and had sent no more messengers, I led the force you were supposed to meet at Balquhan. From there we went directly over to Invergarvane, that's when we found you, badly wounded and unconscious, actually it was True Tam that found you when all others thought you dead, then we brought you back here to Crosbie."

"I don't understand…" says William "It was True Tam who found me?" Ranald shakes his head, stands up and replies, "Aye well, you're safe now, that's all that matters." William enquires, "And my father?" Ranald replies, "He took arrows in his arms and back at the battle down at Buittle, but he's fine and on the mend now, nothing too serious." William enquires, "What of the fighting with de Brix and the Pact?" Ranald replies, "It's over, they've all agreed another treaty. The civil war has ended and we've regained another peace, of sorts, though it's been at a great cost I fear."

William enquires, "What do you mean?" Ranald replies, "Well, the church has invited the King of England to keep the peace, for the lord knows we cannot keep it ourselves. The English King has already sent his peacekeeping forces into Scotland, disbanded our armies and now Longshanks has begun to garrison English soldiers in all our castles fortifications and all the main towns in Ayrshire, Galloway, Carrick and the borders. He's sending more troops into Scotland each day in order to secure the entire realm from further outbreaks of violence until the maid takes the throne."

"Fuck," exclaims William. But it's all becoming too much for him; he enquires, "How long have I been here at Crosbie?" Ranald replies "You've been in a fever and in and out of consciousness for nigh over three months." William exclaims, "THREE FUCKIN' MONTHS…" His head drops as he pulls the crib covers over his head, for this cannot be real of all that he has just heard from Ranald, everything is insanely unrecognisable… "Yie awake now Wallace?" Came a familiar voice from the door. A grinning Stephen carries some hot meal from the kitchens and sits beside William and hands him the hot food. "I was sleepin' by the fire me boy when I heard you go out the door, so I thought to get up me'self and go fetch yie some hot porridge, for I know yie would not yet be feeding yourself. Are yie feelin any better then?"

"Naw, am no'…" replies William, "Fuck Stephen, I've been laid out for near on three months, Ranald here has been telling me things beyond my ken or understanding." Stephen speaks in a lighthearted voice, "Ach well, yie will be fine when yie are up and after moving about a few days Wallace, It will all make good sense when yie have had time to take it all in." Lifting the wooden spoon, William struggles to take a mouthful of porridge from the bowl. Stephen clasps his hands, lowers his head; then he says, "Ah wish ah'd been wit yiez Wallace, but in a way ahm glad ah wasn't, or we might not be here sittin together right now." William looks at his friend curiously, "What do yie mean?" Stephen glances at Ranald who simply shakes his head. There's another moments tense silence, then Ranald says, "William, I'll go and see if your aunt Margret is awake, she's been tending you since you were brought to us, Margret will be overjoyed to hear that you're awake, and looking so much better." William smiles weakly and just nods his head as Ranald leaves him to talk with Stephen. William enquires "I thought I heard Affric's voice earlier, not Margret's?" Stephen replies "Aye Affric, she was here tending to yie with Margret up until yesterday, but when she knew yie would be recovering, she just packed up her things and left…"

"To go back to glen Afton?" enquires a puzzled William. "Naw" replies Stephen "She said she was going north east to find family in a place called Saint Johns Toun." William is still puzzled, "Saint Johns o' Dalry? Affric has no kinfolks there that I know off, and she wouldn't go back to the Corserine on her own." "Naw," says Stephen "She said it's up north-east near a place called Perth, ah think." Stephen continues with a smile, "Here Wallace, stop you're feckn talking and eat some solid bleedin' porridge would ya to be getting your strength back."

The two friends sit in silence while, William vainly tries to feed himself, then Stephen says, "Yie know Wallace, yer uncle Ranald has put his life on the line to save you, did he tell you that? Ah brave man if yie ask me." Totally confused with this information, William enquires, "What do you mean?" Stephen replies, "He gave his word to the English and the Guardians that you are not an outlaw, but had simply been caught in a perilous situation at Invergarvane not of your own making. Even though the English wanted to hang you, they relented when Ranald said he would be responsible for your good conduct, that's why you're here in Crosbie and not in Glen Afton or worse, lying stiff in a paupers midden fattening the rats with your meat and bones."

Glancing at Stephen, William is completely taken aback by what he's just heard, he exclaims, "Me... an outlaw? What the fuck is it you're talking about Stephen... I'm no' a fuckin' outlaw? All I remember doing was my duty as ma father requested, then we ended up fighting some English invaders and their treacherous allies o' Aslikkør Ranald's clan making to attack us without provocation. How could it all come to this? Fuck off Stephen, I think yie must be dreaming all o' this shit up." Exhausted, William is still very confused. Stephen says "Wallace, yie have been sleepin for way too long ma friend. There's a terrible feeling in the air o' yer auld Scotland I be telling ya, and it seems as though there may be far worse to come, this civil war you Scots have been fighting has already been a bleedin' tragedy, but it feels now like its only just the start o' black days yet to come."

Suddenly remembering his friends, William enquires, "Where's Bailey, Coinach, Lihd and the rest o' the Wildcats? We need to get out o' here and back to glen Afton and Wolf and wildcat forest..." Stephen looks at William, slightly confused, then he realises there is something that William doesn't know. William stares at Stephen awhile; he can see by the expression in his friends face that there is something badly wrong. "Well..." demands William, "What the fuck is your problem Stephen, answer me, it's no' like it's a hard fuckin' question?" Stephen shakes his head, "Wallace, ah have to tell yie this but, they're all gone..." William looks into Stephen eyes, he's perplexed..."What are yie talking about, what do yie mean they are all gone... gone where... gone fuckin' where?" He demands impatiently, "Where have they gone… Glen Afton?" Stephen clasps his hands and looks down at his feet, then he looks back at William, who could clearly see emotion well up in his friend's eyes, but this only angers him, for it's a simple enough question. "They are all gone Wallace… they're all dead…" An involuntarily wave of cold revulsion sweeps through William's body, he slams his food to the ground and staggers back a pace, his head and mind swimming. He growls at Stephen, "You have much o' a bad humour Irishman…" Shaking his head, Stephen replies, "There is no humour Wallace." The realisation and gravity of Stephen words begin to sink in, "Everyone's dead?" William staggers back then doubles over nauseous and dry wretches; he slumps on his heels, puts his head in his arms and leans against the stone cold wall. He wants to run away or turn back time that has been only moments ago in his world, but a great weakness overwhelms him, feeling faint, he slumps to the ground sobbing, he repeats Stephen's words with a forlorn pathetic voice, "Everyone is dead?"

Defiantly, he finds the energy to stand up and glare at Stephen, "Naw I won't believe that Bailey, Coinach, Lihd and all the Wolf and wildcats are all dead, you're a fuckin liar Irishman." Stephen does not react or reply… William looks up at the clouds, "All the Ceitherne and youngblood too, naw Stephen they're not dead, they can't be…" he shouts at Stephen, "You're wrong… they cannae be dead, what about Andra, Tam, and Seamus? I saw them with the Youngblood only moments ago…" Again he looks to the heavens, searching the sullen grey skies for an answer. Stephen grips William by the shoulders and cuts through his friend's vain hopes by looking directly into his eyes, he says firmly, "Ah told yie Wallace, they are all fuckin' dead…" Collapsing back to the ground, William drops his head into his hands, "How could Bailey be dead? How can any of them be dead?"

He feels his brain is tearing itself apart trying to wish it so that this had never happened. He looks at Stephen in shock realisation and resignation at the same time. His waking reality is now crushing him. He stands up again, unbalanced and weak, then he questions Stephen desperately, "If they're all dead, then how is it that I'm alive, you must be wrong, please God Stephen, yie have to be wrong about this... not all of them dead surely, I remember..."

Grabbing Stephen, William shakes him violently, expecting an answer that he can understand, for nothing will make him believe that this is anything other than a frighteningly real nightmare. Stephen suddenly slaps William's wrists down with such force, it almost knocks him to the ground. He staggers back unbalanced because his strength is near gone. Stephen catches him as he collapses and helps him back into the seat. "I'll tell you why you're alive Wallace and why our friends are not when you calm fuckin' down." says Stephen gruffly. "Until then, I will not discourse wit' a fuckin' madman." William's head is raging with confusion and frustration, flashes of terror and chaotic reality is his alone to deal with. He begins pleading for any deity that will listen to heal his grief or bring some control to his thoughts, that he may face Stephen with any semblance of limited calmness. For a long time the two friends sit in silence beneath the dark grey skies of early autumn.

After a while, William enquires, "Stephen, will you just tell to me plainly... what the fuck happened at the Duibh Hill?" Stephen replies, "I will tell yie. It was True Tam who found yie Wallace, when yer uncle Ranald's force rode to Invergarvane, they were met by two of the Islemen who had been charged with burning the dead." William buries his face in his hands at the thought of his friends bodies being thrown onto some fire to be burnt, yet only moments ago, in his mind, they were all fighting and so full of life… Stephen continues, "The Islemen recalled to Ranald what had happened the morning o' the fight, the Islemen with Irish and English troops noticed what they thought to be a spy watching them down near their Birlinns, when they saw him leaving, they armed and followed him back up the Duibh Hill towards your camp, they thought you were Baliol or Comyn spies and they set out to trap you."

William thinks a moment, then he realises "Coinach, Fuck…" Stephen continues, "The English say it was you who attacked them first. There were more than a hundred and fifty men and cavalry sent out to trap yiez, but it was the shock of your attack from such small numbers that set the fight in motion before they were ready. The two Islemen told Ranald that yiez all fought with such ferocity and bravery, that they could have nothing but respect for you and your men." William enquires with great angst in his voice, "Aye, that may be so, but why the fuck am I still alive?"

Stephen replies, "They said that when you fell, the big men Bailey and Seamus stood over your body and then they were joined by wee Lihd and all others, exceptin' Coinach and his Ceitherne who'd all been badly wounded trying to kill some De Percy fella. The Islemen said it was like watching the fabled Spartans protecting the body of Leonidas, they also said that Bailey and the Wildcats fought with such ferocity over you and would not leave your body, that the only way to bring them down was by arrow-storm and bolt, for they would not surrender nor give you up Wallace." Shaken by this account, William enquires, "But me Stephen, how can I still be alive when they're all dead?" Stephen replies, "When all was done and the skirmish over, they thought you dead already beneath the rest o' the bodies o' the slain Wildcats. The two isle-men said the Wolf and wildcats had killed and wounded so many of de Percy's and Aslikkør Ranald's forces, they heard word from their own outriders that more o' your kinfolk were quickly closing in on their position, they thought the Wolf and Wildcats must have been a small forward patrol for a much larger unit, so they deemed it prudent to consider they'd lost whatever cause they came to play and didn't want to take on any more mad fuckers like you. They said the back stabbin' shite Aslikkør, the cowardly De Percy and English survivors all fled to the safety of Brus castle, which was not that many by all accounts. The survivors o' Angus óg's Isle-men quickly took to their Longships, leaving the remains of all the dead to be disposed off by the two fella's who found you, and some local fisher-wives."

"So where was I?" William enquiries "I mean, did they say how they found me?" Stephen replies, "When the two Islemen and some local levies were shifting the bodies for the pyre, they found you underneath the bodies of all your men. Apparently Bailey had fallen on Lihd, True Tam says she was holding his hand… and yours, but when they pulled her hand away, they heard a groan, then they pulled you out and found you were still breathing, and by the house markings on your leather battle-jack, they saw that you were Guardian or from Ceil Aicé stock." William Enquires, "Why didn't they just kill me?" Stephen replies, "Well there were a number of reasons they gave as to why they just didn't cut your throat. First they thought you would fetch good money for a ransom. Second, many o' the folk of the northern isles still have loyalties to the Ceil Aicé too, through Scáthach their ancient queen, and the last reason is that they respected the fight that you and the Wildcat Ceitherne put up." Still confused, William enquires, "But how did I get here, and what is this shit about me being an outlaw?" Stephen says "Well Wallace me boy, by the time Ranald, True Tam and their detachment arrived on the scene, the demeanor of the Islemen was favorable towards yie, so they gave you over to your Kinfolks who then brought you here. But the English also knew you were alive and who you are, so they put a bleedin' bounty warrant out for your capture as an outlaw." William is puzzled, "But why? I didn't attack anyone, I was following orders from the Guardians." Stephen smirks, "You attacked English peace keeping troops." William exclaims, "English what?" Stephen continues, "Aye, exactly… the punishment for attacking any English is a death by slow hanging; some fella called Sir Henry de Percy will soon be the acting Sheriff of Galloway and Carrick, and he wasn't very happy that you fucked up his plans and killed most o' his retainers."

Stephen grins, "It was his personal bodyguard that were all but wiped out in the fight, along with quite a few gutless Irishmen that I am sorry to say were acting much out of character, and much to me own personal shame. But anyways Wallace… yer uncle Ranald and Wishart convinced de Percy that it was enacted during a time of civil disturbance and that you had warrant to act on behalf o' the Guardians. Satisfactory compensation was forwarded to de Percy for the loss of men and equipment and also Ranald's surety of house parole that saved you from the axe-man or the hangman's rope." William queries, "So that's why Ranald has me here?"- Stephen replies, "It is. There's another piece of information you should be knowing too." William enquires, "What's that?" Stephen replies, "One o' the isle-men told True Tam that he overheard some drunken English talk of wanton murder and butchery by one of De Percy's nephews, some wee cunt called Marmaduke de Percy they reckon. He said the English talked of great slaughters at the Corserine, Dunveoch, Balquhan and many other massacres they had performed on the Scots and Ceàrdannan. The loose tongues of the English did not think the ears of the Islemen as Scots, but quite a few of the Islemen are good Scots, that's how we found out about who perpetrated those massacres." William says thoughtfully "Then Coinach was right…" Stephen replies "He was. And by all the accounts o' the isle-men, Coinach and his Ceitherne slaughtered many English, Irish and Islemen before they were brought down. Brave men all he said, unfortunately our Coinach did not get De Percy or his nephew, for they had already escaped to the Brus' stronghold at Turnberry castle." William had now been given some relief by what Stephen had told him, though he feels deep grief and a haunting guilt begin to envelop him once more, but he knows now he is not going mad. Stephen stands up, "Wallace boy, I'm going to take you back to your crib now, for yie look se' feckn sick an' terrible to be true, and then me boy I'll be heading to Glen Afton to let all there know of the welcome news of your return to better health."

"Stephen …" says William, "Ah thank yie for telling me this, though I feel I may be consumed by a grief that already gnaws viciously at my heart and senses. Ever since I woke up I thought I was losing my mind or just going fuckin' mad. Maybe I would prefer to be mad rather than face the reality of what's happened." Stephen smiles, "Wallace, oi will be leaving for Ireland very soon, and now that you are back with us… why do yie not come over and stay wit me'self and Katriona, and yie could be seeing yer brother Wee John and Rosinn too? Ah reckon yie should get well away from here, though none if this terrible tragedy was your fault or by your making at all, there is nothing but evil intent abroad in this auld country o' yours and its only going to get far worse, let me tell ya. Yie should think long and hard about me offer brother." William replies, "Naw… ah don't think so Stephen. I'll think about it though, but really, all ah want to do is just to go back to the land o' the Wolf and wildcats and hide myself away, for that's all I feel I want to do just now, for ma head is fucked." Stephen says " Here Wallace, let's be going in now, for we cannot change what's happened but we can be aware of what ails Scotland and be more guarded by this experience." Stephen helps William back towards the main house, then he remembers something unusual "Oh aye Wallace, listen up, ah meant to say to yie, it's an odd thing, but do yie remember that odd auld fella True Tam... well, when everyone had given you up for dead, but that wry auld feckr wouldn't give up at all, he kept lookin for he just knew that you were still alive..."

*   *   *

Many days pass by since Stephen had left for Glen Afton with the good news. William stayed in bed a few more days, regaining his health and strength. It was at a breaking fast one morning that he talks of leaving and going back to the Glen Afton. Ranald speaks to him, "You have to wait a few weeks yet William, there are too many English patrols arriving and they have imposed a severe martial law. You cannot risk any event that would see you brought to the hangman or headsman's pleasure. You must wait awhile till we know it's safe for your return to the Glen Afton to see the family, and only then you must carry a passport issued by the English Sheriff."

"An English Sheriff?" exclaims William. He enquires, "Can I not simply travel when am well again?" Ranald snaps, "No... you would be risking all our lives should you be so foolish." William accepts this stern rebuke from his uncle, though it wrankles his peace to be so confined with him being a wilderness hunter. Ranald continues "Anyone in Ayrshire or Galloway who does not have a free or travel pass from an English Sheriff, is to be arrested and thrown into prison without trial or even executed on the spot for sedition if they so deem. And you William, you have already been marked down by the English as a troublemaker and many English soldiers want your head in revenge." Thumping his fist on the table, William demands furiously, "How the fuck can those English bastards impose these things upon us uncle?" Ranald replies, "It's because the warring lords of the southwest have proved that only martial law will keep the peace. And though we might not like this English martial imposition placed upon us, they have established good order, and now peace returns to this part of Scotland." Angered by this information, William enquires, "Do the English think to hold these barbarous laws above our heads in all of Scotland?"

"They do for now," replies Ranald. He studies his nephew and sees the frustration and his confinement has left him greatly troubled, the lack of interests has William dwelling on the events and terrible experiences he has endured. Ranald could also see these thoughts are taking its toll on him as the sole survivor from Invergarvane. Knowing the guilt William now feels and carries. Ranald also sees this situation is turning William's usual carefree spirit into a sullen broody character. The closed environment of Crosbie is starting to make him behave like a mad circus bear. Ranald understands what this is doing to the mind of the wild young woodland hunter. "William?" enquires Ranald. "Aye uncle, what is it yie ask?" replies William. Ranald continues with a hint of a smile, "Take my horse and go for a ride-out on my lands, you need to grow your strength back and it would be good for you to start getting about more... but mind that you keep to my lands and don't be strayin' across any boundaries, for it's far too dangerous for yie right now." Elated at this offer, William jumps up with such a big grin on his face, "Your no' jestin' with me uncle, are yie…? For I'm goin' feckn mad pacing about the grounds here, though I cannot tell you how much gratitude I have for your help and succor. By the Aicé… even as I speak, the feeling of shame engulfs me at my selfishness and thoughtlessness in not repaying you in good humour for all that you've done for me."

Looking at William, Ranald could see he is genuinely considerate and seeing beyond his own feelings. He replies, "Ach aye, away with yie now boy, we're Clan, and it's about time yie got that famous smile of yours back on your face." Rushing towards the door, William calls back with a grin, "I'm gone…" Ranald smiles, then he calls out, "And remember, stay on Crauford land, do not stray from it or go near anyone at all… and in particular, if you see any English patrols, do well to avoid them, for if they know who you are, they may wish to remedy a mistake in their eyes letting you live after Invergarvane, and they might just hang you or stick your head on a stake. And knowing you so well William Wallace, I really think it's best just keeping your distance, a very big distance." Ranald pauses, then he smiles again, "I'm only saying this for their safety you understand." William stops at the door and laughs hearing his uncle's words, "I will uncle… trust me." William grins and bounds down the stairs on his way to the stables. Sitting back in his chair Ranald thinks, *'Trust me…? Fuck… ah wish he hadn't said that.'*

Leaving the confines of Crosbie castle, William rides hard and fast for many hours over the lands of north and east Ayrshire. He finally stops to rest his flagging horse near the small deserted Balloch of Auchencruive, not many miles from his uncle Richard's Riccartoun castle. Letting the horse graze awhile, he starts a small pit fire then walks to the dip of the small glen where a deep flowing burn (Little river) forms a still pool in the shade of a large hawthorn bush. He knows it well from his youth and he's sure there will be good trout and young salmon resting under the boulders in the shadows cast by the thick hawthorn. Removing his boots and breeks, William wades into the flowing burn where he sees a large round boulder rolling out above the water, he tentatively leans over the boulder and gently feels underneath for spaces with his fingers between the boulder and burn floor where he knows fish will rest.

He guddles about gently awhile, till the smooth feeling he recognises as the underbelly of a big fish brushes his fingertips. Pausing for a moment before he makes to grab his catch, he's still amazed at how it could be that when you gently stroke the underside of fish they apparently freeze for a moment, just long enough to grab them and throw them onto the bank or into a net. *A bit like Wee Maw's chicken magic.'* He laughs to himself, remembering how Wee Maw would turn a chicken on its back then tickle its wattles above the vent. Curiously the chicken would go rigid, like it was asleep or in a blissful trance; then she explained to both him and wee John, that this was a kind and thoughtful way to treat a chicken before you chop its head off. He laughs remembering how he and wee John used to wait till Wee Maw was bringing the axe down beyond the point of no return towards the chicken's neck, they would clap their hands to wake the chicken up... just as Wee Maw dropped the axe and cut the chickens heads off. William chortles, *'Boy she went feckn crazy...'*

Still laughing to himself while thinking about the look on Wee Maw's face, William continues to fish with his hands a while longer, already he has caught and flung five fair sized salmon, trout and a few long eels onto the bank nearby. All the troubles that had recently passed have disappeared from his thoughts; the simplicity of fishing for his dinner with naught but his hands has lost him to all awareness to the outside world. As he wades back out from the burn, he wraps a small salmon in clay and leaves it beside the fire to cook, then he lies down on the bank and watches the clouds drift slowly by. He lay there a long time thinking about Invergarvane and his friends; then he feels a wave of great sadness overcome him, and guilt too at being the sole survivor. He rests his arm across is eyes as though trying to hide away his shame, when suddenly, he is disturbed when he hears a horse whinny behind him, he turns quickly to see an English knight and eight soldiers on horseback staring at him.

'Fuck...I never heard them cause o' the noise of the flowing water over the rocks...' He looks frantically about to see where his horse is, but he also tries to remain outwardly calm and innocent of any thoughts in front of these Englishmen. The knight, dressed so fanciful on horseback as though attending a gay pageant, enquires, "You... Scotch simpleton... I am Sir Arnold De Ferrier, quartermaster to sir Henry de Percy, soon to be sheriff of these lands, who are you and who gave the likes of you permission to take these fish?" Watching the obese knight while the English soldiers dismount, William scrutinises De Ferrier, he also keeps his peripheral vision on the soldiers who are slowly surrounding him with swords drawn. "My name is William Wallace my Lord," replies William, "This land belongs to my uncle, the sheriff of Ayr." De Ferrier enquires menacingly, "And who might that be?"

"Sir Ranald Crauford my lord." William continues, "These are his lands and estates. I've but left him this morn and now prepare to return to his house at Crosbie with my catch, I've merely stopped to cook some vittals as I have not eaten since early morn." De Ferrier says nothing by way of reply. William can sense things are not good. He makes the English knight and offer. "I'll share this catch with you my lord, as I have too much for one meal anyway."

"Not good enough," replies De Ferrier "Men, remove the fish from this thief and hold him fast." Two soldiers immediately grab William by the arms and wrists; another grabs him from behind by his long hair, puts an arm around his throat then begins to choke him. William struggles to get free, but his right arm is still weak from the shoulder wound, suddenly, he is violently struck from behind, momentarily knocking the fight out of him, then they begin beating him to the ground, till they eventually knocking him senseless. William wakes to find two of the soldiers pissing on him, much to the amusement of their colleagues, lord and master. De Ferrier, in seeing William coming to his senses, orders him to be pulled back up on his feet. De Ferrier dismounts and calls out a command... "Hold out his right arm, we shall cut off his thieving hand and make an example plain for all to see what happens when we catch these Scotch thieves. We must be setting by good example to these filthy Scotch that they may not poach on the lands of their betters. Hold him fast men, I will do this chastisement myself." The English soldiers force William's right arm out for De Ferrier, who now holds a long-sword ready to cut off William's hand.

De Ferrier wanders about swinging the sword fancifully in exaggerated circles while preparing for the final cut. William watches him in silence, he knows he will have to act fast, he has only seconds to act. Confidently, De Ferrier approaches William and raises the sword high to bring it down with a swift cutting force on his wrist when suddenly, William appears to faint and goes limp dead weight on the restraining soldiers. De Ferrier pauses and glares, which is all the time William needs. Before the sword can be dropped, William kicks out as hard as he has ever kicked, striking De Ferrier squarely on his brightly garnished groin, crushing the knights unprotected testicles and instantly dropping the red faced knight to his knees. As De Ferrier hits the ground, the soldier's grip of William eases for a mere second, as the surprise at what has just happened shocks the soldiers holding him. William immediately takes the opportunity to break free from their grip and kicks the blustering red faced De Ferrier under the chin, knocking him over onto his arse. Simultaneously he grabs the knight's sword, spins around in the same movement and brings the blade down on one of the English soldiers outstretched arms, cleaving the arm off at the elbow. William moves at speed and with such aggression, the English soldiers are momentarily indecisive… De Ferrier screams "KILL HIM…"

This is the moment William has been waiting for. He quickly turns towards De Ferrier who is struggling to get back on his feet, in an instant, William brings the sword crashing down on De Ferrier's bare head with such a force, he drives the sword down through Englishman's head from forehead to breastbone. While De Ferrier's body shudders in its death throes, the soldiers immediately rush William, he rams the sword into the leading soldiers face, easily piercing through the back of his skull. In the same movement William spins around, pulling the blade out of the soldiers head and chops it down into another soldier, biting deep into the corner of his neck, he pulls back and thrusts the sword deep onto another approaching soldier's stomach. He pulls back again, and drives the blade deep into another soldier's lower gut almost to the hilt. He ducks a swinging blade and rushes forward, pushing the dying soldier in the face, shoving him backwards. William quickly retrieves the sword blade and spins around with such ferocity, he breaks an incoming soldier's sword clean through and buries his blade deep into the side of the assailant's head. Fighting for his life, William is using his peripheral sense of vision as his master tutor old Leckie mòr had taught him so well to rely on, and his instinct. Facing off the two remaining soldiers, they immediately turn and run for their horses, William quickly spins his sword and grabs the end of the blade with both hands, he arcs it behind his head and in one swift motion, he throws it hard and fast nearly twenty feet with such torque, it sticks deep between the shoulder the blades of the farthest running soldier, with most of the blade exiting through his chest, spraying hot blood over his comrade as he runs past him trying to flee. The last surviving soldier flings himself at his horse and clutches at the saddle desperately, clinging on for dear life as the horse gallops away towards Glasgow dragging the surviving English soldier who is still gripping the saddle.

Turning back to see the carnage he has dealt these English soldiers, William looks at an Englishman kneeling on the ground, holding his stump arm and screaming out in great pain while staring wildly at his dismembered forearm lying beside him. William picks up a discarded sword and walks over to the soldier who is crying in agony, then he looks into the eyes of the soldier he had chopped in the neck and sees that his heart is pumping the last few beats of blood out of his body as he lay twitching, with just an occasional flicker from his eyes. Other than spurts of blood pulsing and gushing from the Englishman's open neck wound and getting weaker by the second… he is a dead man.

Turning to speak to the wounded soldier, William enquires, "Why the fuck did yiez make me do this?" The bloodied soldier looks up at William, who is drawing back his sword to rest it on his shoulder, the English soldier pleads for his life, "Don't kill me… please don't kill me… I have a wife and children… please, I beg of you." William rests the sword on his shoulder upon hearing the cry for mercy, at the same moment the English soldier, holding a hidden dagger in his left hand, stabs at William's groin, catching him on the inside of his thigh. Screaming in pain, William screams at the soldier, "Ya stupid English fuck, I wasn't going to strike you..." Without a second thought, William instinctively whips the sword down, then in an vicious upward arc, he catches the Englishman on the side of the head, slicing easily through flesh, bone and brain. William brings the blade around in a sweeping motion and cleanly separates the man's head from his body. William staggers back, covered in the blood and brain tissue of the dead soldier. He stares almost in disbelief at the twitching body, spraying out the man's bloody life force from the gaping stump in his neck. The gargling, rasping noises from his lungs gasping for air and the spasms of life shaking the soldiers body violently is all that is left of this Englishman, who has brought this horrific end upon himself... and more great misery to William.

Standing in own his timeless space, William's thoughts are cold and indifferent to the bloody scenes around him. He drops to the ground, where his entire body begins to shake and tremble with all that has happened. He feels shock draining his body of strength and begins to feel sick to his stomach. Hardly noticing the slashes and cuts about his own body, he looks at the bloody bodies of dead or dying Englishmen. For no reason that he could understand, they had beaten him, pissed on him and were going to cut his hand off. This brutal reality makes no sense to him.

After sitting a long time amidst the carnage in a daze and completely bereft as to knowing why the English soldiers treated him thus, the pain of his many wounds begins to bite deeply, with adrenalin ebbing; weakness is threatening to overpower him, he can also feel fatigue pulling at his waking consciousness. He picks himself up and saddles his horse, knowing there will be great trouble for what's happened. He thinks maybe it's best that he should ride away as far as possible, he could go the opposite direction from where the surviving Englishman had fled, perhaps he could get lost in the crowds of Ayr town or deep in the Wolf and wildcats. In time, maybe he would not be recognised as the assailant of these soldiers, suddenly he remembers, *'Fuck... I told them my name and that my uncle Ranald is the sheriff of Ayr. The one that escaped will soon be in Ayr or Glasgow to tell of what has happened here.'* The thought of this and the dire consequences of his actions merely adds to the sick feeling fermenting in his mind and body. As he mounts his horse, he decides it best to make haste to Crosbie and warn his uncle Ranald of what has happened, then get as far away as possible to thwart any pursuit from the English garrisons stationed in Ayr, Kilmarnock or Glasgow.

It's late in the evening when William wonders through the unmanned gatehouse of Crosbie Tower and walks his horse across the cobbled yard into the ground floor stables of the tower-house. He slides painfully from the horse, removes the tack, then ambles over to the horse trough and submerges his head deep into the chilled waters, trying to wake up his numbed senses. He looks down into the black reflecting surface of the water, he realises he is only wearing his léine; in his haste, he left behind his breeks and boots. William laughs at the insanity and bizarre image reflecting back at him from the black water surface. He drags his aching body over to the smithy forge to seek out the Blacksmith's temper churns, he knows that bathing wounds in water used by blacksmiths has amazing healing properties and also if it is drank too, it infuses healing iron into his body. He finds one such churn, cups his hands and scoops some water out and drinks copiously, slaking his thirst, it's metallic and bitter... just what he needs he thought. He fills a nearby horn goblet and gulps the water, then bathes his cuts and wounds awhile. Having washed and drank his fill, William wearily makes his way up the inner staircase to the first floor, thinking of how he could ever explain this day's events to Ranald. As he enters the door chamber through to the main hall, he sees three men who jump up from their seats, startled at the sight before them, Ranald enquires, "William... what's happened to you? And where are your breeks and boots boy?"

The other two men William recognises as Bishop Robert Wishart and True Tam of Ercildoune. When they see the battered and bruised condition of William, they all rush over and help him to a seat beside the fireplace. True Tam fetches William some hot whisky to heat him up, then William begins to recount to them what has happened, he also accounts for the skirmish at Invergarvane in detail, till sleep and exhaustion takes too great a toll on him. Ranald helps William to his crib chamber. On entering the chamber, William says, "I'm so sorry uncle, but they were going to take my life, I had no other choice." Ranald appears very grey in pallor, knowing that the repercussions for what has happened will have serious consequences, perhaps his own execution at the hands of the English, as he had pledged his life and property bond on behalf of William keeping the peace. He replies, "Get rested son, we shall talk of this on the morn."

Waking early next morning, William makes his way down the stone stairs of Crosbie tower and into the main hall. He sees Ranald, Wishart and True Tam are already awake and discussing the state of the Kingdom, but more importantly, William's current dilemma. Ranald bids him to sit with them, "William it is no longer safe for you to be here, you risk too much for yourself and for us all should you stay any longer." Not really having a care, William replies, "I understand, would you wish me to go to Glen Afton?" Wishart replies abruptly, "You must leave Scotland…" William is stupefied to hear what Wishart is proposing, but something inside him knows that because of what has happened it would mean he could find no peace in Scotland, not for a long time. He enquires, "Where do you suggest I go… France?"

"No…" snaps Wishart "you leave for Ireland, we feel it best served for all if you go to the safety of old Stephen ua H'Alpine in the lands of Connaught." Studying the face of Wishart and seeing the solemn faces around the table, William knows this is a unanimous decision, and most likely the right one. But he also feels he has lost all his friends and has no real care what or where his future would be. Wishart speaks, "The English will hunt you down Wallace, if they know not who you are at this moment, the fact that you told them who you are and then you let one escape, means that it will not be long before they are combing this country till they get their hands on you." William enquires with not much of a care, "When do I leave?" Wishart replies, "Now… I've sent riders out already and we only need get you past Glen Afton, from there you'll travel through the Wolf and wildcat forest into Galloway. There you will have safe passage from Baliol's people to Glen App then on to Pádraic a'carsaide, from there, a ship will carry you to Ireland." Ranald says, "I'll go to Ayr this morn and try to convince the English Sheriff that as I am still the Sheriff of this shire, it's my duty to seek out the perpetrators, not theirs. The English will be looking for someone to make them pay dearly for the killing of this knight and his men. William, we are all agreed that you should leave now. I'll confirm that if, or rather when the English come to seek you here, I'll tell them, with the Bishop Wishart's blessing of course, that you had already left the country before this incident took place." Although he already knows the answer, William enquires, "Can I go and see my family before I leave?"

"No," replies Wishart tersely, "Now put this grey cassock worn by the Augustinians on your back, you will be travelling with young John Blair, he will accompany you. And you Wallace, you will be his mute Irish assistant, for we are all at risk if you're discovered. I will make arrangements with my old friend Bishop Donough O'Flanagan to get you from Antrim safely through to Connaught. Do not speak to anyone, do not say anything or indicate that you have any wit for anything other than the church till you leave these shores." True Tam speaks, "We've also arranged for young Stephen of Ireland to meet up with you at the old crannog at Loch Dhuine, from there you will travel south with him to your destination." It appears to William as though all is prepared for his immediate departure when True Tam comes over and looks at him. He says nothing while he gazes deeply into William's eyes, then True Tam puts his hand on his shoulder. "Walk with me to the stables young Wallace."

True Tam talks to William on route to the stables, with words that only he and William will ever share. A little while later, William embraces Ranald and climbs onto the wagon beside Wishart for the journey to loch Dhuine. True Tam speaks to him one more time, "Wallace, do not return to Scotland unless we send for you. You must not return on any account till you hear from us, is that understood?" William nods in agreement as True Tam continues, "We'll send note to you and it will be only from myself, Ranald or the good Bishop Wishart here who will send for you in person. You know the mark of our three signets for that to be true in all that I have said. Mark my words carefully Wallace, we will need good men like you one day... for it is in your destiny to return to us, for Scotland will need your likes again." William nods his head as True Tam continues. "Trust us Wallace, for when that day comes, and it will, you will hear our call, when war comes again to this realm it will be a war to the death between two ideologies and two cultures..."

*　　　*　　　*

"Wallace... Wallace... William WALLACE..." says the voice harshly. Broken from his deepest thoughts, William replies angrily, "What is it?" He turns to see his friends Stephen, Katriona and John Blair preparing to disembark from Morrison's Blue Angel Birlinn. Blair says, "The boat has been beached on the shores of Ireland awhile now Wallace, you've been standing there looking at the coast of Scotland for ages." William replies, "I was thinking..." Blair smirks, "Yie've been thinking since we left the bay of Pádraic a' carsaide." Turning to pick up what little he has brought with him, William makes his way to the front of the longboat beached on the shores of Domhnach Daoi. (Donnachadee) Looking back across the sea to Scotland one last time, he enquires, "Do you think we will ever return Blair?" Blair replies, "I think so... I know I will, but I don't know about you." William turns to walk up the beach when Blair calls out from the Birlinn "Oh... I nearly forgot Wallace, this sealed message came for you before we left Scotland."

"Who's it from?" queries William. Blair replies, "It came from France, I think it's from the Maid Marion." he throws William the sealed velum letter. Blair enquires as he clambers over the side of the longboat, "Are yie going to read it to see what she says?" Stephen enquires, "Aye Wallace... what is it the bonnie lass is writing to us all about?" Stephen winks at Blair, jumps ashore; then he lifts Katriona gently to the beach. He glances at his big Scots friend who carries a greatly troubled heart. He knows William has been deeply affected by everything that's happened. In a forced but jovial voice, he calls out… "C'moan Wallace ya big miserable feckr yee, come and be tasting the wonderfull fresh air of Irish Freedom."

Taking time to study the sealed velum message in his hand from Marion, William tucks it away inside his jack without reading it. He looks back across the sea towards the blue hued mountains of Scotland, he thinks… *'While I will bide my time waiting for the call, if there are English forces here in Ireland who would wish me harm…'*

Four Years Later...

Norway, September 1290, Margaret's Drekar: A dark grey sky hangs heavily over a grand fleet of Norse royal Longships as they sail away from the port of Bergen in Norway. The enormous billowing sails are fully dropped and all gunnel-tacked to catch a steady easterly wind, driving the fleet of Longships purposely through the slate green Hyperborean ocean. Occasionally, a glimpse of the sun breaks between the grey clouds to reflect off the magnificently ornate gold-leaf and silver lions, snakes, sea monsters and host of other wonderful pagan symbols etched onto the sleek gunnels of the Longships, gloriously complimented with beautifully carved hollow spirit-eagles pivoting on the topmasts to ward off evil spirits and indicate the movement and wind direction of the thunder and storm-gods, Taranis and Thor.

On board the King of Norway's enormous Drekar, (Dragon head Longship) is Princess Maighread Magnusson, the Maid of Norway, escorted and guarded by the Norse Kings Väringagardet (Bodyguard) and King Edward of England's chaperones, all protecting the maid on her long journey to fulfill her destiny as Domina and rightful heir by proximity of blood, to be crowned Queen of Scotland. After four years of delay, the maid Maighread is making her journey from Norway, but heavy seas and North Sea storms drive the ships off course and the young princesses' fleet seeks shelter at the islands of Orkney in the natural harbour of South Ronaldsay. Many who fled Scotland into exile as outlaws from punitive English martial rule during the interregnum, patiently bide their time waiting for the maid Maighread to arrive at Leith docks near Edinburgh, followed by the swift departure of the English army from their beloved realm, that the exiled Scots abroad may all return home.

Finally, news reaches Ireland the Norwegian fleet carrying the Maid of Norway is en route to Scotland. The expatriate Scots receive a call for their return to Scotland, pardoned and welcomed as freemen, in that they may attend her forthcoming coronation at Scone Palace of their new Queen, Margaret.

William Wallace, falsely branded an outlaw by Lord De Percy, the English Governor of Ayr, has also sought refuge in Ireland, residing at the home of his friend Stephen ua h'Alpine in Carraig Mhachaire Rois Muineachan, under the protection of Bishop Donough O'Flannagain for nigh on four years, William has impatiently bided his time while honing his craft as a master archer with Rory O'Conchobhair's Gallóglaigh of Cuige Chonnacht. William had also joined with the Ua Neil's and MacSuibhne's, serving with them as a master archer in their violent disputes against English rule. Then, one day, a sealed velum letter arrives for him, stamped with the signet impressions of his uncle Ranald the former Sheriff of Ayr, sir Thomas of Ercildoune, and Robert Wishart, the Bishop of Glasgow... It is time for William Wallace to come home...

THE RED EARL

Robert Bruce, son of the Robert Brus, earl of Carrick and Grandson of Robert de Brix of Whittle Essex, waits impatiently with a small entourage near the old chapel of Domhnach a' Daoi on the Antrim seaboard of Ireland. He watches anxiously for the Scot's Birlinns of Morrison mòr's Blue Angel fleet, sailing across the Irish Sea to take him back to the Brus family home of Turnberry Castle on Scotland's west coast.

"There they are now." calls out one of Bruce's aides. Bruce replies excitedly "I see them…" He looks into the eyes of a beautiful young flame-haired Irish noblewoman standing nearby with her ladies in waiting. He calls out "Come Elisabeth… Come see the blue sails that will take us to our new home."

Picking up her skirts from around her ankles, Elisabeth runs and joins Bruce on the shoreline. She puts her arm lovingly around his waist and clings to him as young lovers do, then she looks to the horizon with a thrill in her heart and growing sense of anticipation sparkling in her emerald-green eyes. Elisabeth glances up at her bo' Robert de Bruce. She blushes, "My love, where are these ships that sail to carry us away to Scotland?" Bruce points directly across the sea. "Look straight across at Scotland Elisabeth, then you will see them."

Elisabeth strains to see the Birlinns; then after a few moments, the Longships of Morrison Mòr eventually become apparent with their distinct blue-tacked sails and the foaming white wash springing from their proud high bows that forge their way through the dark green Irish Sea. The vivid contrasting colours are now making the Blue Angel Birlinns distinctly visible as they sail relentlessly onwards from the black inch Rhinns peninsular of Galloway, a mere seventeen miles away and a four hour sea journey by fair wind from the coast of Scotland.

"It wont be long now my sweetheart." says the Bruce as he shelters Elisabeth from the chill autumn winds with his royal crimson coloured mantle. The two young lovers huddle together, comforted and protected from the cold sea breeze in their soft Irish linens and waxed felt brats, worn exclusively by the Noble class of Norman aristocracy… and occasionally an Irish outlaw Chief. Pulling Elisabeth close, Bruce points across the sea to Scotland, "Look you now to the blue sails my love… then look away to your left and you will see a great island that sits between Scotland and Ireland… that's Creag Ealasaid, stepping stone of the giants Ben an Donner and Fion Mac Cumhail." Elisabeth queries, "That funny looking island over there?" Bruce replies with a smile, "Aye my love, now look a little further northward on the mainland coast and you will see the tall lime-washed walls of Turnberry Castle, that's the ancient castle of my mother Marthoc and my father Robert." Holding hands with Elisabeth, he looks deeply into her eyes. "They will be so pleased to meet you at long last." Bruce puts both his arms around his love and holds her close to his heart.

Members of Bruce's entourage stand apart from the young couple, watching keenly as the Blue Angel sails gain closer. Two of the entourage are men of the Bruce clan who had travelled with him from Scotland four years earlier as his aides and bodyguards. The two others are native born Irish; both are ladies in waiting to lady Elisabeth. Brona, an elderly lady who wet-nursed Elisabeth from birth, says, "Sure now, it's a fine sight to be seeing such unrequited young love on this cold fall day." Cloda, the younger lady in waiting, grew up in Elisabeth's household, she is also her closest friend and confidante. "Aye Brona, it is a sweet thing to be seeing those two together." Then Brona calls out, "I see them now, there's the blue sails over there." They all huddle together and watch as Morrison mòr's Birlinns gain ever closer, forging relentlessly towards the treacherous channels of the Domhnach a' Daoi headland. They are less than an hour from landing when Bruce and his retinue hear the sound of many horses riding towards their position on the landward outcrop.

Bruce quickly turns to see approximately forty riders approaching at full gallop. As the armed horsemen close in on the small group, Elisabeth realises who the lead rider is, she grabs Bruce in a panic and screams, "NO…" She throws herself behind Bruce, pulling frantically at his heavy crimson brat, desperately trying to shy away from the incoming riders… Another of Bruce's bodyguards calls out, "It's Sir Richard De Burgh my Lord, the Red Earl of Ulster."

Both bodyguards draw their swords and unceremoniously push Elisabeth and the two ladies in waiting behind Bruce. They then place themselves firmly in front of their charges as the armed squadron gallop hard and fast without easing their pace directly at the Bruce and his entourage, only pulling their horses aside at the last moment. With weapons drawn, the riders encircle the small group, intimidating them with the sounds of excited sweating horses brusquely snorting, whinnying and brushing up against the small group. Their hooves stamping at their feet and tails lashing their faces.

A large and bulky knight in red surcoats with the three red leopards of England emblazoned upon his chest dismounts and approaches the group aggressively. He simply reaches out and grabs the first guard and throws him aside to reveal the cowering Elisabeth. The bold knight stares with maniacal determination into the face of the other guard, in one swift movement, he reaches behind the guard, grabs the Bruce by his long hair, pulls him violently and throws him to the ground like a half-full sack of wet corn near the hooves of the knights horse. The Knight glares menacingly into the eyes of the guard's who uncertain of what they should do.

De Burgh commands, "Put your swords aside, both of you... and you may live." This is a desperate situation fraught with danger coming from this aggressive belligerent knight. De Burgh appears almost beside himself with rage as the two guards look to Bruce, who signals that they must comply with the De Burgh's command, and do as they are bid. The guards momentarily look at each other then sensibly; they drop their sword points and back away from the knight. Soldiers of De Burgh quickly wrest away the swords from Bruce's guards and then force them to kneel on the ground. The remaining soldiers train their lances on Bruce's guards.

Bruce raises himself from the ground and approaches De Burgh from behind; he reaches out and touches the Earl on the shoulder, "My Lord..." De Burgh turns quickly, and with the back of his armoured hand, he slams Bruce full in the face, knocking him to the ground. Immediately De Burgh's soldiers retrain all their weapons on the guards and Bruce with ominous aggression, making it clear that any further rash movements will result in serious injury or even possible death. De Burgh moves menacingly towards Bruce, Elisabeth screams, "Father... stop, please stop, it is all my fault, it was my idea father, not Robert's."

Elisabeth drops to her knees weeping, "Please father… please I beg of you my lord, please do not harm him." She pleads and clasps her hands as though in prayer, looking to the heavens, weeping for intervention. She wails, "Please God, do not let my father kill him."

De Burgh stands towering over the Bruce now lying prostrate at his feet, all present can see De Burgh is so enflamed that his next decision is hanging in the balance. Suddenly, De Burgh pulls his sword partly from its scabbard; it appears he is about to commit execution upon the young Scots noble. Elisabeth screams hysterically and beats the ground with her fists in such a frenzy her hands begin to bleed. De Burgh turns his attention away from Bruce and looks at his daughter with utter contempt. He stands in silence watching her hysterics; then he pushes his sword firmly back into its scabbard and walks back towards her. He stands for a moment looking down at Elisabeth, unexpectedly he reaches out to his daughter with an open hand, as though in a gesture of reconciliation. Without warning, De Burgh grips Elisabeth savagely by her hair; violently pulling her close, then he walks away a few paces, dragging Elisabeth behind him screaming in pain and terror.

Elisabeth clutches desperately at her father's legs, her head cowering against his shins. "Father please… I beg your forgiveness…" In desperation, she reaches up to try and take the pain away from his tight grip upon her hair, but De Burgh smashes his open hand mercilessly across her face with such force, blood instantly flows from her nose and mouth, he then starts beating her violently without any indication of mercy, striking her repeatedly about the head with an open hand as she vainly tries to fend off the cruel blows. It's obvious to everyone her frail and slight young body cannot take much more of such a powerfully delivered assault, but De Burgh continues the beating for what seems like an eternity, then he releases his grip and she falls to the ground, stunned and in a daze. Much of Elisabeth's beautiful red hair is torn from her head and now lies about her feet, ripped from her scalp by her father's furious onslaught.

As Elisabeth lay helpless, the sickening assault begins once again as he brutally slaps her about the head with both hands. It isn't long before her hair is a bloodied tousled mess, tangled in the bloody iron grip of her father's fury. While Elisabeth lay on the ground sobbing, the enraged Earl glares at his daughter; he's not finished with her beating yet. He pulls her roughly to her knees and raises his hand to smash his open hand into her upturned face, when Cloda rushes forward and grabs on to his arm and holds on with all her might, De Burgh releases his grip on Elisabeth's hair and grips Cloda tightly by the throat. Brona tries to rush forward to aid her young friend but is held firmly by two of the Earl's soldiers. De Burgh looks menacingly into the eyes of Cloda and spits out the words in her face… "I trusted you both with my daughters life and her chastity… I, sir Richard De Burgh, placed my trust in you… you filthy Irish whore." De Burgh stares maniacally at Cloda, almost in disbelief. He continues in a menacing tone, "You dare think to steal away from me my daughter? De Burgh looks at Bruce, "My God sir, she is but thirteen summers of age…"

Slowly and deliberately De Burgh pulls a dagger from his belt and leans the needle-point gently against Cloda's breast, he puts his other hand around the knap of her waist and pulls her close, trapping her arms by her sides. He pulls her ever closer till her face is next to his. Cloda can see his eyes are bulging and bloodshot red, with a rage nearing insanity, then without another word, he slowly pushes the point of the dagger through the thin material of her dress, the needle point blade causing a stinging sensation in her breast that makes her recoil. Cloda screams and struggles to break free, but De Burgh holds her fast and continues to push the dagger slowly and methodically deeper into her breast till the blade tip pierces her heart. De Burgh looks strangely fascinated as he holds Cloda firm and close to his face. He watches intensely with evil grimace as the overwhelming shock and disbelief becomes evident in the eyes of the young maid. De Burgh suddenly releases his grip on Cloda and quickly pulls the dagger out of her breast; then he wipes the bloody blade on his sleeve.

Cloda stands for a moment looking at the small hole in her breast, the red bloodstain enlarging dramatically against the wheaten colour material of her dress. She looks at De Burgh then pathetically she looks to Elizabeth, as though waiting for an answer to a puzzling question. For a few moments, Cloda stands bewildered, then slowly she drops to her knees and rests sitting upright, "My Lord..." pleads Cloda, looking up to De Burgh, she glances to Elisabeth and gasps "My lady..." but there is no response. Sitting in her own surreal world as though picking wild flowers for the magical fairy sídhe, Cloda flutters her fingers about her breast to chase away an annoying imaginary sprite. Occasionally she clutches at her bosom while making small pitiful sounds as she keeps looking down at her breast. She frantically pats at the dagger wound with her small hands, vainly trying to stem the pulsing blood spraying a red mist outward with every beat of her ailing heart.

Cloda looks around at the faces of everyone, who are collectively observing her struggle in grim silence as an audience watches a macabre Greek tragedy. Cloda's expression is that of confusion, accompanied with gentle moans and little whimpering noises of pathetic despair. The inevitability of death begins to invade her young mind and body, soon to be taking her life as everyone waits patiently. "You try and steal my heart you Irish bitch? Then I will have yours," snarls De Burgh, "I want you to know you are dying, I want you to feel death slowly take hold, you common Irish whore." Cloda is no longer worth a second glance to De Burgh as he turns and walks away.

Suddenly she shudders and jolts upright—then slowly, she falls backwards to the ground. Her body begins to shake erratically with the throes of death closing in to steal her soul from this life. She regains a moment, then with much effort, she pushes herself up from the ground, supporting herself with one hand while pressing her free hand against her breast as the erratic blood spray caresses her face like a misty summer sun shower. Cloda looks at the blood soaked palms of her hands then holds them out with fingers outstretched towards her lady... but no help is forthcoming from the sobbing Elisabeth. Cloda falls backwards like a drunken reveller, her head falls limply to the side. She looks to Brona, then to Elisabeth... pitifully urging them to save her from this chilling moment. She has only just begun her young life and not yet tasted the fruits of love or passion as the rattles of death gain fast. Cloda's eyes scream for life, though no sound escapes her lips. Brona finds the strength to break free from her guards and runs screaming hysterically at De Burgh.

Without a hint of a thought, he pulls the dagger from his belt and in one quick sweep, slices across the front of Brona with absolute precision, slicing her throat from ear to ear. Brona falls to her knees grasping at her throat as the blood sprays from the open wound, filling the air with a pulsating thick red mist. The unnatural gargling noises emitting from her lungs desperately trying to breathe are horrifically audible as Elisabeth screams and wails like a demented woman. De Burgh scowls at Brona then kicks her under the chin, instantly she flops onto her back. He moves forward then repeatedly plunges the dagger into her heart.

Appearing satisfied, De Burgh picks up Bruce's mantle and throws it over the dying Irish women. Their legs are left exposed, sticking out from underneath the mantle while shaking in some bizarre ritual in their death throes. Without a care, De Burgh steps over their twitching legs to where Bruce sits in complete shock in reaction to the scenes he is witnessing. De Burgh nods towards his Captain, instantly six of his soldiers draw shillelaghs from their horse packs. These long heavy clubs are fearsome weapons made from the thick root of the hawthorn tree, hollowed out at the heavy end and filled with lead to increase the weight and striking power. They are smeared with butter and cured by fire, giving these deadly war clubs their infamous shiny black appearance. De Burgh's men turn on the two Scots bodyguards with the deadly clubs and beat them viciously, till both the guards lay sprawled on the ground unconscious in bloodied heaps.

"Bruce, if it were not you are the grandson of my dearest friend lord Brix and under the protection of my liege King Edward, for this betrayal of my trust in you I would have your skin slowly flayed and your peg and balls ripped from your body by my starving wolfhounds before your very eyes, I swear Bruce… I will commit you to this mercy if it is found you have defiled my daughter." He grabs Bruce by the chin, twists his face upwards and digs his fingernails deep into Robert's jaw. De Burgh sneers like a rabid wolf, "My men would take many months of pleasure keeping you alive as they slowly tear you apart for my amusement." Suddenly De Burgh explodes in anger, he viciously backhands Bruce across the face, "You Scotch bastard, I give you shelter then you betray me…" Reaching out towards one of his men,

De Burgh pulls an axe from the soldiers grip and moves on the Bruce, raising the weapon to smash it down on Bruce's skull… "NO MY LORD…" screams De Burgh's captain. He rushes forward and grabs De Burgh's arm before he can deal the fatal blow. De Burgh looks at his man with shock and disbelief at his audacity.

"My Lord…" gasps the captain nervously, "If you kill the Bruce, you will certainly risk the wrath of King Edward and that of Bruce's fathers family and their allies here in Ireland and also those in Scotland and England." The expression in De Burgh's face is that of simple curiosity as the captain continues, "My Lord, look you to Scotland to where the Brus power is greatest. Observe you all on that mainland across the water that is north of the island over yonder, then to all that you see north of the Rathlan Island, that is but a mere fraction of their dominion my lord. The formidable power and reach of the Brus clan and their allies is too great, and it is most certain that King Edward's displeasure and wrath would also be in attendance, killing the Bruce would bring you no gain and nothing but harm. Chastise Bruce if you must my lord… but do not kill him." Pausing for a moment, De Burgh thinks long and hard on the words spoken to him by his captain. He is also considering the implications and nerve of this soldier who has spoken to him thus, but finally he relents, "You may be correct,"

"Strip this Scotch bastard of his brat and léine, then lay bare his back." Bruce is forced to the ground and firmly secured by four of De Burgh's shillelagh men. "Bring me a horse whip." His orders are carried out immediately. Two soldiers hold young Bruce firmly on his knees with his arms twisted behind his back till he resembles a naked hawk diving to earth. His long black hair hangs over his bowed head for such is the forceful grip and twist on his arms he can't raise his head, leaving his shoulders and lower back bare and open for chastisement. The captain of De Burgh's troop holds out a hazel switch. De Burgh snatches it from his hand and walks behind Bruce and begins to thrash Bruce viciously with the hazel whip, marking deep bloody welts into his back. Bruce cries out from the shock and intense pain searing through his body as each new whip strike cuts deep into his flesh. Elisabeth screams hysterically at her father, who stops his whipping of the Bruce and looks into her eyes, "Shut up screaming Elisabeth, or it'll be worse for Bruce." De Burgh vents his anger upon the Bruce and resumes whipping him with a vengeance, "My Lord…" shouts a soldier of De Burgh's troop… "My Lord… there are many riders coming towards us, and they are making great speed." Halting his chastisement of the Bruce, De Burgh looks to see what it is the guard is so excited about. "Who is this that rides upon us?" The soldier calls back with fear evident in his voice, "They fly no colours my lord, I think they're Gallóbhet, there's about twenty of them, but they may be vanguard for a' Gallóglaigh Corrughadh."

"Quickly… to arms." commands De Burgh. His men hastily prepare themselves with weapons defensively drawn, but even at a distance, the aggressive appearance of these approaching riders sends waves of fear throughout the party of the Red Earl of Ulster. It takes only moments for the mounted Gallóbhet to arrive on the scene astride their little hablar war-ponies. These small, strong and supremely surefooted bog-horses are much favoured by their infamous riders and equal to the ferocity of duty required of them. The giant men on such small steeds appear farcical, but for the air of cold retribution emanating from these apparitions of an antiquated warrior caste. Their array of fantastical weapons belay the fact that these men are perhaps the most feared independent class of Scots-Irish mercenaries in Christendom. A young mounted squire recently arrived from England to serve with De Burgh, speaks quietly to a soldier standing nearby, "Who are these dreadful looking beasts good man?" The soldier replies, "Gallóglaigh my Lord, they're Scotch Irish mercenaries, the females are called Gallóbhan, collectively they're known as Gallóbhet." Completely unaware of the true danger he is in, the squire replies, "I see... my lord De Burgh will soon have these unholy barbarous fellow's scurrying away from here with their tails between their legs." The soldier mutters, "Good sir, we will need all our wits about us just to get out of this place alive." The squire looks at the soldier with contempt "You dog, don't you know we are professional soldiers on mission for the King of England. I will personally flay the skin off your back for this display of such cowardly impertinence." Shaking his head in despair, the soldier ignores the squire and scans the roads and ridges of Antrim for any escape routes.

Bruce raises his head and observes these bizarre looking warriors arriving fortuitously. He has heard about the infamous Gallóbhet, but never has he seen them in the flesh. Through the mists of pain, he sits up and watches these strange looking warriors with their great bunches of peculiar styled hair sticking out from below large ill fitting conical helmets protecting heads and ruddy faces adorned with big bushy beards. Some of the Gallóbhet have their great beards pleated with amber beads mixed with dainty little bows of saffron material and pieces of what appears to be grizzly finger bones attached in the weaves. Bruce is taken aback at the bulk and size of these wondrous men and their curiously bizarre appearance on such small sturdy horses. To Bruce, these are men with physiques demonstrating that they have spent their lives in hard physical and martial training, so obviously committed to their skills in the arts of war. He notices there are two mounted archers who appear slightly different, wearing what looks like brats made from the feathers of crow or raven, then he realises that these are the female Gallóbhan, warriors from the old kingdom of Galloway in Scotland, feared hunter scouts of the Gallóbhet and notorious assassins.

Staring at their unusual garb and style of armour, reminds Bruce of the description his grandfather gave when talking of the crusades about the Persian Turkic and Magyar warriors. The Gallóglaigh wear long leather topcoats with ring chain armour worn over a Haubergeon chainmail sleeved vest that reaches down to their knees. It would take a strong horse just to carry their wardrobe and weaponry. The Gallóbhet Chieftain and his bodyguard dismount and walk directly up to De Burgh to stand towering in front of him, but the chieftain simply looks over De Burgh's head towards Scotland. Bruce can see the Chieftain is young, but carries an attitude about him as the natural leader of these notorious warriors. The Chieftain eventually looks into the face of De Burgh, but says nothing. Slowly and deliberately the Chieftain removes his helmet. Through his matted hair and a decorated beard, Bruce can see the giant warrior is grinning like a simple. De Burgh demands an answer from the ancient looking warrior standing before him. "What is your business here?"

The Chieftain looks around as though it were someone else De Burgh has questioned, which incenses De Burgh. The expression on the warriors face appears as though De Burgh is not there at all or that the Chieftain hadn't noticed the red Earls presence. The Chieftain lazily strokes his big beard while scanning the seaboard; then looks to his men, "Did any o' yiez hear a kitten cry out for some titty milk?"

The Gallóbhet all laugh sardonically. De Burgh is inflamed with this apparent slight, "I asked you a question you Irish bastard. Answer your superior, don't you know who I am.... are you deaf? I am somebody, I..." Before he can finish his sentence, the Chieftain puts a finger to his lips, frowns and whispers "Shhhhhhh..." De Burgh is now beside himself with rage, he raises his horsewhip to strike the Gallóbhet, but the Chieftain deftly grips De Burgh by the wrist and wrenches the whip out of De Burgh's hand then throws it away as though taking a stick from a spoilt child. The Chieftain casually lets go the wrist and looks into the red Earls eyes, then he points over De Burgh's shoulder towards Scotland.

De Burgh appears slightly confused and feels drawn to turn his head to look in the direction the Chieftain is pointing. As he peers into the distance to find what the Chieftain is looking at, the Chieftain leans down and close enough to whisper behind De Burgh's ear, "Its big Scottish bastard, if yie don't mind..." The Chieftain straightens up, grinning proudly; then he resumes looking out to sea over De Burgh's head. The wiry woolly-haired Ceannard of the Gallóbhet who had dismounted with the strange disrespectful Chieftain, spoke, "Aye me foin Lord... believe me this, he really is a big Scottish bastard... and you may be taking me word on that sur, for sure now."

Looking into the face of the giant Chieftain, De Burgh is perplexed by his disdain and insubordination. He glances over his shoulder once more to see what this wild man is looking at. Squinting his eyes, De Burgh peers out to sea in the same direction... then he sees the Blue sails of Birlinns coming round a nearby land spur and fast approaching the headland. He quickly turns back to see the Chieftain is looking down into his face with a threatening intensity, "See those ships over there..." the Chieftain says as he points at the Birlinns

"Those are my ships coming to take me and my Gallóbhet back home to Scotland…" The Chieftain pauses to take in the look of bewilderment on De Burgh's face, it's obvious that he can't truly grasp this surreal situation he is in. De Burgh exclaims, "Your ships? What do you mean, your ships?"

"Aye… my ships…" replies the Chieftain with a humorous menace in his voice. He glares with severe intensity into the face of De Burgh, feigning a silent but cheerful challenge. "Would it be going around in that tiny Norman fuckin' head o' yours, to be thinking otherwise?" Suddenly a short gust of autumn wind blows the mantle partly off the bodies of Brona and Cloda lying behind De Burgh, it's then the Chieftain sees the bodies of the women, and noticeably, the twitching of their last spasms of life. The giant Chieftain glances at De Burgh's sword-belt and sees telltale bloodstains on his dagger. Before De Burgh knows what's happening, the Chieftain head-butts him, destroying the bridge of De Burgh's nose and stunning him instantly. The Chieftain grabs De Burgh and throws him to the ground, knocking him breathless; he quickly sits astride De Burgh with his dirk drawn and cutting into the skin of his throat.

The fresh squire from England immediately draws his sword, raises it in the air and yells, "Men, to me…" he is instantly struck by an arrow thumping deep into his neck, in the same moment, another arrow strikes his cheek and exits the other side of his face as another arrow slams under his arm, through the sidewall of his chest and rips into his heart while De Burgh's men desperately try to hold on to their spooking horses. Bruce sits stunned as the hapless squire falls off his horse to the ground dead. Bruce had seen the two Gallóbhan pull and loose their deadly arrows in the time it takes to blink an eye. The Gallóbhet Chieftain calls over to the Gallóbhan archers, "Nice flights…" Eochaidh Gunn and

Fiónlaidh reply simultaneously "Se' do bheatha." De Burgh's men, although outnumbering the Gallóbhet two-to-one, are helpless to come to his aid as each individual soldier is absolutely certain they will not breath another moment longer on this earth if they do, the glare from the Gallóbhet is enough to quell any thought of possible intervention. The confidence and natural arrogance of these fierce warriors becomes even more apparent as it is only now they lazily draw their own weapons. The enraged Chieftain growls, "I think it is you who should be telling me what your business is here my lord fuck…?"

Bruce notices the Anam Crios fixed around the Chieftains waist, then he remembers that only one Scots Clan use that type of rank insignia. Suddenly Bruce recognises the Gallóbhet… "WALLACE… DO NOT HARM HIM…" Bruce immediately rises up from the ground, ignoring the searing pains that wrack his body. William keeps a firm grip on De Burgh as he studies the bloody frame that's limping towards him, then his eyes open wide in surprise. Grinning, William exclaims, "Robert Bruce… Is that you?" Bruce replies, "Aye it's me Wallace." William laughs, "Jaezuz, look at you Bruce, yer no' looking se' much like a noble in the making this day. What the fuck has happened to yie?"

"I will tell you all Wallace," replies Bruce "but first, you must let this lord go free, for you do not know what has happened, nor who he is." Hanging his head shamefully, Bruce continues, "This scene you see before you is of my own making." William enquires curiously, "Well Bruce, tell me then, who is this fine specimen of chivalry that lies bleedin' in horse shit below me?" Bruce replies, "Wallace, this is sir Richard De Burgh, the Lord of Ulster. He's a friend of the English King and companion to my grand-father Lord de Brix." William exclaims, "The Red Earl…" immediately he turns his attention back on the injured man. With utter contempt and hatred in his voice he growls, "I should cut your Norman fuckin' head off, right here right now ya murderin' Norman fuck…" Bruce pleads desperately "Do not kill him Wallace, for peace is coming to Scotland and to Ireland. If you should harm De Burgh, you may jeopardise that peace, then there would be nowhere you or your family could ever find shelter from retribution, he is too important a noble. If you kill him, you may ruin everything for the many, because of just one?"

Glaring at De Burgh with well-founded hatred in his eyes, William says, "This bastard is responsible for the cruel deaths of hundreds of innocents in Ireland… and Scotland, including many who have relatives here with me this day. He commanded the cursed Ranald bastard who murdered my friends and kinfolk a few years ago." Gripping De Burgh tightly by the throat with both hands, William squeezes De Burgh's throat until his eyes are almost popping out of his head. Bruce pleads once more "Don't kill him Wallace, I beg of you, let him be…"

Reluctantly, William releases his grip on De Burgh, pushes his dirk back into his belt, stands up and steps back from the prostrate semiconscious lord. William speaks to Bruce, "Then tell me what this business here is all about? What's this fuckin' madness we've come across before I consider what to do with this Norman bastard?" Bruce replies, "I'll tell you Wallace, but first you must give me your word that you'll leave this lord in peace?" With anger rising in his voice, William demands an answer "And what of these poor women who lie at our feet, is their existence any less important than this Norman fuck? What's happened to them? Who speaks for them?" De Burgh raises himself up on his elbows, coughing and spluttering, then he glares at William, "Yes it was I who bled them you heathen brute." He sits up and spits out mouthfuls of clotted blood, "Those filthy Irish vermin betrayed me, and as such they are my property to do with as I please, as will be your fate when I am finished with you… Wallace? That is your name is it not?"

De Burgh looks up at William as though he's burning the memory of William's name and face into his memory for future retribution. He wipes the blood from his bleeding broken nose while staring with absolute hatred at William. Then he looks at the two Irish women beside him on the ground and spits his clotted blood upon them. William curses in a rage at De Burgh, "Ya Norman bastard…" He lunges forward and boots De Burgh under the chin with such ferocity he breaks De Burgh's jaw and knocks him senseless. Before anyone realises what's happening, William jumps on top of De Burgh and pounds the Earl's head and face with his mighty fists. Bruce runs at William, grabs him by the neck and tries to pull him away from De Burgh. Stephen of Ireland grabs him too and helps wrestle him away from the unconscious De Burgh. "WALLACE… William me boy," says Stephen calmly, "Steady on there now boy, you must be cooling your hot fists. To be sure he's a Norman fuck, but he is not worth the killing. I know this man and what his friends are capable of doing by reprisal upon innocents." Bruce agrees, he pleads, "Let him be Wallace, or the suffering upon the people here will be too great a price to pay."

A bloodied Elisabeth screams as she runs over and throws her body on top of her semi-conscious father, protecting him from any further assault. "Leave my father alone you great beast, he has not harmed you." Bruce rushes to comfort Elisabeth where she throws her arms around his neck and holds him close, sobbing and crying. William is bemused and puzzled… "What the fuck is going on here?" An equally puzzled Stephen pushes his wild tresses back and exclaims,

"Oi'm feck'd if I can make any sense out of this lot Wallace." In all the commotion, no one had noticed the two Scots Birlinns had beached and the captain approaching the scene, "Aye, and what's been going on here then?" says a lone voice. William turns to see the Birlinn captain standing beside him. "Morrison mòr, how are yie doin this fine mornin'?"

"I'm fine Wallace, aye, a lot finer than this lot laying about the place by the looks of things. What's goin' on here?" Morrison mòr smiles as he looks at the unconscious body of De Burgh and Bruce's bodyguards, spread-eagled and moaning on the ground. William replies, "I'm no' sure what the fuck is happening here myself." Morrison mòr says, "Well, you'd better get your Gallóbhet on board Wallace, the tide is on the turn and we have only moments to get off these feckn sandbanks." William calls out orders, "Stephen, get the Gallóbhet boarding straight away, and make sure your bonnie wife Katriona and wee Stephen get a comfortable berth before any other. And you'd better get some o' the lads to throw those two poor feckrs lying over there onto the Birlinns too, they're wearing Bruce colours so they must be his." Morrison mòr enquires, "Is young Robert Bruce here too Wallace? We're charged by his auld Maw Marthoc to take him back to Turnberry castle with us." William sighs, "Aye, that's him over there with that wee lass holding onto him like a low-tide limpet on a high-tide rock."

"For fucks sake…" exclaims Morrison mòr, screwing up his old wrinkled face, "that's Robert Bruce? Would yie look at the feckn state o' him? I've baited hooks for fishin' wie better meat on them than what hangs from that pale bachle." William laughs "Ah know. Aome example o' a Scots noblehood that, eh?" Morrison Mòr turns to go back to his ships, he calls out, "Better get him on board quick then." William walks over to Bruce and Elisabeth then squats down beside the couple sitting beside the unconscious De Burgh. Bruce is still consoling the dazed and battered Elisabeth when William speaks to them "We have to be going Bruce, the tide is turning and we've moments to leave or we'll be fuckin' stuck here on this headland for half a day, and by the look of things here, we don't really want to be doing that."

"I'll be there in a moment," replies Bruce "Please… just give me a moments time in private with my love Elisabeth."

"Your Love?" exclaims William. He smiles at the thought, then he says compassionately, "Don't make it too long then Bruce, for everyone's boarding the Birlinns and Morrison mòr cannot wait much longer." As William walks away towards the Longships and boards, Bruce turns to a weeping Elisabeth… "My love, come with me to Scotland, I fear for your safety should you remain here. Your fathers wrath will be beyond any reasoning because of this day's calamity." He raises his hand and gently sweeps Elisabeth's blood-clotted hair away from her swollen tear stained face. Elisabeth replies, "I cannot leave now Robert, too much has passed my love. We cannot bring any further disgrace or shame upon our families name than we have already brought by our thoughtless actions this day." Pleading with her, Bruce exclaims, "But your father will beat you severely Elisabeth, he may even imprison you. God forbid, he may even bury you in some convent for the rest of your life, I may never see you again… my heart could not stand such a pain as this."

"I cannot go with you Robert," replies Elisabeth "I love you with all my heart, but I must stay with my family and live with the consequences of our folly. This is my decision." Tenderly, she catches a tear rolling down the Bruce's cheek. He states in painful defiance, "I wont leave you, I shall stay here and we will both face your father together." Elisabeth says, "I love you dearly Robert Bruce, but the danger is very

real for the many if I leave with you for Scotland." Bruce
Stammers "But…" Elisabeth put her finger to his lips, "You
must go home Robert, there is no knowing what my father
may do to you if you remain here. If you stay in Ireland then
I may lose you forever my love, this way at least we may meet
again one day."

"Bruce," shouts Morrison mòr from the lead Birlinn, "We
must be leavin' the beaches now, get yer skinny fuckin' arse
on board this ship or you'll be left behind." William exclaims,
"Fuck… I think Bruce means to stay here, the young fool."

Suddenly, William jumps over the side of the Birlinn,
followed by Stephen. Both run at speed through the tide and
up the beach towards the Bruce, who still holds Elisabeth
defiantly in his arms. At that moment, three more Gallóbhet
riders come around the headland at full gallop, it's obvious by
the reckless determination of their hack, that trouble follows
them. On the Birlinns Wallace's Gallóbhet reach for their
spartaxe', swords, skieves and bows and prepare to immediately disembark, but they are held to order by Morrison mòr.

The three riders storm up to the little gathering, where one
rider quickly dismounts and runs beside his horse directly
at William, it's his Irish friend Gormlaidh. William sees
the other two riders hastily dismount, a large redheaded
Scot called Torrance, and Faolán, the Aicé of the Galloway
Gallóbhan, the rearguard of the Gallóbhet. Gormlaidh gasps
trying to regain his breath, calls out, "There's about a fifty
mounted English soldiers not far behind us…" Big Torrance
calls out as he stomps across the sand towards him, "What
dyie want us to do Wallace? Do yie want me, Faolán and
Gormlaidh here to go back and hold them off, there is only
about fifty of them… that shouldn't be much o' a problem for
the three o' us." Gormlaidh cxclaims, "Awe fuck." still trying
to catch his breath and looking forlorn at his big friend

with Faolán standing nonplussed beside him. Torrance says, "Faolán has already seen off about twenty o' the bastards with her flights." Faolán laughs, then she says coyly, "It was nuthin." William laughs out loud as both he and Gormlaidh know that Torrance actually means what he says. William also knows the three of them would execute that command without a thought if he gave the order.

"Naw Torrance," replies William "Lets just say it's their lucky day, just like that Norman bastard with the broken face lying over there." William continues, "Torrance, we need to take Bruce and get him onto those ships, they're already drifting from the shore and we don't want to get stuck here, even if we do fancy a farewell hop with the English that suits our taste." Elisabeth glances at William and Stephen. William understands, he immediately signals his outriders who know what is required of them… Torrance and Gormlaidh lunge forward, grab the Bruce forcefully then carry him away from Elisabeth. Bruce struggles, cursing and fighting to break free as the two Gallóbhet manhandle him out to the ships then unceremoniously throw him on board, where other Gallóbhet quickly secure him in the bilges. Faolán picks up their weaponry and follows them onto the Birlinn. William feels his hearts emotion well up as he looks at the bloodied young woman who sits weeping and sobbing quietly beside her unconscious father. He kneels beside Elisabeth and puts his hands gently on her shoulders; then he speaks to her with an understanding and kindness in his voice...

"We'll look after your fella Bruce bonnie lass, don't you be fretting. I've no doubt you'll see your sweetheart again." William stands up beside Stephen, they look long and contemptuously at the prostrate De Burgh. William says, "I'm sorry that's your father, but he's lucky to be alive for the taking of life as though it were nothing more than…"

Elisabeth interrupts "William Wallace... that's your name?" William replies "Aye, darlin' that it is." She continues "I thank you for sparing my fathers life, but you must leave now or you may be caught." Studying William's face, Elisabeth enquires, "May I ask a question of you Wallace? I don't know you nor have I the right to plead, but there is something about you I would trust; of that I have no doubt." Curious to hear this young woman's request, William replies, "Aye darlin' you can trust me, so ask away." Elisabeth continues, "Will you personally take care of my bo' Robert till he is safely back home in Scotland, for I know there is great hostility towards his family amongst your people?" William laughs heartily at this unusual request. Then he looks at Elisabeth, he can see in her a quality in spirit that reminds him of Marion. Whatever initial thoughts he had of not babysitting the Bruce, is quickly dispelled. "I'll take good care of him bonnie Elisabeth, I give yie ma word... But you must promise me one thing by return?"

"What would you wish from me?" enquires an intrigued Elisabeth. William looks once more into the beautiful emerald eyes of this young woman, then he speaks to her with a care, "I want you to promise me that you'll take care of yourself, and however long it may take, you will find a way to be back in the arms of the one you love?" Surprised at this request from a barbaric looking stranger who speaks to her so intimately, yet with the understanding of a lifelong friend. Elisabeth smiles and nods her head in agreement. She is immensely thankful hearing William's kind words. She looks into his eyes with affection and an understanding that flows warmly between them, she replies, "I promise you I will do this dear Wallace, I do promise." At that moment, De Burgh's captain approaches... William quickly pulls out his dirk as Stephen pulls out two vicious looking skieves.

The captain is startled and jumps back and well away from the reach of William's lethal dirk and the wiry Stephen with his deadly skieves. The captain holds up his empty hands high in the air as his only defence, he quickly explains, "I have come to tend to the lady Elisabeth Wallace. You will have no malice offered from me or my men."

"GET A MOVE ON…" calls out Morrison mòr from the Birlinn. A groan nearby signals De Burgh is starting to come round. He struggles to raise himself from the ground while fumbling at his broken jaw and nose. William glares at him; it's obvious what he's thinking. Stephen says with a cautious tone, "Don't do it Wallace… don't feckn do it…" William looks at Stephen in silent but reluctant agreement; then he turns and smiles at Elisabeth. William and Stephen gain a silent acknowledgment of friendship from young Elisabeth, then the two friends turn and run for the Birlinns. On their way down the shore towards the Birlinns, Stephen calls out with great urgency. "WALLACE… WAIT…"

The two companions halt. William looks at his friend then enquires, "What is it, we have to get going or we'll miss the feckn Birlinns, what the fuck is it you're thinkin?" Stephen enquires, "Did yie not be noticing that De Burgh's men were just sittin' on their horses when there was but the two o' us?" William replies curiously, "Aye, ah did, and what of it?" With a glint in his eyes, Stephen says, "A moment if yie please…" Stephen turns and runs at speed back up the beach towards De Burgh. William calls out to his friend "Stephen, what are…" But it's too late, he watches as his friend runs at De Burgh who is struggling to sit up and raise himself when Stephen rushes into him with a mighty flying kick to the head, breaking the unfortunate earls cheekbone, William, standing on the shoreline, hears the sickening crack of breaking bone. De Burgh's men watch but they do nothing as the unfortunate red Earl flops over once again, groaning in severe pain. Stephen by this time has run back at great speed and is now passing William. He calls out "Come on ya big Scots bastard or yie'll be having us both missing the feckn Birlinns."

"Ya mad Irish Feckr…" shouts William. He smiles to himself as they both race down the beach and rush through the tide toward the last Birlinn, only just managing to clamber aboard over the gunnels before the ships fully pull away from the shore. The Birlinns crew haul up the ships great blue canvas to full sail, catching the fair easterly winds to take them home to Scotland. The Gallóbhet and ships crew's look back towards the headland chapel of Domhnach a' Daoi as a large English cavalry troop arrive on the beach and circle around De Burgh and his men in a great commotion. Some of the soldiers ride to the waters edge, dismount and loose their arrows towards the Birlinns, but to no effect, the famous blue sails of Morrison mòr's Blue Angels lazily billow as they catch the winds and fill to full tack, pulling away from the east coast seaboard of Ireland and setting sail across the Irish sea towards their beloved Scotland… William looks back at the coast of Ireland, thinking of the love so evident between Elisabeth and the Bruce; then he thinks of his own love… Maid Marion…

THEE BRUCE

ailing away from the Irish mainland, the Gallóbhet happily settle into any and all available deck spaces in the Birlinn, when William notices near the bowhead, Katriona tending to the painful wounds the Bruce had received at the hands of De Burgh. As William makes his way towards Bruce, Katriona sees him walking up from the stern-deck towards them. She quickly wraps Bruce with a heavy sea brat then stands up and walks toward William, she stops in front of him and puts her hand on his chest, she says, "It's for the best you leave him for awhile Wallace." Curious at Katriona's request, William enquires "And why would I be doing that, what's wrong with him?" Katriona replies, "It's not an ailment of the body that pains Bruce, it's a malady of the heart."

William studies the huddled body of young Bruce; he also notices that he's sobbing beneath the heavy sea brat. William grins then enquires curiously, "Fuck, is the wee boy weeping?" Katriona snaps at back him, "WALLACE... his heart is broken; he's just left his sweetheart behind to a fate unknown and doesn't know if he will ever see her again. Bruce feels the deepest remorse for leaving her behind and tells to me he would rather have died than to have abandoned her like a base knave." William looks at the pathetic shivering heap that is Robert Bruce, he thinks *Men shouldn't cry... But they do...*

He knows that emotion only too well himself, thinking of his own love and how Bruce must be feeling. No-one has a right to comment on affairs of the heart, except those who have gone through the nightmarish pain of enforced separation.

Having this compassionate understanding could only ever release feelings of sympathy from William, not criticism, cynical judgement or revelling in the despair of another's aching heart. He smiles when he looks down at an impatient Katriona as she stands there defiantly before him, her arms folded and motherly instinct protecting the heart of young Robert Bruce of Carrick. She reminds him so much of his notorious wee granny back in Ach na Feàrna. William relents, he smiles at Katriona then says, "I'll talk with the Bruce later..." He smiles again in seeing Katriona's matriarchal heckles pricking up once more, "don't you worry yer bonnie head Katriona, I'll not be adding to his pains and woes." Katriona observes William, she knows him well enough and remembers how he too had felt such heart pain for the Ceàrdannan princess Affric, and more so for his true love, maid Marion Braidfuite. Katriona looks at him; then she hugs her big friend, relieved and thankful for his compassionate response. "Thank yie Wallace, your Wee Maw would be so proud o yie." Katriona smiles then she returns to comfort Robert Bruce.

As the Birlinns heave in the seas while gaining good speed towards the coast of Scotland, William is fixated for a long time on the Duibh Hill gaining ever closer, beckoning him as a dark angel, his mood is morose thinking of all his friends who had died there, brutally and needlessly, he thinks... *'If it were not for the reckless ambitions of Robert de Brix, all ma friends would still be alive and I wouldn't have been sent into exile...'* A voice nearby interrupts his thoughts, "Wallace, what were you doing in Ireland?" William turns to see

Robert Bruce, still wrapped in the sea-brat but now looking a little better than when they had first set sail. He has moved down the Birlinn near to where William is leaning against the gunnels, Bruce says, "I thank you for your timely arrival upon the headland of Domhnach a' Daoi, if there is any way or anything I could ever do to thank you or to repay you, please, never hesitate to ask…"

William says nothing by way of a reply, he simply glares at Bruce, the silence and intensity between them is palpable. Bruce realises something is wrong but he stands firm and will not look away, he isn't intimidated by the much larger and physically stronger Wallace, though he couldn't begin to comprehend that William's mind is in absolute turmoil and anguish thinking about the personal devastation and grief brought about by the actions of Robert Bruce's grandfather de Brix and his allies.

Big Torrance approaches and gauges the situation easily, knowingly he breaks the silence, "Wallace, dyie want some scran; for we've eaten fuck all but maggots, eel meat an' shellfish for three days?" William replies, "Naw ta. I'll stay here awhile, ah'll catch up with yiez later." Torrance knows that William is seething at the presence of the Bruce, he enquires, "What are yie thinkin' Wallace?" William replies, "I don't know." He glances at Bruce then he says, "Invergarvane… and huntin' down the bastards responsible for the deaths o' ma kin folks and ma friends there… Once ah know who really is responsible for all those massacres and killings for sure. I reckon its time I'll send them to a better life, fuckin' sore and soon." Torrance laughs, "Ho Wallace, don't be using ma words." William queries Torrance, "Your words?" Torrance laughs, "Aye my feckn words, sure I'm the one who sends the bastards away to a better life to try again and come back as a half-decent bastard in the next."

"Awe me poor bonnie darlins'" Quips Stephen sitting close by with Gormlaidh. He stands up and tries to get past William and Torrance who are blocking the gangway with their large frames. Stephen mimics a kiss and blows it towards Torrance the big tough red headed warrior, much to his disgust. Stephen laughs and pushes past them, shoving both in the chest and scrunching William's cheek on his way through towards the galley. Stephen looks back at them with comic disdain…"Why don't you two love birds just kiss and get on with it?" Gormlaidh covers his head as he ducks underneath both William and Torrance on his way past, "Ahm fuckin' off outo here…" Stephen calls back to them, "We're away to join Faolán Fiónlaidh and Eochaidh up at the galley, are yiez comin?" Torrance laughs, "Aye Wallace, are yie coming for something to eat?" William replies, "Aye fine, in a wee while maybe." Torrance replies "Ah'll see you up there then." he turns and follows behind Stephen and Gormlaidh.

Again Bruce speaks, "I've not seen you for many years Wallace…" Ignoring Bruce, William leans once more on the high gunnels of the Birlinn, taking in great breaths of the fresh sea air while gazing at the mountains of Kintyre. Bruce, now getting agitated, enquires, "Wallace, what's wrong with you, why wont you talk with me?"

William turns his head and looks menacingly at the Bruce, he studies Robert Bruce now standing before him. He wants to strike him and throw him overboard to make his grandfather pay dearly for the devastation he has caused and to know the pain of loss, but for some reason he thinks of young Elisabeth and his own feelings of empathy for them both, and that he gave her his bond word that he would look after Robert Bruce till they are safely returned to Scotland. Relenting from his darker thoughts, William begins smiling, he sees his charge is looking much relieved. William relents and greets Bruce warmly, "Look at you young Bruce, yie've grown from a skinny wee runt into a bit o' a man ah see." William laughs as he continues, "Aye Bruce, the last time that ah saw you, yie were heading away from Scotland not long after King Alexander died and the civil war had broke out, but you couldn't have been more than fourteen summers then, what age are yie now?" Bruce replies, "Nearly nineteen summers." William enquires, "So where have yie been young Bruce, how did yie end up in Ireland?" Bruce replies, "I was sent to reside awhile at our ancestral home in Normandy. When I returned to England, I spent a few months at my grandfather's estates in Essex; then he sent me to De Burgh in Ulster. He said since the troubles began, it wasn't safe for me to be in Scotland or England during the interregnum, I've been in Ireland for the last few years under De Burgh's protection and service, learning the arts of chivalry."

"De Burgh…" exclaims William "That Bastard chivalrous, ah don't fuckin think so? It's lucky for you that we never met before this day in Ireland, for if we had Bruce, I reckon we would not be having this conversation now." Bruce exclaims, "Why do you say that Wallace? De Burgh has never harmed you."

"Yie think not?" scowls William "Maybe not personal injury to me, but his troops attacked the defenceless families of the men of Connaught Monaghan and all over the north lands of Ulster, butchery and the slaughter of innocents was his bloody trade. Long before that, troops of De Burgh and a fella called Marmaduke de Percy were party to heinous murder upon many in Scotland at the time your grandfather tried to usurp the throne for himself." Bruce is taken aback; he instinctively thinks to defend the honour of his grandfather, but Wallace's dark almost crazed expression causes him to quickly change the subject, "And what about you Wallace?

The last time I saw you I thought you were training for the priesthood in Paisley," Bruce continues with a hint of a smile, "I can see that you haven't turned to the priesthood then?" William had prepared himself for a tense debate he believed he would easily win, but he's caught out by the simplicity of the response from Bruce.

Calming down slightly, William thinks perhaps now is not the time to lash out at Bruce for something that he is clearly not responsible for. William replies, "Naw yer right Bruce, I sure wasn't cut out for the priesthood. Though Bishop Wishart and auld Leckie mòr tried to convince me to stay, but soon they became even more convinced to get me to leave." William laughs at the thought of them trying in vain to tutor him in the graceful ways of the religious establishment, "Ah much prefer my auld bow and huntin' the Kings Kyle and the Wolf and wildcat forests with my father, rather than getting big blisters and a fat arse sittin' in some fuckin' religious establishment."

Glancing towards Invergarvane, William speaks softly, "After Alexander died and a wee incident when English fuckin' soldiers wanted to cut my hands off for fishing the river on my uncles land, I decided…" William laughs, "Well it was decided for me, that I should go over to Ireland to stay with some of ma kinfolk in Muineachan, When I arrived there, ma Irish kinfolks were having so much fun fuckin' with the Norman's, ah just couldn't resist but to join up with them and refine my fighting skills against those Norman bastards and yer English fuckin' nobles." Bruce recoils at the thought of the wild Irish Gallóglaigh and Scots Gallóbhet allying… and Wallace's evident disdain regarding his bloodline and Norman nobility. Bruce speaks, "Wallace, I heard you personally murdered many innocent English soldiery, men who's only crime was to come Scotland to protect us, and that you had fled away as a coward to hide in exile as a famishing murderous outlaw." William turns aggressively towards Bruce who knows nothing of the pain burning in his heart, nor could Bruce have any knowledge of what had happened to have him branded an outlaw. Spitting the words out, William counters, "If your grandfather Rober de Brix in all his arrogance had kept the fuckin' peace, then I would still be a hunter with my father in the Kings Kyle and many of my friends would not be dead."

Scowling aggressively at Bruce, William continues short of a rage, "Your fuckin grandfather, the lord chief justice of England…" William glares at the young nobleman; thinking how easy it would be to throw him overboard… but that would not bring his kinfolks back.

Bruce easily sees anger evident burning in William's eyes. "What's wrong with you Wallace?" William glowers at the young soft-palmed noble, barely resisting the urge to grip him by the neck and snap it like a twig, but there's something, just something that he likes about the cut of this defiant young Norman. William's anger ebbs… "Ach it's nuthin' they're all just stories…" Bruce senses something is still amiss with William, but he thinks it prudent to change the subject once again, "Then how is your father sir Malcolm and the family in Ach na Feàrna?" William replies curtly, "Malcolm is no' ma father, though ah love him so."

"What?" exclaims Bruce, "I thought Sir Malcolm was your father?" William replies, "Naw. My father is Alain Wallace of the Black Craig and Glen Afton, he's my real Dá. Everyone who doesn't really know us seem to think Malcolm is my father, but he's my uncle from me fathers side. When my birth mother died, my father lost his wits awhile, so my Uncle Malcolm and his wife Margret fostered me and ma wee brother John, that's how I ended up in Ach na Feàrna and tutored in Paisley." Bruce says, "I didn't know that about Alain and your uncle Malcolm?" William sighs, "Not many do." Bruce enquires with a sense of mischief, "So Wallace, what have you been doing in Ireland… apart from killing Norman's, tell me how you became a Gallóglaigh?"

Grinning at the humour of Bruce, William replies, "When I left Scotland with ma uncles Davey and Jamey Wallace and ma cousins from the Rhinns and Machars o' Galloway, the call went out for all Gallóbhet going to Ireland to be joining with the Gallóglaigh army of Conchobar Ua Suibhne, to fight with the Irish chiefs against the Norman occupation of the Pale down near Baile Átha Cliath, (Dublin) Tir Eóghain (Tyrone) and down around Corcaigh awhile." Bruce exclaims, "You fought for silver and not for a cause?" William laughs, "Both… when I saw what was happening to my Irish cousins, I joined the Galloway Gallóglaigh to fight with alongside the Irish, and I've been learning a fine craft with them ever since." Bruce enquires, "You really were fighting against Norman and English rule then?"

"Aye, that I was," replies William, "And ah mean no real offence to yie young Bruce, even though your grandfather is a proper Norman English prick." Bruce immediately retorts, "Why do you goad me by implication of my Norman birthright Wallace, but I say to you that no offence is taken, you being a from the loins of some lowly witless Welsh cunt after all is said and done." Bruce smiles, thinking he has easily countered William's slight with a birthright insult of his own. "Ha…" sneers William "You're big mouth just gave away your Norman English fuckin' tongue Bruce." Appearing bemused, Bruce enquires, "How so?" William smiles then he replies, "Welsh is not a Scots, Irish, Gaelic or even a Cymran word. It's Norman or Saxon, meaning a foreigner or a slave in those tongues… and I'm not your slave.

And if I'm foreign to you Bruce, then its not Scots blood to the fore in your heart." Listening, though he's a little confused, Bruce shakes his head then replies "That may be your humble opinion Wallace, but I'll tell you, my mother Marthoc is kin to the house of Canmòre from the dynasty of Dunkeld, and she's a direct daughter of Gilla Brigte mac Fergusa of Galloway, a pure pedigree of the Gall-Ghàidhil queens and direct true bloodline to the ancient Cruathnie Kings, that's why I return to Carrick and Scotland Wallace, its my birthright. My grandfather makes a legitimate claim for the throne of Scotland as a descendant of King David the Lion and our late King Alexander through Marriage, that is his right."

"Not any more it isn't," replies William tersely, "Not with the Maid coming from Norway to gain her rightful throne." Bruce replies, "Aye Wallace and I pray that everything will settle down by her return, for as I said, and you may have noticed if you had been listening, that I too follow the faith of the female lineage of my blood, as do you and all who carry the true calling and faith of a Scot."

This totally unexpected reply from Bruce perplexes William's thoughts. He hadn't expected a Bruce to be a genuine supporter of the Aicé, and also in favour of the Maid becoming the reigning Queen of Scotland. Bruce enquires, "Are all the Scots Gallóglaigh and Gallóbhan coming back to Scotland?" William replies, "Aye, well most that can do are coming back. Many will be making their way to Domhnach a' Daoi, Manaan or Rathlan to catch Birlinns to journey homeward. As far as I know, everybody has been recalled to witness the confirmation by the Olambh Rígh for the crowning of our new Aicé the Queen, and then to escort the English out of our realm." Bruce sighs, "Aye Wallace, Alexander's death has sure been a mean and sombre blow to our realm, he's been dead for nigh on five years now, yet still he's sorely missed." Bruce suddenly beams with a great smile, "but I am certain great days will return when the maid is crowned our new Queen."

Hearing these unexpected words, William looks at Bruce thinking that this is a Bruce who warmly welcomes the maid as his Queen. He believes the sincerity Bruce is espousing in favour of the Maid. William says thoughtfully, "It really is good to be meeting yie young Bruce, maybe I wont be throwing you overboard after all." Astonished at what William has just said, Bruce drops his sea-brat and steps back a pace. William grins as Stephen approaches the two young men, "Wallace, I've brought yie some very fine fish gruel, for you've no' eaten in awhile." Stephen looks at Bruce then says to him "And here is a bowl for you too young Bruce." Cold and shivering, Bruce picks up his sea-brat then reaches out and accepts the bowl of much needed nourishment. He looks at Stephen then says with conviction, "I am Robert THEE Bruce, Irishman."

Stephen is surprised at the thoughtless way Bruce has spoken to him, but he shrugs it off with a sly smile, "Then it's pleased to be meeting you then, Robert 'THEE' Bruce. And for yer noble fuckin' information before yie ask, ma name is Stephen "OF" Ireland. Anyways, eat yer gruel ya skinny wee noble bastard, and get wrappin' yerself up in that sea-brat, it'll keep ya warm." With mirth in their eyes, William and Stephen glance at each other as Stephen continues, "Sure now young 'thee' Bruce, don't you be looking as if you have never been eating, at all... EVER. Could it be that you're still suckling on your poor auld Maw's flaggin' titties by the looks o' yie, ah don't feckin' know, and at your age too." Nonchalantly, Stephen shakes his head and grins as he sits down with his own fish gruel. Bruce ignores the verbal challenge. Instead, he observes in fascination these two wild looking madmen, no one has ever addressed him as they both have and there is something fascinating about their uncouth manner that appeals to him, after a life of courtly and chivalric formality.

Bruce huddles against the gunnels, sheltering in his sea-brat while supping his gruel. He observes William and Stephen as they converse. Bruce thinks about what Wallace had said to him a few moments ago and shakes his head, in disbelief, *'He was pleased that he had decided he was not going to throw me overboard?'* Bruce laughs thinking... *'And that's supposed to be a good thing. Then this mad Irishman just said I look as if I am still suckling on my mother's titties?'*

The private world of Bruce and his thoughts are abruptly broken by a gruff command from Stephen, "Fuckin' EAT..." Bruce realises Stephen had noticed his incessant gaze. William is grinning too; then he makes a proper introduction, "Bruce, this fella here is Stephen Ua Mac h'Alpine... or Stephen 'OF' Ireland as he likes to be known." William and Stephen smirk at each other as he continues, "Ma wee brother John married Stephen's sister Ròsinn, Stephen is now married to Katriona Graham, a kinswoman of mine. It was she who tended your welts and wounds earlier, bonnie Katriona hails from glen Afton too." Bruce smiles, "Well I'm pleased to be meeting you Stephen OF Ireland." Stephen grins, "I sincerely wish I could be sayin' the same back to ya Robert THEE Bruce, but sure then, wouldn't I be just be lyin to ya."

For a moment it looks as though Stephen's slight would be the cause of an incident. Then Stephen suddenly grabs Bruce by the hand and begins shaking it profusely, "Sure now, wasn't I just jestin' wit ya little fella Bruce, it's pleased to be meeting a Norman noble, and us both knowing yee will be the first of that kind to leaving me fine company... alive. Aye, there sure is a first time for everything ah'll be tellin' ya."

Once again there is a long pregnant pause… then all three begin laughing heartily. They sit together awhile eating, deliberating and it soon becomes obvious to Stephen that both Wallace and the Bruce have found a liking for each other. Though they may represent different political and likely religious views on Scotland's future, there is a camaraderie growing between them that nurture's a growing friendship.

Feeling settled with these two wild Gallóglaigh, Bruce begins to enquire more about their return to Scotland. "I can understand why all the nobles are being recalled to Scotland… but why are so many mercenaries and miscreants of no account like you two returning?" Both William and Stephen spit out their fish gruel when they grasp the content of Bruce's question. In all innocence, Bruce enquires, "Is it something that I said?" Stephen exclaims, "And you fuckin' Norman cunts wonder why we want you fuckers out of feckn Ireland?" William laughs, "No-a-feckn-count?" He punches Stephen solidly on the arm; "You've certainly came up in the world since ah first met yie… Stephen-of-no-account Ireland. Ha, you'll need to change your name now."

Bruce is slightly confused "I… I… but, I meant both of you…" William blusters as Stephen punches him on the arm and laughs aloud with great gusto. William demands, "What the fuck did you just say Bruce?" Stephen laughs again on seeing the change on William's face. "Ha, its you who should be moi Ceitherne, William-of-no-feckn-account-Wallace." William glares at the Bruce, but he quickly relents and begins laughing too, then he enquires, "Could you be explainin' exactly what you meant by no account folk like us, before we feed you to the fuckin crabs, Robert-thee-about-to-fuckin-die-Bruce?" Bruce realises he has perhaps made an error in the way he spoke to them and tries to correct his mistake. "I simply meant, why do so many return who have no say in the matters of state or offer any obvious benefit, such as soldiers, traders, simples and the likes, I honestly meant no offence." William and Stephen look at each other for a moment; then they decide to let Bruce's indiscretion pass. William speaks candidly, but with concern in his voice, "Bruce, I'll tell you, we are aware many Norman Scots nobles will not support the Maid, and they're threatening all out war if she lands to claim her throne. And after your grandfathers previous exploits in Galloway, it's fallen to everyone who supports the Maid to be in Scotland for her homecoming. Bruce, do yie not yet understand? We are not like your Norman societies where men are bonded in servitude." Bruce enquires, "What do you mean?"

"Fuck," sighs William. Then he smiles at the thought of educating this ignorant Norman Scots noble while on their journey across the Irish Sea to their homeland.

"For many of us outside your noble cabal Bruce, Scotland is family, and contrary to what you fuckin' nobles think, we don't hanker for a man to dictate to us like some wee man—God in Rome or the king of England. Och, maybe on the surface it may look that way, with us having a Christian church structured to scare souls into self-denial and self-sacrifice to be lining the pockets o' the priests. Scots like my brothers and sisters here, we thrive on our faith in the Céile Aicé and life's blessings through her and Magda Mòr. Didn't your own father marry an Aicé in Marthoc to inherit her lands and grand titles, as did your great grandfather down in Annan?" Stephen laughs, "Sure Wallace, even your bleedin' country is named after an Aicé is it not?" Bruce remains silent but listens intently, he has never heard or even considered the feminine perspective of Scotland's faith and culture, closeted by his noble upbringing in Whittle Essex and so far removed from that of a native born Scot.

William continues, "That Bruce, and the Maid returning, is why all the Gallóbhet and Céile Aicé are being called back to Scotland from abroad, to join the Garda bahn Rígh and support our Breitheamh Rígh to protect our hereditary Aicé." Bruce replies, "I don't know of this Céile Aicé and Breitheamh Rígh as you call them, but I tell to you that there are so many against the princess' investiture that Margaret's father, King Eric of Norway and many Scots Magnates have already made approaches to king Edward of England to continue with his peace keeping in Scotland, this is to ensure her safety. I have also heard the maid is to be sent to England as a ward of good King Edward Until Scotland is a safe enough realm for her to reside in."

"What?" Exclaims William. Stephen sighs, "Feckn Norman's Wallace, didn't I warn yie about them." William is confused, "I know there are a few who would reject the Maid, like the other claimants, but who else would dare raise arms against our rightful Aicé? And you say she is to be sent to England for her own safety?" Bruce replies, "Yes Wallace. King Edward has agreed that she must reside in England awhile till it is proven beyond doubt that Scotland remains at peace, for the maid is his blood family to him too, he is her grand uncle after all."

"The English can't do that." exclaims William, "She's the hereditary Aicé of Scotland; nothing can change that. Certainly no man can change her blood claim, it's the law of our land, but more than that, it's the law and very order of nature, blessed and protected by our people since time began." Bruce says, "Eric of Norway and the Guardians have long since dispatched official ambassadors to King Edward at his residence in France, everything is agreed, you're out of touch Wallace." William and Stephen look at each other as Bruce continues, "The Norwegians were so disgusted with the Scots continually bickering and arguing in regards to her claim, they've long since carried legitimate charters and presented them to Longshanks, who does refer to the maid as the true Queen of Scotland, as do you. The meeting was led by our own Bishops, were you not aware of this?" Totally taken aback, William enquires, "What happened at this meeting of which you speak?"

Bruce looks at the two friends as though they should have already known this. He explains, "After much pleading by the Scots Bishopric, the charters of the claimants were accepted by King Edward, finally securing Scotland's future. Everything from that time onwards is to be approved between Edward and Eric. They decided to excluded the Scots until Edward had met with my grandfather and a few Scots magnates and they agreed to debate at Salisbury in England." William exclaims, "I cannae believe what I'm hearing…"

Bruce continues, "Wallace, you must understand, the Scots are in a very weak and vulnerable position. It now exists within Scots law, that Edward can legally arrange Margaret's marriage to the future King of England, prince Edward or any other if he so chooses, and without any reference to the Guardians or recourse to any Scots institution. After meeting with my grandfather Rober de Brix, he has graciously invited the Guardians and the Scots clergy to have a future say in the matter, but that decision was influenced from Rome by his Holy Father in all his wisdom." Clearly surprised to be hearing this, William enquires, "So what was the decision between the Norse, the Guardians and Longshanks?" Bruce says, "Well… It would appear as though the Guardians managed to gain some time for Scotland to stop Longshanks taking over the realm completely, but they could only do so by signing an agreement proposed by Longshanks, called the Treaty of Salisbury, where all present representing the best interests of Scotland pledged upon agreement, the maid Margaret should be sent to England from Norway before November, and any proposals on her potential consorts would be deferred until she is in Scotland and as Queen, oh, and that Edward is now our sovereign overlord."

"Fuck what?" curses William. He looks across the sea as the Birlinn gains sail and speeds towards the shores of his homeland. Bruce continues, "King Edward has given his word on oath, should Scotland remain peacefull and establishes a quietness in the realm, he will send the maid North, free and quit from any marriage contract obligations, but with the sole proviso that she is not be married without his consent and approval." William enquires, "And what do you think about all this political manoeuvring by our nobles, this is a madness that's already brought such chaos and senseless killing to Scotland? Surely you must be in support the maid's legitimate claim, is this not what you said earlier?"

Bruce replies, "Wallace, I simply don't know, my grandfather is almost maniacal about our own legitimate family claim. He says that should the maid ascend the throne, Scotland will merely be a vassal state tied by chains to the English crown, and he will not suffer that, this is the very reason he raises arms. I am personally content for Margaret to be on our throne, even my father would be satisfied, but my Grandfather will never accept it." Bruce looks at William, "You may have rejected the church as a calling Wallace, but if it had not been by the efforts of the Scots clergy that were present and resolute at Salisbury. Those like Dunn Scotus, Robert Wishart, Laurence de Ergadia, Robert de la Provendir and the likes, then both of us would be now going back to Scotland as English subjects to a new Shire of England." William retorts, "Fuck off Bruce. Why would I ever want to be English? The only English I've ever met have all tried to kill me, and for what? The English treat me like something so base beneath their feet, yet I cannot understand why, though now I'm no longer that interested in finding out why. It seems that whenever I have extended a courtesy or a welcoming hand to any English I have ever met, they wish me dead. So why would I want to be fuckin' English? And as for our Bishops, they're only looking to soften their palm skins and procure padded cushions for their fat arses, they are independent of the crown in Scotland and want to keep it that way, unlike the English church who pay homage to three gods, Longshanks, the Pope and your God in the heavens. Those Bastards have a famishing need to continually enslave more believers to sustain the riches of the servants o' their three Gods. No wonder our fuckin' world is always at war with those religious bastards and Norman nobility ruling over us? What chance does anyone have, fuck them, fuck all you noble bastards…"

Bruce exclaims, "Wallace, have you lost your wits? You blaspheme, this is too much…" William towers above Bruce, "Where was your fuckin God when all the forest folk of Galloway were being cut to pieces or fed alive to the hunting dogs of the English nobility? Where was your fuckin God then Bruce? Where was your God in Ireland when that bastard De Burgh let his henchmen burn and rape their way through Ireland and then they murder those two poor Irish women on the shores of Domhnach a' Daoi, and all with the blessing of the fuckin' church?" Shrinking back a pace, Bruce begins to fear for his safety. William is almost out of control. But suddenly he becomes acutely aware of the ominous silence in the Birlinn. William quickly regains his senses and begins to calm down, a little while the Gallóbhet and crew wait till they see William and Bruce sit down together before the chatter and noise of a crew at work returns to normal. Glaring at William, Bruce speaks solemnly, "Wallace, you have a vile temper, and though young and biased as you may think I am, I too have my doubts. I've seen awful things enacted in the name of God, but ultimately there is the greater scheme of things to be taken into account, so much more than our own personal thoughts are to be considered, for the sword alone will never bring us peace, nor God, only man may bring us peace. And I tell you this Wallace; my chivalric training has gained me a deep understanding of world politic and a comprehending of the cohesion required by the ruling lords of the Christian world. I also understand the importance of Scotland being a contributing part of it all, it's the only way we will ever have any peace in these islands. If we are always chained to the crown of England, we will always be their lapdog, but if we remain independent and have our own trade partnerships with all of Europe, then we will carry forward the great legacy of out late King Alexander."

William thinks… *'Wise words from such a young head.'* He considers it might be best to speak strategically with Bruce, for he talks freely with interesting information when he's under a point of conflict. But William also knows he has to inform Bruce of a reality that he would not want to enact upon his new young friend… "Bruce, you must heed what I say to you here and now, for I gain a fondness for you, of sorts." Bruce laughs as William continues, "Bruce, if your family tries to reject our hereditary Aicé, our Queen, be it the Maid or Devorguilla, and de Brix tries once again to usurp the throne, then you and others who follow your banners, will tear Scotland asunder, and a war most brutal will then break out between brother's fathers and sons, then Bruce, we may find each other on opposing sides. Mark my words, for if that be so, I will find you and your kind and

I will kill you all. If you or your kinfolks are ever to gain the throne through base treachery by ignoring our ancient customs, then you will never be safe. And if by chance you or yours kill me Bruce, then others will follow me, and should you survive awhile, then the legions of the Céile Aicé will descend upon you as you or yours sit upon the throne of Scotland, and they will utterly destroy you." Bruce looks at William, not with shock or defiance as William expected, but with a look of an old soul in his young eyes.

Bruce gazes at this giant in front of him who has probably just saved his life on the shores of Erinn. "I understand what you say Wallace, believe me I do, but I fear what happens next is beyond our control, and be assured, should my family go to war, then that is where you will find me, standing with my blood and my kinfolk. If God's will is that we should be opposed in our calling, then believe this of me Wallace, I will be looking for you, and when I find you, I will kill you."

William smiles, for he understands the impassioned words of Robert Bruce. He laughs out loud then slaps his big hand down on Bruce's tender shoulders. Bruce yelps and immediately recoils in agony. William instantly pulls his hand away as Bruce winces in pain. William exclaims, "Sorry Bruce, I forgot your welt's are still fresh and raw." He continues, "Though I cannot do anything but admire and have respect for your last answer, had I been in your boots I probably would have delivered the same." Bruce laughs, "Then let us pray it never comes to that Wallace, that we may enjoy our friendship, limited as it is." Bruce pauses and studies the smiling face of Wallace. Bruce says as he reaches out his hand, "Then shall we shake hands as friends then Wallace and pledge an honest friendship." William replies, "Aye, I'll shake hands with you on this pledge Bruce." The two young men stand up on the deck of Morrison mòr's Birlinn and shake hands on a genuine and reciprocal feeling of friendship. Speaking to Bruce as they shake hands, William says, "Yie are some fine young man Bruce, I think that I might be liking you right enough." Bruce enquires, "So you wont be throwing me overboard after all?" William laughs, 'Ah'v still no' made ma mind up about that, yet…" Both of them laugh at their honest conversation. "Wallace?" enquires Bruce "Aye, what is it?" queries William. Bruce replies, "I think we've just had our first political debate." William laughs, "Aye and we didn't kill each other, that's another first for Scotland. I knew there must o' been some reason not to throw yie over the side of the Birlinn to feed the fish, ach, there isn't enough meat on yie anyway." The two unlikely friends laugh again; then they rest on the gunnels of the Birlinn looking eagerly landwards, both savouring the closing shores of Scotland. William comments, "Yie have a fine tongue and a strategic brain on yie there young Bruce, I see that. I think that I'm liking you more right enough." Raising his hand to slap Bruce on the back again, William suddenly freezes as Bruce screams, "DON'T…"

Bruce is relieved when he sees the human missile is not going to strike him, he regains his composure and continues, "Anyway Wallace, it might come to pass that the angst we feel this day may never unravel." William enquires, "How so is it are yie thinking that may be young Bruce?" Bruce exclaims, "Wallace… Why do you keep calling me young Bruce? You're not much older than I." William replies, "Well you're young Bruce to me, and there are three of yiez called Robert Bruce, Brus, Brix or whatever the fuck it is. At least when we say young Bruce we know who we're talking about." William queries "Is that a good enough for yie?" Bruce replies, "I would prefer it if you address me as Robert THE Bruce." William looks at him then laughs again, "Aye, fair enough then, I am liking you even more now that we have had the rime to talk, Robert THE Bruce." Smirking at the bravado of his young charge, William enquires, "Now what is it you were going to tell me about not something coming to pass young Bruce?" Shaking his head in feigned dismay, Bruce continues, "I was going to say, it would likely not come to war now that King Edward is involved, and you may still have your Queen or Aicé to guard and protect. I am informed that Edward has asked the Pope for dispensation for Edward's son, the prince of Caernarvon, to wed the princess Maighread." A curious William enquires, "The Prince of what?"

"The Prince of Caernarvon." replies Bruce "Now that the Welsh no longer have a royal bloodline of their own, Edward is going to name his son the Prince of Wales."

"That doesn't sound right," says William "The Cymrans have their own bloodline, the Llewellyn's of Cundda and Aberffraw, then there is lord Duncan MacDuff, Mormaer of Fife, he's married to Ellen Verca, a Llewellyn daughter of royal blood." Bruce exclaims, "No Wallace. The royal Llewellyn's are all dead or branded as despotic outlaws. The Llewellyn name will never return to rule Wales, and most certainly not through the loins of the clan MacDuff. Anyway, didn't you know? Duncan MacDuff was murdered by his own kinsmen only last month"

"Fuck, I have been away for far too long," exclaims William "The English branded me an outlaw in my own country. For fuck's sake Bruce, isn't that what happened to the Cymrans by your fuckin' Norman nobility, they too were also all branded outlaw? Is this not the same pretext Longshanks may use to take over Scotland as he did in Wales by destroying the royals of the realm, first through marriage, then war?" Ignoring William's slight, Bruce continues, "ANYWAY Wallace, as I was saying, Edward asked for dispensation from his Holy Father to marry Maighread to his son prince Edward, but I wanted to tell you, the Pope refused, saying he would only permit dispensation for marriage if the Scots did agree to it, for the Pope sees Scotland as his Favourite Daughter, as he calls our realm. Then, if we Scots do agree to the marriage, there will be no civil war, and you will still have your Queen or Aicé as you call her to guard. If later she chooses Prince Edward as her husband or another is chosen by the church and Guardians, your ancient laws will still be upheld and modernity comes to Scotland, everybody will be happy." William says, "So Bruce. Yee who knows so much, do you know when the maid is due to be arriving in bonnie Scotland?"

"Aye Wallace, if she is not here already, she is due to be in at the docks of Leith about now, or by the end of the month. This is also why I return home." Stephen, who has been quietly and patiently listening, interrupts. "Are you two going to be eating your fish gruel or talking all the way back to Scotland?" William and Bruce laugh and resume eating their gruel, though still engrossed in the strength and mutual interest of their conversation. Bruce enquires, "Wallace, can I ask you something?" William replies, "Aye Bruce of course yie can, what is it you would like to know?" Hesitating slightly, Bruce then enquires, "What is it like to kill a man?" Stephen splutters out his fish gruel, laughing, he says, "Fuckin' answer that one Wallace."

William smiles, but deep inside he wishes he didn't have an answer, but he does, and It doesn't seem so long ago that he had asked the same question. Bruce waits patiently on a reply as William thinks on an appropriate answer. "Well Wallace, what is it like to take a life?" William replies, "It's not that simple to reply Bruce, it will likely be different for each man to answer, I reckon it would depend on who, why and what are the circumstances or particular reasons." Bruce agitates William for an answer, "You Wallace, I'm asking you, I want to know how did you feel when you killed your first man?" William replies, "Bruce, I will tell you of my first time. It was so fast and there were so many coming at me, I wasn't really sure what had happened. What I will tell you is that, the body of a man is soft and doesn't offer much resistance between the bones, yet it can also be difficult to actually kill a man, it just depends on so much." William sees the look on the face of Bruce and knows he is sounding vague,he says, "You can hit one man in the heart and he'll drop, hit another in the heart and he can fight on awhile like nothing happened."

"But you're still not answering my question." says Bruce. William replies, "Ach Bruce, its no' se' easy to explain." Bruce, now getting frustrated; enquires once more, "You've told me of what you did, but I asked you how it feels, what were your thoughts afterwards?" William thinks long and hard, then finally he replies, "There was probably the first time I was thinking before I killed a man. I gave the bastard a chance to live, but still he tried to kill me for no reason that I ever understood, or ever will understand, but I knew just before I struck him, that once I had crossed that line, and believe me Bruce when you are thinking before you strike, knowing that when you kill a man there is no return from that place you now enter, the feeling of taking a soul from this earth cannot be explained, it's eternal, it's with you every waking moment... and only those who have crossed that line could ever know."

"I don't know," says Bruce "That's why I am asking you." William pauses, then he explains, "It's not a good feeling Bruce, you don't want to ever go there... If you can avoid it then do so, if you can't, then it's an eternal duty to accept and have to live with. Only you will know if it was the right or wrong thing you have done. And if you believe it was righteous, that is the sole justification that keeps the nightmares at bay." Thinking about William's words, Bruce says "I hope I never have to kill anyone."

"You'll kill all right," utters Stephen emphatically "And you Bruce, you will kill many." Bruce enquires curiously, "Why would you say that, you don't know me?" Stephen looks at Bruce before finishing the last of his gruel, he replies as he throws his gruel bowl onto the deck, "Because you are a Norman fuckin noble Bruce, that's why, you fella's can't bleedin' help yourselves." Bruce looks at Stephen as though his words are impossible to comprehend. "No I wont..." Stephen laughs, "Oh aye Bruce, but yie will kill, for deep down, yer still a dirty Norman bastard." Bruce is angry and confused "How can you say that to me Irishman?" Stephen continues "Like ah said ya little Norman prick ya..." suddenly a voice calls out, "LAND HO..." Morrison mòr calls out to William, "That's us sloping towards the shores o' Invergarvane Wallace. We'll be beachin' there shortly, be getting your men prepared to disembark, for we will no' be stopping long on this high tide."

"Stephen, get the Gallóbhet ready," orders William "And look to the landings, there should be folk already waiting there for us there with horses and provisions." Stephen replies, "Right yie are." As William goes forward to prepare the Gallóbhet for disembarkation, he looks to the river mouth of the Garvane and could see a camp flying banners. Bruce enquires, "Is that your friends Wallace?" William replies, "Aye, ah think so, that's the banners of John de Graham of Dundaff, he must be our escort, and I see there too the banner of my uncle Ranald Crauford too." Bruce says, "That's some fine reception waiting for you Wallace." William replies thoughtfully, "Aye... so it would seem." The Birlinns gracefully slide up the beach onto the shore where William's Gallóbhet hastily throw their kit over the side. William and the Bruce bid their farewell as the Birlinns push away from the shore to continue their journey north. William looks along the shore to see John de Graham riding toward him.

"WALLACE..." shouts de Graham, "I've urgent news for yie." William watches the Birlinns drop sail to forge north, he sees Bruce wave to him, bidding farewell. William acknowledges Bruce as Graham arrives beside him and dismounts, he enquires, "A friend?" William replies, "Aye I suppose so... That there is young Robert the Bruce of Carrick." Graham exclaims, "Young Bruce? You were on the same Birlinn as him?" William smiles, "Aye, Robert 'THEE' Bruce to be precise."

"What?" enquires Graham. "Why didn't you just throw him overboard, you would o' did us all a favour?" The two young men laugh and warmly greet each other. "Anyway Wallace, how are you? It's been such a long time." William replies "Ach it's so good to be standing in Scotland once again I'll tell you that Graham. So what is this news you have for me?" Grahams face takes on a sombre countenance. "It is grim news I bring you Wallace..." suddenly a voice calls out, "William..." He turns to see his uncle Ranald approach. William greets his uncle and sees that Ranald too appears ashen faced, he speaks abruptly, "William, it's the maid of Norway... she's dead." William is instantly struck dumb. Then he utters "How... I mean, how can she be dead; she was so young? Did her boat sink, what happened to her?" He looks at the faces of the men who have come to greet him, and they too are burdened with a heavy countenance. Ranald replies, "None are sure yet as to the why, though it has been said that she died from some sickness of the sea." William turns his head away to watch the blue sails of Morrison mòr's

Birlinn sailing north towards Turnberry castle, taking young Robert the Bruce homeward. Ranald lays a hand on William's shoulder,"There is more bad news William, Devorguilla is also dead, some say the good lady of Galloway was poisoned, but this cannot be proven."

"What the fuck is going on Ranald?" queries William. "First it was the death of the great Canmòre and his entire family, then it's the MacDuff and the Maid… now it's the lineage of auld King Fergusa with Devorguilla's death… it's as though both Royal lines of our ancient past are being wiped out for some reason, so what will we do now…. Another civil war?"Ranald replies, "It would seem that the King of England will be choosing the next regent for our throne…"

"This is too much Ranald, why do we need a foreign King to choose for us who shall govern our realm, what other realm in the known world does such a thing by asking a foreign power to choose who rules them. Perhaps its time that the people of Scotland should choose who will be our next Queen or King, someone who we elect…" Graham laughs, "That would be something else to see Wallace, a King or Queen of Scots elected…' William replies, "Aye, a King or Queen of Scots, not of Scotland, for the land should belong to the people who till it, believe in it as do all of us who respects and nurtures the great Magda mòr…" Ranald sighs, "A very fine theory indeed William, perhaps for another time though, but would you like to hear some good news?" Ranald continues, "You've been completely pardoned."

Astonished at this good news, William exclaims, "You mean I can really go home without prejudice?" Ranald replies, "You may go home in peace." William sits down on the shore, gazing at the Minch panorama, greatly relieved at this news of his pardon, but he's also saddened at the news regarding the deaths of the maid and Devorguilla. Graham puts a hand on William's shoulder; "It's good to see you back home again Wallace." William stands up and looks around the long shores, sweeping slopes and the craggy vista of Invergarvane. "I'm glad to be home Graham."

"So Wallace," says Graham, "What's your thoughts now your home?" William replies, "I had thought I would spend the rest of my life in exile in Ireland, or at the very least as a hunted outlaw here at home. But now, all of that time ah spent away from my home, and all of those that were killed... for what...?" Graham replies, "Well at least you can walk this land as a free man again Wallace." William smiles weakly as he grabs a handful of sand from the shore. "Fuck, it's good to be home." Stephen enquires, "Where are we going now then Wallace, the Bonnie glen Afton?" William replies "Feck Stephen, where else?" Ranald enquires, "When will you be going to Ach na Feàrna William? Yie know that Wee Maw and the family will be so excited by your return, it's been a few years now and there will be a time Wishart and the Guardians will need to be speaking with you about joining the Garda Bahn Rígh." William exclaims, "The Garda Bahn Rígh?"

Ranald walks a little way up the beach in discussion with William till the time comes for them to part ways. Ranald says, "You mind and be seeing your Wee Maw and the family soon, they miss you up at ach na Feàrna." William replies "Soon uncle, very soon." Ranald and William bid farewell as Graham picks up William's kit and walks up to him and Stephen, "C'mon Wallace, you must be telling me all about your time and ventures in Ireland." William replies, "Aye Graham. But first, tell us about the maid and Devorguilla's demise and what you think is going to happen in Scotland because of it, this must be a serious quandary we now find ourselves in?"

Graham explains his own thoughts as the little group and escort make their way to their horses. Soon, they all gather with their horses, preparing to leave. William bids farewell to Gormlaidh, big Torrance and the rest of the Gallóbhet who are now heading to their homes and loved ones. Faolán walks over and looks into William's eyes, they have shared much as friends, companions, warriors, and on occasion, lovers. William says, "I owe you a great deal Faolán…" She squeezes his hand and smiles then turns to join her Gallóbhan to be returning to Galloway down the west coast. Faolán glances at William, they both acknowledge each other then she turns her horse with Fiónlaidh waves and smiles then with Eochaidh, they canter southward. William turns, packs his horse and mounts ready to leave, then looks up the Duibh Hill. He thinks of Bailey, Lihd, Coinach and all the Wolf and Wildcats… Stephen notices and says, "Aye Wallace, they're all now gone to a better place." William says nothing as they walk their horses forward and on towards Glen Afton.

THE BOWRIE

Months pass as William and Stephen settle back into a normal life in Glen Afton, resuming their craft as hunters of the great Wolf and wildcat forests in southwest Scotland. Although peace had came to that part of Scotland, many blood feuds are still sparking vicious reprisals as a legacy from the violent warring between Baliol, Comyn and Brus, making the old Gallgael Kingdom of Galloway an extremely volatile and dangerous place to be for those not allied to one or the other of the claimants.

Stephen lay basking in a warm mid-morning breeze, surveying the beauty of glen Afton from the summit of S' Taigh am Rígh mòr, when he notices William is pounding up the hill towards him. He watches as his friend with his long wild hair flowing out behind him, runs and jumps from boulder to boulder, surefooted at a fast pace using the weight of his long-bow in one hand while clutching his quiver full of arrows in the other, assisting his balance as he stealthily speeds up the steep sided Corrie crag, moving with the agility of a pride wildcat attacking its prey. It's not long before William bounds over the edge of the small plateau and dives to the ground, barging heavily into Stephen and knocking the wind out of him, leaving him pained and breathless. Stephen groans holding on to his chest as he rolls over in the grass.

"For fecks sake ya big clumsy bastard, I think you've broken me feckn ribs." He sits up trying to catch his breath, William wipes his brow, "Sorry about that Stephen, but I think they're coming from the north road?"

"You think so?" Enquires Stephen. "Aye, ah do," replies William. Stephen sits beside his friend then they both peer into the distance looking towards the northern pass drove road of the glen, scanning for horses and wagons. Stephen enquires, "I don't see anythin' yet, are yie sure they're coming this day?" William wrings his hands, then using his sleeve he wipes the sweat of his brow, "I was told they are coming this day for sure." Stephen can feel William's nervousness and sees a look of fear in his face, "Are yie all right there Wallace? Are you really sure about doin' this?" William replies, "Aye, ah'll be fine, don't worry about me." Stephen continues, "Well I don't think you are fine. I think you're shittin' yourself. For years you've been learning your trade in Galloway and Ireland, and now yie think to call yourself a Gallóglaigh? Oi don't feckin' tink so," Stephen spits on the ground with obvious contempt, then he laughs, "You could just admit defeat and walk away yie know."

"I'M FINE..." States William, with anger and tension evident in his voice. Stephen enquires, "What will yie do when they get here? What's your big feckn plan then o' great leader o' the porridge Goblins?" Glaring at Stephen, William replies, "Are you gonnae fuckin' shut up so that ah can think?" Stephen enquires, "So you don't want me to be talkin' to yie then do ya?" William growls in reply, "NAW..." Stephen declares, "All right I won't, I'll just be talkin' to me bleedin' self then." The atmosphere is tense between the two friends as William watches and scrutinises the North pass for any signs of movement. Stephen lay back down quite unconcerned, chewing on a stock of grass. Then, he starts whistling to himself... "Don't..." commands William. Stephen stops whistling, sighs—then starts chewing on his grass stalk again, all the while glaring at William. A few moments pass then Stephen mutters, "Arse..." William curses tersely, "Fuck off Stephen..." Another few moments pass, "Prick..." mutters Stephen. "Ahm warnin' yie..." says an exasperated William while studying the drove road into the Glen. More time passes by as William continues to watch and search intently. Stephen smirks then he enquires nonchalantly, "Is it because yie might be having a liking for men rather than women? Is it because all o' that special religious teaching starting to show its ugly head?"

"Arrgh... ahm gonnae kill yie," growls William as he launches himself at Stephen, grabbing him by the throat with both hands. Stephen grips William firmly by the wrists and looks into his eyes, "Sure now, if it's Roman wrestling wit a man yie like, does this not just prove me bleedin' point?" William instantly releases his grip and sits back down to watch the North drove road. Stephen says "I tink..."

"Don't think." growls William "Don't utter another fuckin' word or I swear to yie Stephen... Fuck me, ma nerves are already wrecked as it is, so don't whistle, don't chew your grass out loud, and don't even speak to me. Just don't do any fuckin' thing at all." Stephen replies "Right then, oi wont..." as he lays back down in the lush green grass chewing on his grass stalk... quietly. After a little while, he starts humming a fine old Irish melody. Another few tense moments pass by, eventually William calms down.

"Are yie goin' to stop hummin' that feckn tune Stephen, you're driving me witless." Stephen snaps back, "Oh for fucks sake Wallace, calm yourself down, he's not the son o' bleedin' Satan, he's but a mortal man like me'self." Rolling over in the long grass, William sits beside Stephen; the stress of waiting has played heavily on his nerves. "Ahm sorry Stephen, its that I just don't know what to do." Stephen smiles, "You'll be fine Wallace, mind now though, if you be needin' my help?" William interrupts; "I'll ask for your help if I need your help." he smiles and put out his hand in a gesture of friendship, "You're like a brother to me Stephen ua h'Alpine." Stephen smiles as the two friends shake hands "As you are to me Wallace, ya nippy big Scotch feckr."

"Ahm so sorry Stephen," says William, "It's just that ah'v never did this before." Stephen looks at his friend, "Remember Wallace, I've only ever done this once before me'self, but ahm here if you need me. At least you know ah'v done it, and look who I had to face, a renowned notorious mad wee killer." A nervous William replies. "Ah know." They resume their vigilant watch of the drove road when they hear rustling noises in the long grass behind them. Stephen whispers quietly "Did you hear that?"

"Aye," whispers William, "don't move, ah think there's someone behind us." Suddenly they hear screaming and yelling as they're attacked from behind. Before William could turn around, two hands grab his hair at the back of his head, pulling him violently backwards. William roars in pain, he reaches back, catches his assailant by the arms and pulls him over his shoulder, he quickly grips the assailant round the neck, holds him firmly, then with lightning speed he drives his fingers into his assailants stomach. "Tickle, tickle, tickle, tickle…" says William. The screams of laughter from little Stephen nearly deafen William. As the child reaches upwards, William shouts out, "No, No, NO… Not the beard, NO' THE FECKN BEARD…" But it's too late, the ten tiny fingers of Little Stephen yanks with all the might a four year old could muster on William's beard. Meanwhile, Stephen has captured his own assailant, William's little half-sister Caoilfhinn; he's tickling her too. The screams from the two children laughing could be heard down the glen. William pleads, "NO Stephen, you must no' be pullin' beards, ever." William lifts young Stephen high into the air, only to be met with dribbling wet slavers slobbering onto his face by the laughing youngster. Stephen fairs no better from William's half sister Caoilfhinn. "Right you wains, calm down..." commands a stern voice. Wee Graham appears from over the grassy knoll behind them, "Will you two put those wains down, if yiez get them durty Auld Jean will feckn kill me."

"Holy feck Stephen," says William "Your wee man just took handfuls o' ma feckin beard and ripped it out o' ma face." But Stephen is too busy with his own hair-pulling problem to hear William. He cries out in pain as Caoilfhinn jumps up and down giggling while clutching great clumps of his tousled hair entangled in each little hand. Stephen pleads, "Caoilfhinn darlin' let me go... please..." Mercilessly she keeps tugging his hair, bringing tears to his eyes. Wee Graham eventually prizes her grip loose. After managing to calm the children down, Wee Graham looks at the two bedraggled warriors with hair lying around them where they sit, "What's you no-users doing away up here anyway?" Rubbing his sore scalp, Stephen points at William, "I'm waiting up here wit that..."

"Awe, ah see," sighs Wee Graham "Are they no' here yet?" William replies, "Naw." Suddenly little Stephen points up the glen "Who dat der grandpa?" They all look anxiously to where little Stephen is pointing, "Marion," exclaims William "She's here." Instantly he jumps up ready to bolt down the steep craggy hillside of the Black Craig to meet her, when Wee Graham steps firmly onto the back of his léine, pulling him to the ground. "What the feck are yie doin'?" growls William as he pulls his léine out from under Wee Graham's foot.

Wee Graham stands over William and wags his finger, "Just be holding yer horses there Wallace, yie cannae just be running away down the hill to see the bonnie maid." An irate William enquires, "And why no'?" Wee Graham replies, "Decorum son, decorum. Yie must never appear too keen, that's fatal wie a wumman. Yie need to be using a wee bit of the auld stand-offish strategy, and yie must never appear too befuddled, just like yie do right now."

Standing up and looking down at Wee Graham, William enquires curiously, "Ah don't know what yie mean?" Wee Graham flicks his long curly hair back, "Listen son, as yie know, ahm ah man o' the world, and with much experience with wumman kind. Now then, there's a certain decorum you must maintain with a wumman, or else you're feck'd before yie start." Stephen chips in, "He's right yie know Wallace." William enquires, "What the fuck are you two talking about?" Wee Graham says, "Well... first off all, how long is it since you got back from dear auld Ireland?" William shakes his head, "Ah don't know, about a five, six months, maybe." Wee Graham scratches his sparse unkempt little goatee beard, "Next question then, have yie washed since yie got back? Look at the state o' yie, yie look as if you haven't even run your durty fingers through your manky hair for ages, never mind a taking a feckn bone-comb through it." William laughs, "Feck off..."

While fighting off another onslaught from the wains. Stephen calls out, "He's right Wallace, yie are a bit ripe there." A shame-faced William sniffs under is arm's, then he retorts, "You can feck off too Stephen." Stephen replies, "Ahm only trying to help, if you're thinkin of asking her father this night for the Maid's hand, you'd better be putting your best foot forward, I mean, look at who I had to ask." Stephen laughs, nodding in the direction of Wee Graham, who glares back at him, "Watch it boy…" Smiling, Wee Graham contin-ues,"William, William me boy, ah have tae be tellin' yie, that yie are that ripe, even for me. Aye, yie smell just fine enough for a woodland hunter in the company o' other men, but the bonnie lass maid Marion is se' awfy refined, she will be wanting you to wash n' be getting that long hair o' yours cut, and ahm certain she'll also be wanting you to be smelling nice and wearing fine townie attire to." Thinking a moment, William gasps; then he enquires, "Do yiez really think so?" Stephen and Wee Graham look at each other and laugh, then they chime at the same time, "We know so." William is curious, "Ever since she came home from France, Marion has never said anything about me being ripe?" Wee Graham nudges Stephen "You tell him Stephen me boy, for your fresh to the sufferance."

Clearing his throat, Stephen offers this advice "William me darlin' boy, first, when you give your heart and hand to a woman it's what men like us are meant to do, of that there is no doubt. Second, when you become betrothed, something very magical and tragical happens at the same bleedin' time… for some reason only known to women, they want to change you from the man they met into something else."

"What are you two talking about?" enquires William "Ah mean, look at you Wee Graham, what were you like before Auld Jean changed you?" Wee Graham scratches his head a moment, then he replies in deadly earnest, "Eh… Happy?" They all laugh heartily as Wee Graham continues, "It's a curious thing Wallace, but when a fella is young and in love, yie are awake all night, excited and thinking about what you want to say and what yie want to do, then, when yie get married, yie fall asleep before you finish saying what yie want to say and can only dream about doin' what yie want to do." Pondering a moment, Stephen says, "Hmm… I cant really explain it better Wallace, but for some reason you start to feel you are in bad trouble all the time, and the closer it gets to the hand-fast, the more you start to believe your beloved hates the very sight o' yie. The funny thing is, you seem to love them even more. Yie will know yie are in real deep shit when she starts dressing you up and telling you to be get your hair cut and wear this and wear that…"

"What?" exclaims William, "Nobody's going to cut my hair, nope, look at you Wee Graham, and you too Stephen, you both have long hair?" Wee Graham replies, "Aye, that's only because Auld Jean finds it useful for grabbing me when I try to run away or when she is dragging me along the floor when am drunk." Stephen continues, "It's true William, me too wit Katriona, for some reason known only to the beautiful creatures, they always want you to get your hair cut for the Trystin'"

"He's right," confirms Wee Graham, "and after me being married to Auld Jean longer than Lilith was to the bonnie wee angel Sammy, once you have hand-fasted with the bonnie darlin, the whole thing goes downhill faster than snow off a dyke on a hot day after that, bless their wee woolly under-breeks." (Knickers) Stephen looks at William with a vacant expression then shrugs his shoulders. Wee Graham calls out to the children, "Right wains, Stephen, Wallace, throw the wains on yer backs and we'll walk down and greet the visitors, ahm sure they must be thirsty with all their travelling. Ah reckon I had better be givin' yie a wee bitty more advice on the strange but awfy lovable bonnie creature… Wumman." Hoisting the children up onto their backs, William, Stephen and Wee Graham begin the slow walk down the hill when Wee Graham stops and says to William "And then there's the list." Stephen laughs, "Aye, the list…" The little group continue their walk down the hill while talking intensely, with Stephen and Wee Graham explaining to William all about the meaning of the list and the virtues of marriage. It's not long before they find themselves standing at the horse corrals of the Craig Darroch and looking at many fully laden bow wagons. "Wallace, ah'm no' sure," says Stephen "But ah think that's your uncle Malcolm's wagons. Suddenly, a grey-haired head pops out from behind a wagon, William exclaims. "Granny..." Wee Maw smiles and holds out her arms to greet her grandson, "William me boy, If I had a favourite grand-wain you would be it, but I don't, for I love yiez all in equal measure, now c'mon son and be giving me a big hug." William bounds over and gives his Wee Maw a mighty embrace, then she notices Caoilfhinn and little Stephen watching her with petted lips and almost bursting into tears. Wee Maw reaches out to them, "Awe ma bonnie wee darlins', come here and give your great granny a big hug." The two youngsters run over to Wee Maw, where she lifts them up and they smother her in kisses and hugs. A jubilant Wee Graham enquires, "Would you be liking a nip of my new season Craitur Wee Maw?"

"I don't mind if I do," replies Wee Maw, "wait Graham, is it heather honey or floral honey?" Wee Graham replies with pride "Queen bee honey Wee Maw, strained through the finest of the craitur clootie by my very hands themselves, nothing but the best for you me darlin'..." With a wrinkly smile, Wee Maw replies, "That'll do me just fine." Wee Graham speeds off to fulfil his noble mission, when Auld Jean comes out the kitchen door with her sleeves rolled up, appearing very tense... "Wee Graham..." she bellows. Wee Graham stops dead in his tracks, then he replies meekly, "Aye dear?" Jean shouts, "Don't you 'aye dear' me. When you've finished with the craitur detail, I want you to come back to the kitchens, I have plenty chores for yie to be doin...

don't you make me come a' looking for yie, if you know what's good for yie." Wee Graham mutters "Aye dear," as he skulks away looking extremely depressed. "William," says Wee Maw as she put the wains down and holds their hands "If you're thinking o' asking sir Hugh for the hand of the Maid Marion, yie need washed, shaved and dressed proper," Wee Maw screws her eyes up looking intently at him, "And get your hair cut." William looks at Wee Maw aghast, he's about to object when he notices Stephen grinning behind her. Wee Maw senses William's possible objection and crushes any thought of resistance by giving him the "Look" He gasps, "But…" Wee Maw growls "William," while giving him 'the look' once more to shut him up. "Aye granny."

"STEPHEN UA H'ALPINE…." Calls out another stern voice from the kitchen door. Stephen stops grinning and quickly goes red in the face. He looks up at the sky, then turns to face Katriona and meekly replies, "Aye me darlin'?" Katriona shouts "Don't you aye me darlin me… get up here, now, and would yie look at the state o' wee Stephen, what on earth have yie done to him?" Stephen stutters, "But… it wasn't me." Katriona glares at Stephen then shouts at him, "It doesn't matter, it's your fault anyway, now get up here right now." A despondent Stephen replies, "Aye ma dearest chittlin." Wee Maw calls out to Katriona "Its all right Katriona darlin' I'll bring the wee fella and Caoilfhinn up soon."

Katriona smiles and returns to the kitchens as Wee Maw gives out fresh orders, "Stephen, give William a hand to unload the vittals, then you're going to get William ready and proper presentable for sir Hugh later this night." Stephen enquires with much gusto "Will I give him a haircut granny?" Wee Maw replies "Of course." Stephen rubs his hands with glee "Now that'll be just grand." William glares at a smug looking Stephen, he's about to say something when Mharaidh came out the front doors of Wallace castle, "William, have you seen your father, Malcolm or auld Tam anywhere?"

"Naw," replies William, "we've just come down from the Craig with Wee Graham and the wains." Mharaidh continues, "Well, if you see them, tell them to finish unloading the wagons and come see us, for we need them to help us up here, we've lots of chores for them to do." Mharaidh turns to walk back into the Keep then she stops, turns and calls out, "Oh William?" William replies, "Aye Mharaidh, what is it?" Mharaidh continues as she disappears back in the door "Get washed and cleaned up, and get your hair cut." William stands with his mouth open trying not to be distracted by Alain, Malcolm and auld Tam, who are all hanging out the back of a bow wagon trying not to laugh and waving frantically not to let the women know where they are.

William watches Wee Maw wander up the path toward Wallace castle with the wains in hand when he hears a noise coming from a bow wagon. A voice whispers, "Wallace, Stephen…" Still perplexed by his recent education and observations about wedded bliss, Willian looks at the covered bow wagon to see Auld Tam waving them over. William and Stephen walk over to the back of the wagon then jump on the back step and peer into the darkest depths where they could just make out many bodies seated tight together and crouching between the flour salt and grain sacks. "Tam," enquires William, "Who's in here…" William gasps, SIR HUGH?" Sir Hugh replies urgently, "Get in here quick boy's, before you're spotted by the women." William and Stephen quickly climb into the back of the wagon, instantly they smell the strong thick aroma of whisky in the air. William looks about then he exclaims, "Dá, sir Hugh, Dáibh (Dave) Donnachaid, your here too?" Dáibh enquires, "How are yie doin Wallace?" William replies, "Good for seein' you Dáibh.

Is the Lady Daun here as well?" Dáibh replies, "Aye, she is up at Keep with the women. I said I would help the fella's down here, and would yie believe it, these fella's kidnapped me." Alain waves his hand frantically, "Sit down boyz, yiez are rocking the wagon, it'll get us caught by the women." Sir Hugh pulls William's léine sleeve to sit down on the flour sacks beside him. "Here, drink this," says sir Hugh as he hands William and Stephen a flagon of honeydew craitur.

Totally bewildered, William finds himself sitting in the back of a dimly light bow-wagon with his father, Malcolm, auld Tam, his old friend Dáibh and unexpectedly, Sir Hugh Braidfuite, his impending father-in-law, and it seems as though they are all getting drunk. William enquires, "What's happening with the women? They seem to be all a' flapping about the place?" Dáibh replies, "We're hiding, for the women have got a real big list, that's why we've jumped into the back of this wagon." Alain says, "We found a cask of Wee Grahams stash o' honey dew Craitur in here so we thought…" Dáibh says, "With the women running about everywhere, dustin' and a' cleanin' we decided to have a wee nip or two till they forgot about us." Sir Hugh laughs, "Doesn't seem to have worked." William enquires, "Why, what's going on?" They all laugh at William's question, auld Tam points a finger, "YOU."

"ME…" exclaims William. "Aye you," replies Alain, "when you and Marion decided you were wanting to romance and that you are going to ask Sir Hugh here for his permission this eve, the women do what women do, and that is to make everywhere spotless, clean and pure…" Dáibh quips, "And our lives feckn miserable." Laughing at the answer, William enquires, "I thought that you were all out here to talk about going down to the conference at Norham with the English?" Alain replies "We are, but with the impending tryst, hand fast and wedding in the air, a realms priorities wither into insignificance as far as women are concerned." Dáibh agrees, "They are, but without strong family ties, how can you have a strong realm?" Malcolm groans, "Its just the way the women go about things son." Alain states, "No man's safe when they want things fixed about the hovels." Dáibh sighs, "Ah, the list…" William enquires, "What is this List everyone keeps talking about?" Everyone laughs as they pass Wee Grahams whisky flagon round for another blessed and much needed drink of the fortifying craitur, Dáibh enquires, "You've no' heard of the dreaded list then Wallace?"

"Naw, well aye… kinda. Only what Wee Graham and Stephen was tellin' to me this morn?" Everyone laughs again, much amused at the innocence of William. Dáibh says, "I'll explain all about the list to you later." Alain laughs, "Aye, Dáibh here is the expert on the dreaded list." Dáibh smiles as though bestowed the highest honour, then sinks another nip of the craitur. Suddenly there is a clattering sound at the back of the wagon, everyone ducks down and tries to hide on the darkened floor.

"Ya durty evil miserable Feckrs…" exclaims a voice from outside the bow-wagon. The inside of the wagon goes deathly still and silent, then there's a collective groan of relief as Wee Graham pops his wiry head into the back of the wagon. Alain sighs relieved, "Awe, thank Feck it's you Wee Graham. We thought it was the women that had found us." Wee Graham exclaims, "Yiez have found me stash o' craitur ya durty theivin' feckrs." Everyone laughs at Wee Graham's Bothy courtesy as he clambers into the back of the wagon, with a hand extended for swift drink of his dwindling craitur. Alain enquires, "What's happening up at the Keep?" Wee Graham replies as he takes a much-needed swig of his craitur…"The women are going crazy lookin' for you fellas,

it's a feckn disaster up there for they are cleaning everywhere."
Alain says "Fellas. Why don't we go down to the William's
bowrie after we visit the Obhainn uisge beg, we can get the
fires started and water heated up then it'll be Hades hot for
the women, they can have a relaxing steamie and we can go
to the bowery, have a wee tune, a song or two and some more
craitur, and maybe help William here prepare for his appeal
of betrothal to maid Marion, then maybe a few more nips o'
Wee Graham's craitur?"

Everyone in the wagon agrees that this is a good idea.
Sir Hugh enquires, "Have you got the bowrie finished
yet William?" William replies, "Aye. There's still some fae
lanterns to put up, but me and Stephen finished making the
swing-bench this morn. It's got a fine overarch trellis o' willow,
with cords of ivy, Lilly, ears o' corn, and we've laid a floor
o' dried bluebell and as many scented flowers as we could
find." Sir Hugh smiles, "You've certainly a sense of making it
just the romantic place for Marion to sit and enjoy the eve."
The men blether awhile in the back of the bow wagon awhile,
safe from the dreaded lists and chores. William asks sir Hugh
a question, "Sir Hugh," says William nervously "I have no'
yet asked your permission to woo Marion and…" Sir Hugh
replies "I know. Why do you ask?" William cautiously replies,
"Because everybody is all talkin' as though you have already
approved."

"I haven't" replies Sir Hugh, before he can continue,
a female voice calls from the outside. "ARE YIEZ HIDING IN
THERE?" Everyone goes silent in the back of the bow-wagon;
then they hear someone climbing onto the back step. William
sees first glimpse of blond hair and thinks its Mharaidh, then
he sees who it is, "Daun…" exclaims William. He springs
up and embraces the visitor with a passion, for Daun is the
cousin of Mharaidh, but William knows her better through

his friendship with Dáibh, Dauns erstwhile husband. "Co'nas William?" says Daun. William grins, "Daun it's great to see you, jings it's been too long." Daun replies , "It has. You need to be coming up to Badenoch to see us instead of hiding away here forever and a day." William replies, "Aye Daun I would like that, once all the harvesting is done I would like to come up and see yiez." Daun smiles, then she enquires, "Is Dáibh hiding in there?" William turns and points, "I cannot tell a lie Daun, he's hiding up there in the front the wagon."

"Oh you men." says Daun with a bonnie smile. Everyone in the back of the bow-wagon welcomes Daun as Dáibh makes his way to the back of the wagon and kisses his bonnie wife on the cheek, "I have news for you men," says Daun, "The women know that you're all in here, and you had better get moving on the chores if you want any meaningful vittals this night, other than lashing's of tongue and cold shoulder."

"Ah the list." sighs Dáibh. Daun gives everyone the "Look" as they listen intently to her words… "Some of you are to get the Obhainn uisge beg ready and the rest are to finish the bowrie for William and Marion. And you William, Marion wants you to be at your best when you seek permission from Sir Hugh," William enquires "Is Marion here?" Daun smiles, "She's getting herself ready up at the Keep." William exclaims, "She's here…" Alain mumbles as he and the others climb out the back of the bow-wagon. "We didn't have time to tell yie." William enquires, "Can I see her?" Daun replies, "No. You can't be doing that William. She wants to be looking her best when the time comes and she'll not be pleased if you go up and see her now." Dáibh puts his hands round Daun's slender waist and lifts her to the ground. He enquires, "Why don't I go with William ma little honey-pot, ma bonnie sweetness and light, I can get him all washed and cleaned up while the rest get the list sorted."

"I know what you're up too" says Daun with a cheeky smile, "Get William ready then, I'll go back and tell the lassies that you men are doing as you are bid." Sir Hugh, Alain, Malcolm. Stephen and Wee Graham come over to William and Dáibh. Alain laughs, "It's on your head now Dáibh." Sir Hugh puts his hands on William's shoulder, "You're a good and fine young man William, and I know Marion loves you, I just hope you understand that I cannot be making this easy for you, for that's what father-in-law's are supposed to do." William looks at sir Hugh, perplexed at the comment, "Right fella's," says Alain "We had better attend to the chores the women want done. We'll see you at the vittal table soon son."

As the bow-wagon cronies make their way to finish their chores, they all wish William good luck as they depart. Daun kisses Dáibh on the cheek then she leaves to go back to the Keep. William enquires, "Dáibh, why are they all wishing me good luck with such melancholy faces?" Dáibh, says "C'mon Wallace. We had better be getting you ready for the asking, I'll explain everything to you real slow so that you understand everything. And if you're late or you mess the Trystin' up, I don't want to be getting' any o' the blame."

William and Dáibh walk down towards William's obhainn, talking about Marion, Daun, marriage, melancholy and the many titbit's of advice as Dáibh, a man of great experience, has to offer. William eagerly soaks up the information like a sphagnum sponge. "Oh Wallace," says Dáibh, "Ah near forgot, I've a message for you from young Andrew Moray. He say's when your father goes to Norham to sign the second Ragemanus, if you could meet with him up in Dundee or Perth in a few day's time that would be great. He wants to ask you something personally. I've brought some homin' Doo's and put them in your father's doocots to send him a reply." William enquires, "What does he want to ask me?" Dáibh replies, "Dunno, he said it's personal?" William sighs, "Ach, maybe I'll go up and see him after the tryst, for ah know that wagons o' winter salt are needed to be brought down from the salt-flats near Ceanncardine. How long does it take to get a message reply to Dundee by pigeon from here?" Dáibh replies, "Ach less time than breakin' fast to mid-day vittals, and you to getting' your hair cut."

William groans, then Dáibh says, "I know Malcolm's wife and Wee Maw are going to Dundee and Saint Johns Toun to see kinfolks soon and if you want to be travelling North with me and Daun, that would be just fine." William replies, "Aye. Marion and Brannah are going to Rosbroch for a week or two, and then Edinburgh for another week. I don't think that a conference of fancy knights down at the border marches is something that appeals to me, so if Wee Maw and Margret are going up to Perth, then I reckon I could travel up with yiez too." Dáibh smiles, "That's good. I'll let Moray know by the morrow." William enquires, "What brings yie down here anyway?" Dáibh replies, "I'm here to escort Wee Maw and Margret up to Dundee for your early year vittals. But if your coming too, when we see yiez off in Dundee, Daun and I will head on up north after that to Badenoch, you'll be fine escorting them back here wont yie?" William laughs, "I'd hate to be any road rat or bog bandit jumping out on Wee Maw asking for her chattel." Dáibh laughs, "True, very true." The two friends arrive at William's obhainn and set about preparing their own list for the vittals and the impending lovers tryst with maid Marion.

The hours pass quickly in Glen Afton, till its time for the gathering of the clan in Wallace castle. Alain a' Dale has journeyed up for the occasion and is playing sweet music on his clarsach. Everyone is settled around the evening feasting table waiting for the two young lovers to arrive, when the hall doors open. William is the first to walk in to face the family and guests. "Woo…" exclaim the women as the men join in with wolf-whistles and hoots of approval. William feels pride as he stands at the door, wearing his finest clan apparel for the occasion, dressed in his fine dark brown léine, made for him by his half-sisters Uliann and Aunia, skilfully embroidered with Cruathnie animals, fantastic beasts of legend and embellished with ochre emblems and saffron coloured knotwork. The centrepiece of this fine garment is the gold veined turquoise Dragon of Wallace totemic heraldry. Around his waist he wears the Anam Crios and Royal dirk of his late grandfather Billy, gifted to him by his father Alain and uncle Malcolm.

Wee Maw sheds a tear on seeing him standing there in all his clan finery, with his long blond-brown hair tied neatly in pleats behind his head and long side locks hanging down tied and braided with golden saffron strips. His long bushy beard is gone, revealing a sharp handsome smiling face with short-cropped goatee beard. "Oh he's my Billy's double," cries Wee Maw; then she blows her nose into the sleeve of Alain's léine as he sits by her side at the head of the table.

Patting the empty seat beside her, Wee Maw says "Come and sit by me son." Sir Hugh, who sits at the left hand side of Alain, is also impressed, "My, look at you young Wallace, I can see that I can soon be putting my feet up by the fireside with such a strong hand as you to hunt and fetch for us." William walks over and sits between Wee Maw and Alain, the empty chair beside sir Hugh is reserved for Marion. Everyone chats while Wee Graham busily serves them all with oversize portions of fine wines and honeydew craitur. Wee Maw becomes emotional and clasps William by the hand, "You're so like your grandfather son, he would be so proud of you." William replies, "I so dearly wish I had met him."

Wee Maw holds his hand tight, when suddenly there is a sharp sound of a Dirk being struck against metal. Everyone turns to see Wee Graham, standing to attention at the door. When all are silent, he makes an announcement… "The maid, Marion Braidfuite, heiress o' Lamington, daughter o' sir Hugh Braidfuite, attended by her gracious honour women, Lady Mharaidh Wallace o' Black Craig, Bellendean and Buccleuch, Lady Margret Wallace o' Ach na Feàrna and Auchenbothie. The Maids Brannah Braidfuite o' Lammington o' that ilk, Uliann and Aunia Wallace o' Ach na Feàrna, Lady Daun Donnachaid o' Angus glens and Badenoch… and Katriona de Graham o' Glen Afton." Wee Graham then steps back and opens the doors. Maid Marion enters the hall first, followed by Mharaidh, Margret, Daun and Brannah.

A stunned silence falls in the room, for the women are all dressed in the finest of silks and linens from the French court, such a wonderful representation of feminine beauty had never been seen before in the hall's of Wallace Keep. Everyone cheers and applauds them. Wee Maw, holding William's hand, whispers, "Aine, Branbhinn, Cliodhna, Magda's Niamh." (Aunia Bronwyn Cloda Ma and Neve) Turning to William, she says "Ach son, the bonnie lassies are the very incarnation o' the daughters o' the Divine Goddess." Marion gracefully walks across the floor as the earthly incarnation of the goddess Niamh from Dá Danann legend. Her gently flowing waist length hair is braided, part of her silken jet hair is bound back, plaited and brought forward in circular fashion, held fast by a gold circlet, silk and flower barbette. Her dress is a light emerald green with her long flowing sleeves slashed over a dark green silken undergarment with cuts of material hanging like little jade-coloured leaves. William is dumbstruck at the sight of her beauty, his visionary princess of love. Marion notices the look of sheer delight on his face then their eyes meet, she blushes seeing her fine handsome warrior dressed in his fine clan léine of knotwork, silver embossed belts, flash pastel brat and wolverine mantle.

Mharaidh, Margret and Daun each wear a cream coloured filet with intricate full gold and green braid barbettes, saffron coloured wimples with silkerchiefs drape about their neck and shoulders, with one corner falling over their left arms. The kirtle fabrics are of yellow and wheaten white with similar leaf slashes in their mantles, all flow freely. Long sleeves and dresses glide exquisitely as they walk with the delicate grace of natures Aicés behind the maid. Stephen smiles as Katriona with Marion's sister Brannah beside Uliann and Aunia, enter the hall as Marion's maids, dressed in a simpler garb of bell sleeve léine, held together by a dark green cross-laced bodice, over a light saffron léine skirting. Their mantles are embellished with intricate vine knotwork and songbirds of legend as they escort the Maid to the side of sir Hugh.

Wee Maw and Auld Jean's eyes fill with tears of joy as they watch Marion, the honour women and the maids sweep elegantly across the hall, accompanied with the beautiful scintillating airs from the clarsach playing of Alan a' Dale. Wee Maw stands and calls for attention, "Mo kith and Kin, I would like you all to gather round the great fire with myself and sir Hugh, for he sure has something to be saying to us all this fine night."

Everyone gathers to form a half circle around the great fire. Wee Maw stands in the centre, with William and Marion on either side, followed by the family kith and kin, till all are warmly shoulder-to-shoulder. Wee Maw joins William and Marion's left hands together, then she whispers, "We good-wives always use your left hands for love, as they are closer to each others heart." Sir Hugh steps forward and turns to face the families to propose a toast, whereupon

Wee Graham rushes around everyone's quaich, filling it with fine wine or Wee Maw's craitur. Sir Hugh raises his quaich… "To the families o' the Wallace and Braidfuite gathered here this special night, to bless and honour the Trystin of Marion and William for the celebration of Ag iarraidh and the Reiteach "(Asking and Betrothal), Sir Hugh pauses and glances at Wee Maw, with a broad grin he says, "I say to yie all, that I have never witnessed such radiant feminine beauty to which my eyes delight upon seeing the women of our clans before me this night."

Everyone smiles and applauds sir High as he continues, "It is said that the wisest of men know not the origins of the Aicé's of Magda mòr or that of the Tuatha de Cruinnè cè, but the scripts of the ancients do tell us they came from the heavens to grace us men with their gentility, beauty, nurture and love. I ask you all to raise your hand and hearts to bless this tryst of William, and my beautiful ward… Marion. I propose we all toast to the love and happiness and the trystin o' William and Marion."

"To William and Marion…" repeats everyone as they raise their Quaich's and drink to the health and happiness of the young couple. Alain nods to Wee Graham, who brings forward a Cruathnie Quaich mòr, a large carved oak vessel with the centre carved out and a lid on the top. This peculiar vessel has five individual drinking spouts from which the contents are to be drank from. Wee Graham proclaims, "The Cruathnie Quaich mòr, that we may drink as one to the health of the bonnie Trystin couple." Sir Hugh invites William to step forward to take his place in front of everyone, while he steps back and stands between Wee Maw and Marion, linking arms, the Cruathnie Quaich is passed around the gathering. William stands in front of his kith and kin, looking every inch a handsome prince of love and devotion. Marion and William gaze at each other, so much in love and so plain for all to see. After a few moments, Wee Maw coughs, "Oh…" Exclaims William. He briskly steps forward, faces sir Hugh then goes down on one knee resting his arm across his leg, bowing and looking at the feet of sir Hugh, as is the tradition of the Ag iarraidh and the Reiteach.

"Sir Hugh," says William "I seek your permission to hold the hand of Marion, your beloved daughter. I humbly ask for her hand in marriage and ah seek your blessing to enter the sacred union of man and wife with her. I declare to you and all present here, that there is only one that I love to whom may gain the best of all that I am and all that I possess and all that I will be. I offer to Marion my love, my heart and my hand in a marriage of mutual esteem, built on the pillars of love, affection and respect. To be crowned by your blessing sir Hugh, and under the guiding light and protection of Magda mòr, the Divine Goddess and by your acceptance of me to her as a loyal husband to your daughter, to serve you as a son, in that, I will endeavour to bring honour to your name and to your house as well as my own. I will seek your wisdom to grant me your hearts approval, that I may walk with her as my true love to the Bowrie of Glen Afton, where I may pledge my heart, eternal love and devotion of duty to Marion, my love, my bonnie Aicé." Pausing for a moment, William gazes into Marion's eyes and sees tears of joy.

Marion smiles as he whispers to her in Ceàrdannan Beurla reagaird, "Le mo ghrasa mise agus liomsa mo ghraidh." (I am my beloved's and my beloved is mine) Marion smiles then replies using the language of love "Tu es ma joie de vivre." (You are the joy of my life) William grins, "Túes mon amour, mon amour pour toi est eternal bonnie Marianne." (You are my love, my love for you is eternal beautiful Marion) Marion giggles, "Je t'aime Wallace, tu' es mon meilleur ami." (I love you Wallace, you're my best friend) William speaks once more in Beurla reagaird, "Tha gaol agam ort Marion, mo shíorghrá." (I love you Marion my eternal Love) "Mhuirnin." Marion says with joy in her voice, (Sweetheart) Then she says "Entre deux cœurs qui s'aiment, nul besoin de paroles." (Two hearts in love need no words) The two young lovers laugh together, for they have become blissfully unaware of anything but the mutual gaze into each other's hearts.

The family kith and kin blissfully look on, being joyously entertained by the banter between the two young lovers. Wee Maw pulls at Sir Hugh's arm and blows her weepy nose on his léine sleeve, "Bheitris..." exclaims sir Hugh, but Wee Maw ignores his protestations, she smiles, "Ach isn't young love just so wonderful Hugh? Isn't this just a sight to behold?" Sir Hugh, who also has a tear in his eye, suddenly remembers decorum. He clears his throat, "Ahem," Looking at sir Hugh, William is startled, then he remembers... "I'm sorry sir Hugh, forgive me." He glances back at Marion, who looks at him with a wicked smile and a twinkle in her eyes.

Sir Hugh clears his throat once again to focus attention on the ceremony of the asking. "I would be proud to have you as my son-in-law William, for I fear it is too late to be saying otherwise ma boy." William throws his arms in the air in pure joy and happiness, then quickly turns and kisses Marion passionately, much to the consternation of Sir Hugh. Everyone cheers the decision of sir Hugh as Mharaidh, Daun and the maids rush forward with glee to the side of Marion, hugging and kissing her. Wee Graham shouts above the cacophony "I would also like to propose a toast." but his voice is lost amidst the celebratory joy. "Order, order..." Commands Wee Maw, "Wee Graham here will be giving us another toast to the bonnie couple." Wee Graham makes sure everyone's Quaich is full then he clears his throat with a wee nip of craitur himself. He addresses the small gathering. "Right, here we go then... Gu bhana íngra linn, iad siud ata i ngra linn, Iad siud nach bhuil go casa Dé a croithe, agus muna casann se a croithe, Go casa se caol na coise acu go n-aithneoimid iad as a bacadail, s' nil aon leigheas ar anngrá ach posadh." A moment's silence passes with everyone gaping at Wee Graham. He lifts his Quaich, and with a big toothy grin... "Slainte a'huile duine, your good health everybody." everyone laughs and cheers then the pipers start playing barrel-jigs.

Dáibh wanders over and nudges William, "Wallace, that's no' any proper Gaelic that I know, I understand some of it, but what did Wee Graham just say?" William smiles, "Naw, that's the Galloway Gaelic Dáibh, it's the old Gallóbhet tongue, with a wee bit o' wolf and wildcat Ceàrdannan twang mixed in." Dáibh enquires again. "So what did he say then?" William laughs, then he replies, "Ha, basically he said, May those who love us, love us, and those who do not love us may the Gods turn their hearts. And if they don't turn their hearts, may they turn their fuckin' ankles so we may know them by their limping. And the only cure for love... is marriage." Laughing heartily, Dáibh raises his goblet, "Wee Graham, he's a man after me own heart."

As the bagpipes play on, everyone commences to Ceilidh and celebrate. Marion walks over to William, reaches out and holds his hand. He looks into her beautiful cobalt dark eyes. Amidst the joyous noise and ruckus trysting celebrations, he says, "Marion, I do love you, I always will." Marion sweeps her arms around his neck, "Oh William, I love you too, more than anything and everything in this world. I want to wake up beside you every day and spend the rest of my life by your side." Marion's eyes sparkle, then she kisses him gently on the lips. "Right you two..." interrupts Wee Maw,

"Everything is to be proper as it should be, everyone is now happily blessing themselves with plenty of Wee Graham's and ma very own special occasion craitur. Mharaidh and sir Hugh have also brought some very fine wines and the pipers are playin' ther' finest, so wains, yie should be getting' ready to be going away down to the Glen Afton bowrie, it'll be a full moon in a wee while, and if you want the blessings of Danu Machu, Magda mòr and Luna, yiez had better be getting' the going the now."

Sir Hugh, standing tall beside Wee Maw agrees, he looks across the busy hall, raises his hands high in the air and calls out over the joy of the Ceilidh, "Wee Graham…"

"Aye sur." replies Wee Graham standing beside sir Hugh. Pulling his mantle aside, Sir Hugh is surprised to see Wee Graham standing almost underneath him. Sir Hugh is lost for words for a moment. Wee Graham enquires, "What is it you'll be wanting from me sur, more craitur?" Sir Hugh shakes his head, "Naw, ahm fine, I've a bucket full of Wee Maw's nectar below my chair to finish off first. But I'd be honoured if it's you and Jean who would be chaperone's for these two love birds, would you be taking them away to the lovers bowrie?" Wee Graham replies cheerfully, "It will be an honour and our pleasure sur."

Wee Maw once again calls for order from the gathering. "Right awebody, Auld Tam and Stephen have been away busy lighting the torches and bowrie braziers to bring warmth and light up the pathway o' love. Wee Graham and Jean will be chaperoning Marion and William down to the bowrie, so we'll be seeing them to the door, now be away and getting all your quaich's filled and your best mantles and brats on, then we'll usher the bonnie couple away with the purest of loving intention in our hearts." Everyone quickly disperses to find mantles, capes, brats, and also to fill their large Cruathnie

Quaich's to keep themselves warm, inside and out as they escort the young lovers to the start of the path leading to the lover's bowrie. Wee Maw pulls William aside, "William, I want yie to have this before yie go down to the bowrie." She produces a little iron box from underneath her mantle then places it on the table and opens it. Curious as to what is in the little box, William looks inside and can see various little silver and gold rings, coins and jewellery, then he notices an unusual looking pair of gold and silver talisman. He sees the impression of a faceless naked woman imprinted on them, and four Oghamic letters…

"What are those granny?" Wee Maw, still fussing about in the box, replies, "Ach son, I want you to see this." Wee Maw pulls out a golden chain with many rings attached, including the talisman. She removes a beautiful silver-gold ring from the chain. "Your grandfather Billy made this ring out of pure Strathclyde gold and silver for me on Leckie mòr's very own anvil for our wedded day." She sniffs with emotion then hands William the ring. He looks at it and sees two tiny outer gold bands embedded with Lewisian diamonds completely filling the outer-face circumference, he can see the ring is also stamped around the third-side edge with the letters WMWM. "Wallace and Morríaghan." says Wee Maw with a smile, "Now it's William and Marion." William exclaims, "Its beautiful…" as he genuinely shows his gratitude. Wee Maw appears pleased, happy and so very, very emotional. "I would wish you to have this ring William," says a tearful Wee Maw "For it's my fingers that are far too small now to be wearing it, but it'll fit the wedded finger o' Marion." He studies the ring, then he looks at Wee Maw, the moment between them crystallises in the love of family emotions. William bows down and puts his arms around Wee Maw and holds her close, she hugs him awhile, then stands back and cups his face in her tiny hands. "William, all you wains are so special to me, but you're the most so like your grandfather. I know he too would want you and the bonnie maid to have our ring of betrothal and I… we, would wish you to share all the love and happiness we ever had that's carried on through this gift of love." William feels an emotional wave sweeping through his heart as he looks into the steely blue eyes of Wee Maw, now softened by tears of joy. He hugs her close once more and thinks that when he is old and happy with his own grandchildren like Wee Maw is now, if he is half the character she is, then his kin and children would always know how it feels to be truly loved. Fighting back tears of emotion he says "Granny, I don't have any words enough to be thanking you or to even explain what this means to me."

"Ach me darlin boy," replies Wee Maw, "Just make sure there are lots o' tiny feet running about for me to hug and little ears for me to be spinning me yarns too very soon, that'll be thanks enough." Laughing at Wee Maw's request, William is delighted at the thought of at least trying to make her wish come true. Wee Maw says, "And before yie ask, I took the ring to Brannah and we tried it on her finger, which is the same size as her sister Marion, and it fits her perfectly. So William, I'll wrap it up for yie then ah'll slip it to yie before yiez go down to the bowrie."

Putting his arms around Wee Maw, he says, "Ah love you granny." So overwhelming are his emotions, he can't utter any more words. Wee Maw replies, "I love you too son." She steps back a pace and dabs her eyes with her own sleeve, "Now William, away yie go I say, before yie have me weeping again, for ah have to think of my standing and reputation yie know. Ah mean, how can ah be ruling the roost if yiez all think am soft in the head and havin' a wee tear every time ahm happy?" Adoring the wrinkly grin of his precious Wee Maw, they both laugh and embrace, then she says, "Right William me bonnie boy, its about time you get yourself hanging off the arm o' your beautiful wife to be, so away yie go now son and I will be wrappin' up the ring for yie." William smiles "I thank you granny, for everything you've ever done for me and wee John." Wee Maw replies; "You'll do the same for your own wains and grandwains some day." Wee Maw grins as William walks away towards Marion, he pauses and turns to see Wee Maw is busily wrapping up the ring and tying a little bow around the wrap. He smiles and thinks of what a wonderful time it is, to be living with such amazing and loving kith and kin.

Later that evening, the young lovers sit on the bowrie love swing beside the Afton water. Marion looks around the bowrie, "William, this just so beautiful, and you built all of this, just for me?" William replies feeling rather pleased with himself "Just for you." They gaze into each other's eyes and hold hands under the watchful attendance of Wee Graham and Auld Jean, who are sitting just a little distance away. Wee Graham looks at Jean lovingly, "Jean me bonnie darlin'… do yie remember when we first met, and you dragged me away by the hair away to the Trystin' tree and the bowrie love swing that ah built for yie wie my very own hands me dearest?"

Auld Jean looks to the stars and full moon that glow serenely and brightly above; then she looks curiously at Wee Graham, tentatively she replies, "Aye, that ah do." He reaches out to hold Jean's hand, "Then do yie remember our wedding night too me dear?" Jean cannot resist a smile as she studies the wizzened old face of the love of her life. Again she replies cautiously, "Aye, that I do my love, how could I forget it…" Silence follows… Auld Jean looks at Wee Graham and she can see he is looking back at her romantically. With a toothy grin he smiles eagerly up at her with an expression of pure hope in his wide-open watery, bloodshot eyes. "Aye Graham, ah do remember it well… You were sick, drunk and finally fell over unconscious, then I had to sit in the kitchens all night all on my own, with a may-butter egg-white poultice on my head after the oak bowrie swing you built broke and the top beam hit me on the head, giving me this big scar…" Jean points to a long and deep furrowed scar on her forehead. Wee Graham takes the opportunity to clasp Jean lovingly with both his hands as she gazes at the stars once more, desperately trying to hide her amusement. An irrepressible Wee Graham continues, "Then me bonnie bonnie lass, do yie remember the next night after the wedding night we missed me bonnie darlin Jean?"

"I do my love, and it was so beautifull." A grand smile appears as she relents to Wee Grahams persistent charm. Jean takes her gaze away from the stars above and looks into the sparkling bloodshot eyes of Wee Graham; then she laughs, for his mongrel puppy dog appeal always got the better of her. Auld Jean enquires, "Are you thinkin of what I'm thinking your thinking?" Wee Graham's eyes light up, "Oh ma bonnie Darlin' ah'v been thinkin about doin' it again for years…"

Unexpectedly, Wee Graham goes down precariously on one knee in front of her, still holding both her hands, as much for balance as it is for romance, then he looks lovingly into Auld Jean's eyes and says, "Me bonnie darlin Jean, ah must tell yie, ah love yie more than ah'v ever loved yie before… and Jean me darlin' I never thought that could be possible. Ah would renew ma vows to yie here right now if ah could just remember what they feckn were." Jean looks at Wee Graham, her husband since time began, then tears of love well up in her eyes. Looking up at Auld Jean as he shakes and hangs on tight, Wee Graham says, "Ah really do love yie darlin' and ah will do so till the end o' days." Auld Jean chortles at her own thoughts of romance, for she too has grown old and very happy with Wee Graham as her Bo. "I love you too Wee Graham, despite yourself. And darlin' I could never live without you." Gazing at Jean with clarity and sincerity, Wee Graham is truly in love. For a moment, Jean can see in him the youth she fell in love with. Wee Graham says, "I love you Jean me darlin, more than words could ever say." Wee Graham then struggles to get up from the ground with his arthritic knees shaking, Auld Jean reaches down and pulls him to his feet, where he stands a moment trying to regain his balance, then he sits down beside her, trying in vain to put his arm around her ample waist. Laughing together, she puts her arm around his shoulders and pulls the little fellow close under her arm and kisses him on the top of his head. *'Tonight's the night.'* thinks a jubilant Wee Graham as he snuggles his head into the comfort of Auld Jean's full and ample bosom.

Meanwhile, the young lovers sitting in the bowrie swing, watch their chaperones. "Oh William, isn't little Graham so cute… I do hope that when we are that age we're as much in love as those two are now." William replies with a grin, "I don't hope so. I know so." Marion looks into his eyes while holding his hands tightly, she whispers quietly in his ear… "Te amo ab imo pectore. (I love you from the bottom of my heart) William smiles, "Numquam te amare desistam Marion." (I'll never stop loving you) Marion giggles, "In aeternum te amo" (I will love you for all eternity) William continues, "Omnia vincit amor… et nos cedamus amori." (Love conquers all things… let us too surrender to love) Marion counters "Amor meus amplior quam verba est." (My love is more than words) William laughs, then with a twinkle in his eye he enquires… "Apudne te vel me?" (Your place or mine?) Horrified, Marion exclaims, "What did you just say to me Wallace?" She feigns indignation, then her eyes sparkle and she smiles her cheeky gorgeous smile. Tantalisingly she leans forward and close, till he can feel her sensual warm breath caress his neck. She whispers, "Yours." William exclaims "What…?" Marion stands up and puts her arm round the trestle and gazes at the moon, then she turns and looks into his eyes, puts a finger to her lips and teases him, "Wallace, audentum forsque venusque juvant." (Fortune and love favour the brave) He thinks about what Marion has just said; in one movement, he rises from the lovers swing and goes down on one knee and holds Marion by the hand. "Marianne, je t'aime de tout moncoeur." (Marion I love you with all my heart) Marion looks down on her handsome Bo' "Moi aussi je t'aime Wallace." (I love you too) Reaching into his a small leather sporran on his belt, he pulls out a small parcel and begins to unwrap it.

Marion, sensing what it could be, holds her hands to her lips with excitement, then he reveals the silver-golden ring. "William, It's beautiful…" gasps Marion as he displays the ring of commitment. He slides it gently onto her finger… "Marion, Veux-tu m'epouser… Will you marry me?" She gazes into William's eyes and could see the same anticipation and feel the same energy of excitement coming from him that pounds in her own heart. She wraps her arms around his neck and kisses him frantically, "Oui, Oui Wallace. Je veux passer la reste de ma vie avec vous. Yes, yes Wallace, I want to spend the rest of my life with you." Pausing a moment, they look into each other's eyes. William smiles then enquires jokingly, "Does this mean you're no' sure darlin'?" Marion giggles and holds her hand high gazing at the ring, She smiles as the moonlight reflects from the tiny Lewisian diamonds, "Maybe…" Marion throws her arms around William "I love you so much Wallace…"

They kiss and passionately embrace, after a few moments of intense passion, William smiles and says, "Marion, I have loved you from the first day we met down at the river Afton. When you left I couldn't eat, I couldn't think, I couldn't sleep…

I felt so sad without you, even though we were not yet together as lovers. When you left for France, it near broke my heart, to love you yet not be able to reach out and hold you, touch you… I missed you so much." Marion rests her head on his shoulder "I felt the same as you William, when I had to leave with Queen Yolande for France it broke my heart too, I thought of you every day. And when my brother and little friar Blair passed me your messages from Lanark, you made me laugh, even though I was so far away from you. Just thinking of you made me happy, I knew we had to be together. I knew that one day we would be together, I prayed to the angels and the Aicé every day to bring you back to me, and you did come back to me."

William reaches inside his léine and pulls out a sealed velum letter. Marion enquires. "Is that…?" They both look at the unopened letter. "This is the letter you sent to me from France Marion, I've kept it with me un-opened for near on five years now." Marion enquires, "William, why did you not open it?" William replies, "Darlin, I feared most of all that it would tell me you did not love me, and I didn't want to see those words. I believed too that one day we would meet again and your beautiful eyes would tell me more than words could ever say." William holds her close as she whispers, "Oh William, I never want to ever be apart from you ever again, I want to spend my life in your arms."

"I love you Marion," says William "I always will…" Their hearts entwine, so much in love under the spell of the moon and stars, completely lost to the world. Suddenly they notice the sound of coughing that becomes more persistent. Turning round, they see Wee Graham standing close by, looking at them with big wide eyes and a toothy smile. "Little Graham…" exclaims Marion. Wee Graham frowns "I am afraid it's time for yie to be going back to the big house darlin."

Auld Jean says, "C'mon with me Marion I will walk you up. I'm sorry to be ending your tryst, but it is right and proper on such a wonderful occasion as this, yiez will understand why when yie have wains of your own some day." Wee Graham takes William by the arm, "Ahm sorry too son, but I have to be escortin' yie back to yer obhainn and lock yie in for the night good and proper."

"What?" exclaims William "How can yie lock me in when ah'v only got a bull-hide door?" Wee Graham laughs and winks, "I am only jesting wit yie Wallace, but its time that you two bid a good night, for it's tradition that temptation should not befall yie both on this night of nights." As they reach the door outside William's obhainn, Auld Jean stops, then she says, "Me and the wee fella here will be turning our backs for a wee while to be looking at the beautiful Glen Afton moon away up above the Black Craig up there. So if you two be wantin' a wee bitty more time to say fair night together…" Auld Jean nudges Wee Graham who is still smiling watching William and Marion. "Oh, sorry ma dear." says Wee Graham.

Marion looks into William's eyes as he holds her close. For a long time they kiss passionately, till Wee Graham could take the tension no longer, "C'mon Wallace, we don't want sir Hugh to be frettin'." The lovers kiss once more then slowly part, never taking their loving eyes from each other. "C'mon Marion me darlin'." says Auld Jean. Marion looks into William's eyes "I long for the day when we may rest together in wedded union William, for I love you like no other." William whispers, "Marion, I do love you… mo bonnie Anam chara." The two young lovers embrace once more and bid each other goodnight. As Marion walks away with Auld Jean, Wee Graham stands with William outside his Obhainn. "She's a lovely lass Wallace, the time will be here soon enough when yie wont be needing me any more, for yiez will be walking into an obhainn o' yer very own the pair o' yie." William laughs, "I don't think Marion is thinking of living in an obhainn." He smiles then he slaps Wee Graham on the back, "And what about you wee man. Aren't you quite the romantic?" Wee Graham laughs, "Ach Wallace, ah just cant help me'self, yie know, its no easy bein' me and bein humble." William and Wee Graham share a moment's laughter. "Right, in yie go." commands Wee Graham as he holds the thick leather door flaps up. William enters his obhainn and sits down beside the central peat fire. He waits a few moments then he pops out to see if Marion is perhaps coming back to him, but he can see the three of them walk all the way up to the front doors of Wallace Keep then enter. He watches almost forlorn as the doors close behind them. The night of lover's bowrie tryst is complete.

Standing a long time outside his obhainn, William hopes in vain that the doors of Wallace Keep would open and Marion would come rushing out and run back to him, but the doors stay firmly closed. Looking up at the moon, William thinks of how many men in the history of the world have done exactly as he is doing now, looking at the moon and thinking of how much in love he is with the most beautiful woman in the world. Suddenly he feels the chill of a typical Scottish summers night touch his bones. He shudders at the biting cold and looks at the moon and stars one more time, then he retires into his obhainn and lays down beside the glowing peat fire.

Unknown to William, Marion has been looking out a window watching her love before he went inside his obhainn. She looks at the moon too, then she retires to her chamber so happy, so enamoured, and so very much in love. William lay beside the peat fire poking it with an grill iron, he can't sleep being so lost in his thoughts of Marion, her touch, her hair, her wonderfull sensual scents, the way she wrinkles her little nose when she laughs and her beautiful smile, then he hears a noise outside…

The door flap pushes open and someone comes in wearing a large wolverine brat and hood. The dark interior of the obhainn makes it impossible to know exactly who this could be. He sits up and looks at the tall strangers outline in the low ochre light of the fire. Suddenly the wolverine brat falls open slightly… William glimpses the sensual nakedness of a female, he exclaims, "Marion…"

Coming Soon

The fourth thrilling instalment in
Wallace: Legend of Braveheart

Milton Keynes UK
Ingram Content Group UK Ltd.
UKHW010639031023
429856UK00001B/9